Shopping Experience and Satisfaction of Outshoppers in Shopping Malls of Selected Cities in Tamil Nadu

Dr.R. Geetha

Published by

Shopping Experience and Satisfaction of Outshoppers in Shopping Malls of Selected Cities in Tamil Nadu

ISBN 978-93-86638-11-3

Author

Dr.R. Geetha

Bonfring

309, 2nd Floor, 5th Street Extension,

Gandhipuram, Coimbatore-641 012.

Tamilnadu, India.

E-mail: info@bonfring.org

Website: www.bonfring.org

Phone: 0422 4213231

Author Profile

Dr.R. Geetha, Prof & Head, Department of Commerce with Computer Applications, Sri Ramakrishna College of Arts and Science (Previously SNR Sons College) Coimbatore has 10 years of Teaching experience and 8 years of Industrial Experience. She has graduated in PSGR Krishnammal College for Women and during her college days she actively participated in NCC activities and passed 'C' Certificate Exam. She was been awarded Doctorate during the year 2017. She has also qualified in Master of Business Management and Post Graduate Diploma in Computer Applications in Bharathiar University. She has passed her National Eligibility Test (NET) conducted by UGC during December 2010. She has successfully completed 2 NPTEL exams with Elite Certificate conducted by Indian Institute of Technology(IIT) Kanpur.

She is a Research Guide for M.Phil Research Programme under Bharathiar university and successfully produced 2 M.Phil under her guidance and as on date guiding 1 M.Phil scholar. She was handling class for the ICWA and CPT students. She was also handling part time MBA classes for ICFAI university, Bharathiar university for past 8 years and been visiting professor for CMS Academy of Management & Technology.

She has attended nearly 28 Conference in which 12 are International conferences. In the area of research she has published more than 15 papers in international journal, ISSN books and ISBN books. She has attended various Faculty Development Programmes and Workshops. She has organised and acted as moderators in 4 National and International Conference and been Editor in the Bonfring International Journal of Industrial Engineering and Management Science. She had been fine arts co-ordinator and organised many inter collegiate cultural events. She is been part of Organizing Committee for various Programmes in the college.

<table>
<tr><th>Chapter</th><th>Contents</th><th>Page No</th></tr>
</table>

CHAPTER I

INTRODUCTION AND RESEARCH DESIGN

1.1. Introduction

Shopping has been part of many cultures across the world for centuries. The shopping culture of people have changed over the years from bazaars (street vending), to small retail outlets to shopping in multiple complex buildings i.e., in shopping malls. In India, outshopping is part of its people's culture for many centuries. It is a common custom among the rural and semi-urban Indian to travel to far distance urban cities for shopping during religious festivals, weddings, other occasions and social activities. Moreover, people are tend to shop at distance urban cities, when they travel to those places as tourist or guest attending any social family celebration. In the modern day, out shoppers consider themselves as the biggest beneficiaries of retail infrastructure available in the nearby city or within the state or even across the nation. With the development of new shopping centers, retail patronage patterns have also changed, and urban malls have become favourite shopping destinations for both inshoppers and outshoppers.

The changing behaviour of shoppers has a deep connection with emerging business models which will change the way 'total retailers' do business[1].Moreover, the Indian demographic landscape has witnessed enormous changes in the past fewdecades. In both urban and rural India the increase in income levels, the priority given toward education and rapid industrialisation coupled with liberalisation policies pursued relentlessly by the Indian government has transformed the Indian economy it in to the path of growth. Changing prospectus of Indian economy to a greater extent have changes the lifestyle status of its citizens, which is one of the key factor that influence buying behavior. With growth in the economy, the employment opportunities are growing, standard of living of the people are increased and consumers purchasing power has increased. Now the consumers look for the better quality and service, so they have started visiting to modern retail stores functioning at malls.

In short, it can be said that consumers are the major beneficiaries of the retail boom in India. Indian consumers are changing rapidly as there is choice of wide range of products, quality and prices.

---

[1] Total Retail A Change is Underway (2014), http://www.rasci.in/downloads/2014/Total_Retail_Change.pdf

Organised retailing is changing the whole concept of shopping in terms of consumer buying behaviour. Shopping today is much more than just buying. It is an experience itself. Shopping has become a pleasurable experience these days. Consumers now value convenience and choice on a par with getting value for their hard-earned money. Consumers are now preferring shopping malls for shopping, as it enables them to shop a variety of products under one roof and offer shopping experience in terms of ambience and entertainment.

A shopping mall is an agglomeration of shops in the commercial area.It has stores assortment, accessibility, convenience, distance, economic advantage, leisure facilities, and these essential factors attract consumers towards shopping malls. Moreover, shopping malls are dynamic business centers that attract a large section of customers for experiencing modern shopping pleasure. A categorically planned assortment of stores in a mall would provide diversity, arousal, and propensity to shop, entertain, dine, leisure, refresh and relaxing environment around the mall. Also the mall concept enable the consumers to the purchase, of branded products expressing their self-identity, personal values, status, and aspiration[2] and help them to move up in their life-style status.

During the course of this study and at the stage of literature review analysis it has been understood that in the Indian context, not much research had been conducted in the past on the shopping experiences and satisfaction of outshoppers in malls. The researcher realised that with the growth of retail revolution in India, the retailers have to focus on the issues of outshoppers i.e., shoppers who prefer to shop outside his/her local retail establishments. In India shopping mall retailers always like to attract customers both from local and far rural and semi-urban distance communities. Based on this theoretical discussion this study aims to analyse shopping experience and satisfaction of outshoppers in shopping malls in selected cities in Tamil Nadu. The study focused on selected shopping malls functioning in tier II cities of Tamil Nadu i.e., in Coimbatore, Madurai and Trichy.

1.2.   Statement of Problem

The escalating consumer trends have led a retail trade growth in India and lend strong support for more research on Indian retailing and consumer behaviour. In future more number of shopping malls would be cropping in the tier II cities. Retail is the fastest growing sector in the Indian economy. Traditional markets are making way for the new formats such as departmental stores, hyper markets, supermarkets and specialty stores. Western style malls

---

[2]Sonu Joseph and Vibhuti Singh, Changing Lifestyles Influencing Indian Consumers: Conceptualizing and Identifying Future Directions, Global Journal of Management and Business Studies, Vol. 3, No. 8, Pp. 861-866, 2013.

have began appearing in tier II cites, introducing the Indian consumers to an unparalleled shopping experience.

Shopping malls play an important part in today's consumer lifestyle. Consumers' views of shopping malls have changed from seeing them as merely a place for shopping to seeing them as a center where different activities, such as shopping, entertainment and eating could be experienced at time. Nowadays, shopping malls face intense competition not only from similar malls in their area but also from other retail formats, such as the Internet or cyber malls or from other types of center, such as power centers, discount chains and category-killers, which provide shoppers with access to almost everything they need under one roof. Given the intense competition between malls, shoppers can be more selective and are more likely to patronise those shopping malls with which they are more satisfied. Therefore, it is crucial for mall managers and retailers operating in malls to understand shoppers' reasons for patronising one shopping mall and not another and to know how far retails in mall cater to the consumers expectation and rising demands, as various shopping malls have differed attributes and their different importance as perceived differently by customers[3].

This study aims to analyse shopping experience and satisfaction of outshoppers in shopping malls in selected cities in Tamil Nadu. The study focused on selected shopping malls functioning in tier II cities of Tamil Nadu i.e., in Coimbatore, Madurai and Trichy.

1.3.   Rationality of the Study

Outshopping is the purchase of goods by customers outside their local shopping area. Generally, cross-regional outshopping is explained from an economic perspective on account of geographic closeness of the two regional areas (implying cost and time efficiency) and thus outshopping is viewed mostly as utilitarian behaviour[4]. Moreover, outshopping as primarily instrumental and functional in nature and argue that cross-border outshoppers do not consider leisure and store atmosphere as important and focus on lower prices due to lower taxes or duty exemptions and a chance to buy brands unavailable in their home country as the main benefits of cross-border outshopping[5]. For cross-border outshoppers, better quality is

---

[3]Mohammed Ismail El-Adly, Investigating the Relationship between Shopping Mall Patronage Motives and Customer Satisfaction Using Importance-Satisfaction Analysis, International Journal of Customer Relationship Marketing and Management, Vol. 3, No. 2, Pp. 33-46, 2012.

[4]F. Piron, International outshopping and ethnocentrism, European Journal of Marketing, Vol. 36, No. 1/2, Pp. 189-210, 2002.

[5]T.A. ,Arentze, H. Oppewal and H.J.Timmermans, A multipurpose shopping trip model to assess retail agglomeration effects, Journal of Marketing Research, Vol. 42, No. 1, Pp. 109-115, 2005.

one of the primary reasons for buying products from urban regions, because they may not have access to high quality brands in their own geographical regions especially in semi-urban and rural areas[6].

It has also be inferred that outshopping is not just a means to satisfy the economic needs of shoppers by way of lower prices, greater variety and convenience; instead, shopping to urban cities trips may give them emotional and social benefits such as shopping enjoyment, innovation and socialization[7].

For many tourists, shopping is a form of recreation making the trip a more enjoyable and relaxing experience and this is particularly true with outshoppers, who tend to be more active, recreation, and sensation seekers[8].

As discussed above, outshoppers are always more concerned about product quality compared to local shopper, due to their primarily utilitarian motivation, hence they may be more sensitive to perceive risk while outshopping and it may affect their perceived value to a greater extent, and their satisfaction level too.

Drawing empirical and theoretical evidences from the above discussion, conduct of this study is considered as rational and significant for the future growth of retailing business across India.

1.4. Conceptual Framework

Officially shopping malls are defined as "one or more buildings forming a complex of shops representing merchandisers, with interconnected walkways enabling visitors to walk from shop to another."[1]

Unofficially, shopping malls are the heart and soul of communities, the foundation of retail economies, and a social sanctuary for teenagers across the world.

---

[6]Y.J. Wang, S.K. Doss, C. Guo, and W. Li, An investigation of Chinese consumers outshopping motives from a culture perspective: Implications for retail and distribution. International Journal of Retail & Distribution Management, Vol. 38, No. 61, Pp. 423-442, 2010.

[7]D. Jarratt, Outshopping behaviour: an explanation of behaviour by shopper segment using structural equation modelling, International Review of Retail, Distribution and Consumer Research, Vol.10, No. 3, Pp. 287-304, 2000.

[8]D.J. Burns, J.M. Lanasa and C.L. Lackman, Outshopping: An examination from a motivational perspective., Journal of Professional Services Marketing, Vol. 19, No. 2, Pp. 151-160, 1999.

In recent decades, the concept of the shopping mall, which has its origins in the U.S. and became full-blown modern retail trend there in the post-second world war years, has proliferated across the globe. The five largest malls in the world now reside in Asia[9].

In the last decade, retailing sector in India has seen a vast transformation from traditional retailing to modern retailing.

As the economy has started growing in India, retail sector has also started modernising and growing. Amongst modern organised retailing, shopping malls are becoming attractive destinations for retailers and shoppers[10]. At present there nearly 255 malls are functioning in India at the top seven cities.

The success rate of mall depends on factors like: design and layout, the mall's brand positioning, location and how well they cater to the needs of their target segments of shoppers[11].

Different types of people visit shopping mall and People visits mall for different reasons. Some give preference to it being situated near to home or home town, while some feel the layout of the mall as well as the shops present within the mall are very good and attractive[12] and some traveller like outshoppers prefer visiting malls as it is good place for entertainments, shopping branded products or those products that are normally not available in their regional markets.

The above discussion provided a required scope and helps the researcher in building the conceptual framework, for the effective conduct of this study.

---

[9]Roberto Fantoni, Femanda Hoefel and Marina Mazzarolo, The future of the shopping mall, 2014. http://www.mckinseyonmarketingandsales.com/the-future-of-the-shopping-mall.

[10]Positioning Strategies of Malls: An Empirical Study,

http://www.jiit.ac.in/uploads/ SYNOPSIS_S.%20SURESH.pdf

[11]Malls face uncertain future as customers desert them (2015), http://www.dnaindia.com/money/report-malls-face-uncertain-future-as-customers-desert-them-2087068, 19th May.

[12]Amandeep Kaur, Shopping Malls: The Changing Face of Indian Retailing–An Empirical Study of Cities of Ludhiana and Chandigarh, International Journal of Business and Management Invention, Vol. 2, No. 5, Pp. 30-36, 2013.

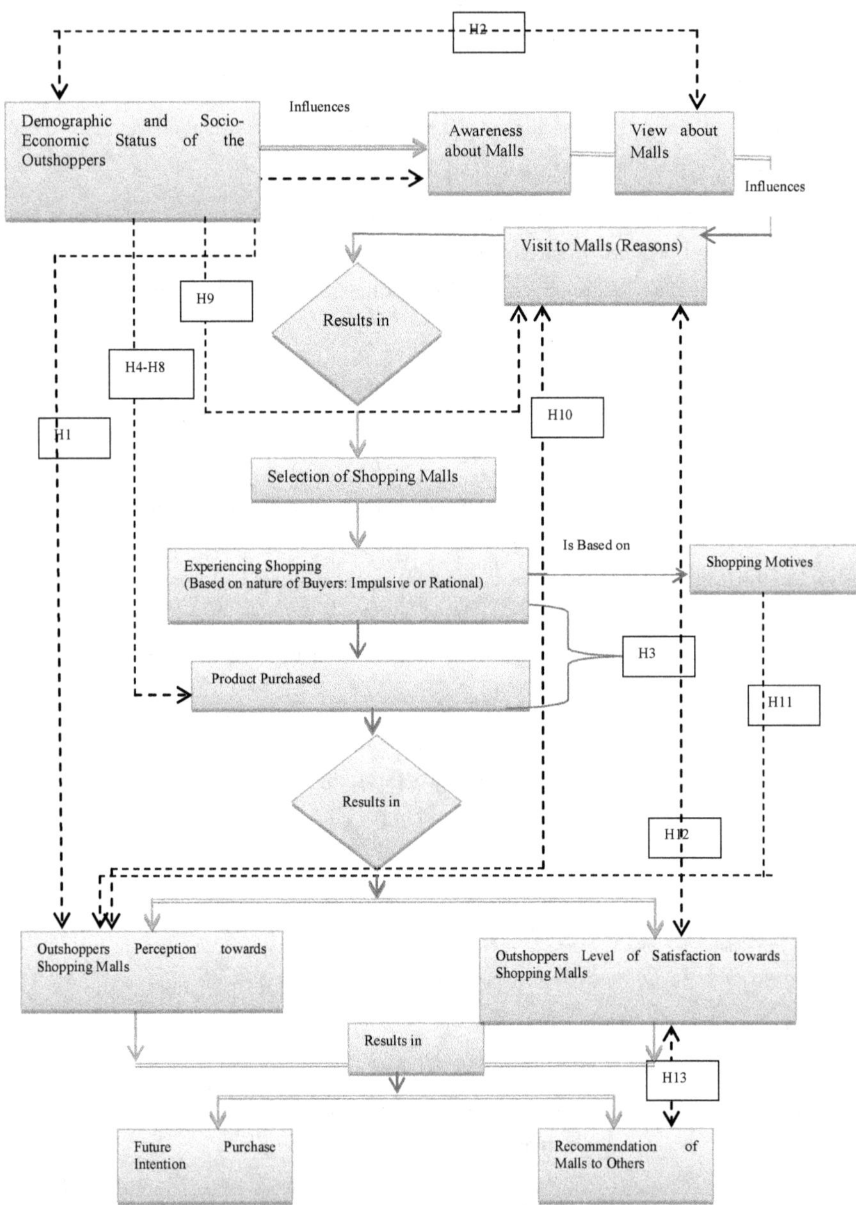

Exhibit: 1.1: Conceptual Framework of the Study

Source: Pictogram Prepared for the Study

Shopping malls attract shoppers by offering an opportunity to learn new trends i.e. opportunities for exploration. Consumers always look for new and upgraded product and their desire for variety can only be met through the process of exploration[13] especially for the outshoppers, who travel for a long distances out of their home town for the purpose of shopping.

This study aims to analyse shopping experience and satisfaction of outshoppers in shopping malls in selected cities in Tamil Nadu. As the buying behaviour of outshopper, their level of perception, satisfaction and intention of repurchases are comparatively different from that of the local or domestic in shoppers. The study focused on selected shopping malls functioning in tier II cities of Tamil Nadu i.e., in Coimbatore, Madurai and Trichy.

1.5. Scope of the Study

Customer's orientation towards shopping may shed light into the way they indulge in shopping and it may also tell the reason why they choose a particular shopping malls. The present study covers some of the important aspects like finding out the outshopper's awareness, perception and level of shopping experience in shopping malls. Also the study focuses on the outshoppers' personality traits, level of satisfaction and their future loyalty towards shopping malls. This would be of great help to marketers in design the malls and set up retail outlets in a way so as to increase the shopping experiences of the customers and coping up with the expectations and needs of the mall customers.

1.6. Objectives of the Study

Detailed conceptual discussion and understanding reveals the importance of analyzing shopping experience and satisfaction of the outshoppers in shopping malls for effective conduct of this study following objectives are framed:

- To study the demographic and socio- economic status of outshoppers in Tamil Nadu.
- To measure the outshoppers level of awareness and perception of outshoppers towards shopping malls.
- To evaluate the level of shopping experience experienced by the outshoppers in malls.
- To critically evaluate the influences of shopping motives on the outshoppers buyer behaviour.

---

[13]Rupesh Kumar Tiwari and Anish Abraham, Understanding the Consumer Behavior towards Shopping Malls in Raipur City, International Journal of Management & Strategy , Vol. 1, No.1, 2010.

- To measures the level of satisfaction experienced by the outshoppers and their future loyalty towards shopping malls.

1.7.   Hypothesis of the Study

To draw empirical justification to the above stated objectives of the study, following hypotheses are framed:

- There exists close association between outshoppers' level of awareness about a shopping mall and their preference of visit to the malls.
- Outshoppers view about malls does not differ from one demographic and socio-economic segment of populations to others.
- There exists close association between impulsive/rational nature of consumers' and products brought by them in the shopping malls.
- There exists rational association between the gender of outshoppers and the products shopped at malls.
- There exists rational association between the age of outshoppers and the products shopped at malls.
- There exists rational association between the educational qualification of outshoppers and the products shopped at malls.
- There exists rational association between the occupational status of outshoppers and the products shopped at malls.
- There exists rational association between the monthly income of outshoppers and the products shopped at malls.
- There exists rational association between demographic and socio-economic status of the outshoppers and the primary reasons stated by them for visiting shopping malls.
- Primary reasons stated by the outshoppers' for visiting shopping mall greatly influence their perception towards it.
- There exist a great influence of shopping motives on the perception of outshoppers towards shopping malls.
- There exists wide gap between the reasons stated by the outshoppers for visiting the shopping malls and the level of satisfaction derived by them.
- Outshoppers' level of satisfaction experienced in the shopping mall to a greater extent determines their recommendation of shopping mall to others in future.

1.8. Research Methodology

The research methodology of the study consists of two stages. First stages of the research were explanatory in nature. This forms the desk research where the reviews of available secondary literature for the study were collected. This exploratory search forms the basis for preparing the questionnaire for the next stage. A descriptive research was carried out at the second stage. Descriptive study is a fact finding investigation with adequate interpretation. The growth and development of the tier II cities in Tamil Nadu have motivated the researcher to select the region for the field work. A well-structured questionnaire has been used as the data collection tool.

1.8.1. Rationality in Selection of Study Area

The mall culture is 50-60 years old across the world. It has just crept into India. Retailing in India is gradually inching its way toward electricity, cold chains and ports which has further led to become the next boom industry. Due to the shopping has altered in terms of format and to these constraints, retail chains have to resort to consumer buying behaviour, ushering in a revolution in multiple vendors for their requirements, thereby, shopping in India. Modern retail has entered India as seen in sprawling shopping centers, multi-storied malls and huge complexes offer shopping, entertainment and food all under one roof[14]. In this context, it can be rightly said that in India shopping malls are not only a shopping place but a place to rejuvenate, socialize and entertain. In big retail stores shoppers get everything under one roof from branded clothes, grocery, electronics to foot wear. Without a doubt malls have changed the shopping experience of Indians. Youth take this as a status symbol. Visiting malls and buying branded products satisfy their thirst for better quality of life. Teenagers do come to show off. Certainly shopping malls are bringing in a new culture in India which is different from the traditional culture as far as shopping is concerned. India offers an immense market opportunity for modern shopping mall, supported by increase in middle class income and changing lifestyle of middle class families[15]. The first shopping mall in India was set up in Tamil Nadu, the SpencerPlaza in Chennai established in 1991. It was then a seven floor

---

[14]V. Lakshmipathy and S. KareemullaBasha, Globalisation-Its Impact on Indian Retail Industry-Opportunities and Challenges, International Journal Of Marketing, Financial Services & Management Research, Vol. 1 No. 2, Pp. 89-95, 2012.

[15]Ramandeep Kaur, Growing Mall Culture in India–Changing Lifestyles, http://www.mapsofindia.com/my-india/india/growing-mall-culture-in-india-changing-lifestyles7thSeptember.

building with a mix of retail, office space and entertainment[16]. Since, then Delhi, Mumbai and Bangalore have received greater economic and social contributions from malls and now the establishments of shopping malls are more in the Tier-II cities like: Coimbatore, Kochi, Madurai, Thirchy, Pune, Nagpur, Aurangabad, and Vishakhapatnam etc[17]. Based on the above discussion Tamil Nadu is chosen as the study area.

1.8.2. *Malls Functioning in Tamil Nadu*

Tamil Nadu is the eleventh largest state in India by area and the sixth most populous state in India. The state was ranked sixth among states in India according to the Human Development Index in 2011. Tamil Nadu is the second largest state economy in India with 4789 billion (US$71 billion) in gross domestic product. The state has the highest number (10.56 per cent) of business enterprises and stands second in total employment (9.97 per cent) in India, compared to the population share of about 6 per cent. Tamil Nadu was ranked as the third most developed state in India based on a "Multidimensional Development Index" in a 2013 report published by a panel headed by current RBI (Reserve Bank of India) governor Raghuram Rajan[18].

Moreover, Tamil Nadu state was once an important business centre in the days of British rule in India and till now it is retaining its same position. Chennai is one of the best trade and business centers of South India where the newer commercial developments can be seen spreading up at a high speed. The most common developments coming up in most of the prime commercial areas of the Tami Nadu are the large, swanky shopping complexes. Thus, it can be rightly claimed that the shopping mall culture is fast gaining popularity in Tamil Nadu to keep up with the international demand of the customers who are looking for an altogether different shopping experience. The concepts of globalization and liberalization have become popular in the Indian markets and as a result there has been a flood of international brands in the top metros of India who are looking for trendy and well facilitated shopping centers to establish their business. It is because of this reason that shopping malls in Tamil Nadu are being planned in large scale to cope up with the increase in requirements of shopping and business centers[19].

---

[16]Chapter 3-Introduction to malls,
http://shodhganga.inflibnet.ac.in/bitstream/10603/7381/8/08_chapter%203.pdf..

[17]A. Mansurali, R. Swamynathan and Umesh Chandrasekhar, Mall Mania:A Study of Factors Influencing Consumers' Preference Towards Shopping Malls in Coimbatore City, The IUP Journal of Marketing Management, Vol. 12, No. 4, Pp. 29-41, 2014

[18]Tamil Nadu, https://en.wikipedia.org/wiki/Tamil_Nadu.

[19]Shopping Malls in Chennai,http://www.pacificacompanies.co.in/shopping_malls_in_chennai.html

Table 1.1(A): List of Shopping Malls Functioning in Tamil Nadu

Place	Name of the Mall	Location	Year of Establishment	Area
Chennai	Spencer Plaza	Anna Salai	1990	530000sq ft (49000m²)
	Abhirami Mega Mall	Purasawalkam	2003	-
	Chennai Citi Centre	Mylapore	2006	117,600 sq ft (10,930 m²)
	Alsa Mall	Egmore	1998	
	Ampa Skywalk	Aminijikarai	2009	650,000 sq ft (60,000 m²)
	Express Avenue	Whites Road, Royapettah	2010	900,000 sq ft (84,000 m²)
	Mayajaal	Kanathur, East Coast Road	2006	30000sq ft (2800m²)
	Chandra Mall	Arcot Road, Virugambakkam	2011	143130sq ft (13297m²)
	Coromandel Plaza	Navalur, OMR	2011	3000000sq ft (28000m²)
	Spectrum Mall	Paper Mills Road, Perambur	2011	160000sq ft (15000m²)
	Ramee Mall	Anna Salai, Teynampet	2012	225000sq ft (20900m²)
	Bergamo	Khader Nawaz Khan Road, Nugambakkam	2011	40000sq ft (3700m²)
	Ten Square Mall	Inner Ring Road, Koyambedu	2012	150000sq ft (14000m²)
	The Laurel Mall	GST Road, Chengalpattu	2012	152460sq ft (14164m²)
	Gold Souk Grande Mall	GST Road, Vandalur	2014	80000sq ft (74000m²)
	The Forum Vijaya	Arcot Road, Vadapalani	2013	636000sq ft (59100m²)
	Phoenix Market City	Velachery	2013	
	MARG Junction Mall	OMR	2015	1150000sq ft (107000m²)
	Singapore 2000	Paper Mills Road, Perambur	2000	-
	Skycity Mall	Marshalls Road, Egmore		-
	Marina Grand Mall	OMR, Sirusery	2012	540000sq ft (50000m²)
	The Grand Velachery	Velachery	2011	250000sq ft (23000m²)
	TVH Mall	Adyar	2012	500000sq ft (46000m²)
	Metrozone Mall	Anna Nagar (West)	2013	1250000sq ft (116000m²)

Source: https://en.wikipedia.org/wiki/List_of_shopping_malls_in_Tamil_Nadu

Table 1.1(B): List of Shopping Malls Functioning in Tamil Nadu

Place	Name of the Mall	Location	Year of Establishment	Area
Coimbatore	Brookefields Mall	Brooke Bond Road	2009	450000sq ft (42000m²)
	Fun Republic Mall	Avinashi Road, Peelamedu	2013	325000sq ft (30200m²)
	Velan Esplanade Mall	Kangayam Road, Tiurpur	2013	Under construction
	Tristar XO Mall (planned)	Peelamedu Airport Road	2014	Under construction
	TVH Kovai (under construction)	Singanallur	2014	Under construction
	Prozone Mall (planned)		2014	Under construction
	Grand Mall (under construction)	Nava India, Avinashi Road	2014	Under construction
	Mall of Joy		2015	Under construction
Madurai	Milan Mal	KK Nagar	2009	90000sq ft (8400m²)
	Vishaal de Mall	China Chockikulam	2012	230000sq ft (21000m²)
Trichy	Mangalam Towers (Vijay Cinemas)	Reynolds Road	2012	Under construction
	Rams Maris	Tiruchirappalli Cantonment	2015	Under construction
	Femina Shopping Mall	Cantonment Road	-	-
	Femina Hyper Mall	Thillai Nagar	2015	172000 sqft(16000m²)
	Jee Mall	Palpannai Road	2016	Under construction
	KGS Trirchy Mall (under construction)	Ramanathapuram Road, NH210	2014	Under construction
Erode	Tex Valley Mega Mall	Gangapuram	2014	1600000sq ft (150000m²)
	Reliance Hyper Mall (under construction)	Perundurai Road	2015	-
Tuticorin / Thoothukudi	DSF Plaza Mall	Victoria Extension Road	2008	-
	Velavan Hyper Mall	WGC Road	2014	-
Nagercoil	Rajas Mall	ChettikulamJn	2012	-
Tiruvannamalai	Vijaya Mall	By Pass Road, Gandhi Nagar	2014	40000 sq.ft
Viluppuram	MaghalakshmiPlaazaa	P.J.N. Road	2015	-

Source: https://en.wikipedia.org/wiki/List_of_shopping_malls_in_Tamil_Nadu

Out of the 46 malls registered in Tamil Nadu, only 30 malls are currently functioning successfully.

1.8.3. *Sampling Framework*

Two types sampling techniques were adopted for the effective conduct of this study. In the beginning stage of the study, for the identification of the geographical region and mall located in the Tamil Nadu clustered based stratified sample technique has been applied. For the collection of primary data from the sample population in the second stage of the study convenient sampling technique was applied to classify the cities located in Tamil Nadu and for identification of very successful and popular shopping malls functioning in Tamil Nadu.

As stated in the above Table 1.1 (A) and (B), there are 46 malls registered in Tamil Nadu, of which only 30 malls are currently functioning successfully. These 30 malls were considered as the sample malls for the effective conduct of this study. The malls operating in the tier II cities of Tamil Nadu were considered as the primary samples. For the identification of the tier II cities in Tamil Nadu, the major cities in Tamil Nadu are listed and ranked based on their population size, refer following Table: 1.2.

Table 1.2: Population Details

Rank	Name	District	Population 2011
1	Chennai	Chennai, Kanchipuram, Tiruvallur	8696010
2	Coimbatore	Coimbatore	2151466
3	Madurai	Madurai	1462420
4	Tiruchirappalli	Tiruchirappalli	1021717
5	Tiruppur	Tiruppur	962982
6	Salem	Salem	919150
7	Erode	Erode	521776
8	Tirunelveli	Tirunelveli	498984
9	Vellore	Vellore	481966
10	Thoothukkudi	Thoothukkudi	410760
11	Thanjavur	Thanjavur	222943
12	Dindigul	Dindigul	207327

Source: https://en.wikipedia.org/wiki/List_of_cities_in_Tamil_Nadu_by_population

Moreover, the Reserve Bank of India has classified the cities across India into 6 tiers cities[20] based on its population size and human index rating. The table below shows the classification.

Table 1.3: Classification of Cities (TIER WISE)

Population Classification	Population Size
Tier - 1	100,000 and above
Tier – 2	50,000 to 99,999
Tier – 3	20,000 to 49,999
Tier – 4	10,000 to 19,999
Tier – 5	5,000 to 9,999
Tier – 6	Less than 5000

Source:http://rbidocs.rbi.org.in/rdocs/content/pdfs/100MCA0711_5.pdf

---

[20] http://rbidocs.rbi.org.in/rdocs/content/pdfs/100MCA0711_5.pdf

Based on the above two table discussions (Table: 1.2 and 1.3) it has been observed that Coimbatore, Madurai and Trichy can be summarised as the prominent tier II in Tamil Nadu. Thus, these three cities are considered as sample geographical regions. Coimbatore is the second largest city and urban agglomeration in the state after Chennai city in Tamil Nadu[21]. Madurai is a major city and cultural headquarters in the state of Tamil Nadu in southern India. Madurai is the second largest corporation city by area and third largest city by population in Tamil Nadu[22]. Tiruchirappalli is one of the oldest inhabited cities in Tamil Nadu; its earliest settlements date back to the second millennium BC. Tiruchirappalli district lies at the center of Tamil Nadu[23].

In total Six malls are functioning in these three regions, i.e., Coimbatore has two shopping malls namely Brook Fields, Fun Republic Mall, Madurai has Vishall De Mall and Millaneum Mall and Trichy has two malls Femina shopping Mall and Femina Hyper mall.. Out of the six mall functioning in these three region, Femina Hyper mall had started functioning only in the mid of 2015, thus, this mall was not considered for sample data collection. The study focused on five mall only: Brook Fields, Fun Republic Mall, Vishall De Mall, Millaneum Mall and Femina shopping Mall.

In the second stage of the study convenience sampling technique was adopted. The date collection was divided into two stages, in the first stage a pilot study was carried with the help of well-structured questionnaire with a small sample size of 30 respondents in each city. Later the primary data required for the study was collected at the exit point of the shopping malls in the above mentioned cities. The purpose of research was clearly explained and those respondents who are willing to cooperate were only participated in the study. The structured self-administered questionnaire was collected by selecting 200 respondents from each city i.e., Coimbatore, Madurai and Trichy. Out of 600 questionnaire distributed nearly 35 questionnaire were found to be incomplete, these 35 questionnaires were deducted from actual sample and thus the study was confirmed to 565 respondents only. According to Orme. B (2010) [24]sample size for conjoint studies generally can ranges from about 150 to 1,200 respondents and it largely depends on the purpose of research. Conjoint analysis is a statistical technique used in Social Science (marketing, management and others) research to determine how people value different attributes (feature, function, benefits) that make up an individual product or service. Based on this concept, the sampling framework of the study is constructed.

---

[21]https://en.wikipedia.org/wiki/Coimbatore
[22] https://en.wikipedia.org/wiki/Madurai
[23] https://en.wikipedia.org/wiki/Tiruchirappalli
[24]B. Orme, Getting Started with Conjoint Analysis: Strategies for Product Design and Pricing Research, Second Edition, Madison, Wis.: Research Publishers LLC, 2010

1.8.4. Period of the Study

The study period of the researcher pertain to three years and four months i.e., September 2012 to December 2015. First six months of the study period was utilized in the desk research where the researcher collected relevant review of literatures pertaining to this study and also this time period was used for questionnaire framing. The second part of the study focused on the pilot survey and in the correction and modification of the questionnaire. Field survey for the primary data was conducted between December 2014 and July 2015. The researcher has made all possible efforts during the course of data collection. Rest of the time period is used for data analysis and in compilation of thesis chapters.

1.8.5. Data Sources

Data base of the study includes both primary and secondary data. Primary data were collected using a structured questionnaire. Firsthand information has been collected from the outshoppers directly. Discussions were held with knowledgeable persons who are experts in the field of Shopping Malls. The secondary data required for the study were collected from published research articles in reputed journals, published documents, thesis works and websites.

1.8.6. Data Validity and Reliability

Kaiser-Meyer-Olkin (KMO) was measured to test the sampling adequacy which ranges from 0 to 1. The reliability of an indicator can be defined as its overall quality of data, i.e. its consistency and its ability to give the same results in repeated measurement. The most outstanding feature of reliability is the test-retest correlation of the specific measure under scrutiny. Correspondingly, the test-retest correlation for most single-item measures is presented in the following table.

Table 1.4: Data Validity & Reliability Test

General Variables	Number of items	Range	Cronbach's Alpha
Outshoppers Level of Awareness about Various Shopping Malls	5	1-5	.865
Primary Reasons Stated by the Outshoppers for Shopping at Malls	15	1-15	.684
Outshoppers Opinion on Level of Influence of Cultural & Religious Festivals Sales Periods on Shopping Behaviour	3	1-5	.732
Outshoppers level of Perception towards Shopping Malls	10	1-5	.698
Outshoppers Shopping Motives at Malls	18	1-5	.764
Outshoppers Level of Satisfaction to Shopping Malls	15	1-5	.711
Overall Score for Sample Adequacy (Kaiser-Meyer-Olkin Measure of Sampling Adequacy)	.665		
Overall Score for Data Reliability (Cronbach's Alpha)	.742		

Source: Computed from Primary Data

The most widely used measure to assess the internal consistency of constructs is Cronbach's alpha. The generally agreed upon value of Cronbach's alpha is 0.70, although it may decrease to 0.60 in case of exploratory research (Hair et al. 2006; pp.137). In this research the reliability measure for the whole scale is 0.782 which is very much acceptable. Again the reliability for all the constructs is shown in Table 1.1; the values for all the constructs range between 0.684 - 0.865, which again fall under acceptable mark. Similarly, the value of KMO's sample adequacy was rated at 0.665. Hence, construct of both validity and reliability in this research is satisfactory. The result of Cronbach's alpha draws a significant amount of correlation between the variables tested. The validity of a test is the extent to which differences in scores reflect differences in the measured characteristic. Predictive validity is a measure of the usefulness of a measuring instrument as a predictor. Proof of predictive validity is determined by the correlation between results and actual behaviour. Construct validity is the extent to which a measuring instrument measures what it intends to measure.

1.9. Statistical Tools Applied

To analyse the data and draw inferences the following statistical tools were used. The statistical tools applied in the study are: Frequency Analysis, Weighted Arithmetic mean, Likerts's Summated scales, ANOVA, Chi-Sqaure, Independent 'Z' Test, Paired 'Z' Test, Multiple Regression Analysis, Discrimination Analysis, Rotation Factor Analysis and Reliability Analysis.

- The frequency distribution of the variables has helped the researcher to calculate distribution value of variables tested.

- Weighted arithmetic mean and Likert's Summated scales helped in interpreting the averages of the variable used in this study, like: Outshoppers level of awareness about various shopping malls, primary reasons stated by the outshoppers for shopping at malls, outshoppers opinion on level of influence of cultural & religious festivals sales periods on shopping behaviour, outshoppers level of perception towards shopping malls, outshoppers shopping motives at malls and outshoppers level of satisfaction to shopping malls.

- ANOVA test was applied to measure whether (i) there exists close association between outshoppers' level of awareness about a shopping mall and their preference of visit to the malls and (ii) there exists rational association between demographic and socio-economic status of the outshoppers and the primary reasons stated by them for visiting shopping malls.

- Chi-Square test was applied to measure whether (i) There exists no difference from one demographic and socio-economic segment of populations to others in the view point of outshoppers of the malls and (ii) there exists rational association between the demographic and socio-economic status of outshoppers and the products shopped at malls.

- Independent 'Z' test was applied to measure whether there exists close association between impulsive/rational nature of consumers' and products brought by them in the shopping malls.

- Paired 'Z' test was applied to measure whether there exists wide gap between the reasons stated by the outshoppers' for visiting the shopping malls and the level of satisfaction derived by them.

- Discriminant Function Analysis was applied to measure the outshoppers' level of satisfaction experienced in the shopping mall to a greater extent determines their recommendation of shopping mall to others in future.

- A set of two multiple regression analyses were constructed to measure whether the:
  - Primary reasons stated by the outshoppers' for shopping at mall greatly influence their perception towards it.
  - Shopping motives of outshoppers' greatly influence their perception towards shopping malls.

- Rotation factor analysis with Kaiser-Meyer-Oklin (KMO) test and Reliability analysis were applied to establish and reveal the correlation between the (i) shopping motives and shopping malls selected by the outshoppers and (ii) outshoppers' level of satisfaction and the shopping malls they had visited.

1.10. Limitation of the Study

The study area is confined to Tier II cities of Tamil Nadu namely Coimbatore, Trichy, Madurai. Hence the study is subjected to geographical limitation since the shopping malls functioning in Tamil Nadu may not represent the features and functioning in other geographic regions across South India or across India.

Yet another limitation is that this study, also suffers unclear information furnished by the sample respondents for certain queries raised by the researcher which may be subjected to bias, which may in turn affect the study findings and conclusions drawn.

1.11. Chapter Organisation Scheme

The framework of this research work has been structured to gain insights into the above purpose and thus includes five chapters, namely the Introduction and Literature Review, Research Design, Theoretical discussion, Analysis and Discussion, Summary, Findings, Suggestions, Conclusion, and Future Research Scope for the Study. The thesis of the study is organized into five major chapters. A brief outline of chapter is discussed below.

Chapter I: The introductory chapter deals with the: introduction, statement of problem, rationality of the study, conceptual framework of the study, scope of the study, objectives of the study, hypotheses of the study, research methodology, study area, statistical tools applied, limitation of the study and chapter organisation scheme.

Chapter II: The second chapter of the study focuses on the reviews of the relevant literature of studies in this field carried out by various researchers in the past.

Chapter III: The third chapter focuses on the growth of retailing business in India and mall culture among consumers.

Chapter IV: The fourth chapter deals with analysis and interpretation of data collected from the study region.

Chapter V: The final and fifth chapter summarises the findings of the study, suggestions and conclusions of the study.

CHAPTER II

REVIEW OF LITERATURE

2.1. Introduction

The review of literature guides the researcher for getting better understanding of methodology used, limitations of various available estimation procedures, data base, lucid interpretation and reconciliation of the conflicting results. Besides this, the reviews of earlier studies explore the avenues for present and future research related to the subject matter. The researcher of this study had understood that in the past both at national and international level intensive efforts has been made to find the relevant studies on consumer behaviour of migrants shopping habits (outshopping) in shopping mall .However, only a limited study is available in this field especially in India. A summary of literature reviewed is reported here.

2.2. Consumer Behaviour

Consumer behaviour is a complex, dynamic, multidimensional process, and all marketing decisions are based on assumptions about consumer behaviour. Consumer behaviour can be defined as "the decision-making process and physical activity involved in acquiring, evaluating, using and disposing of goods and services[1]. Few reviews on various dimensions of consumers buying behaviour is discussed in this segment of the study.

Gupta (2006)[2] study aimed to examine the extent to which different promotional measures attract shoppers' towards product and service to make a positive buying decision. The study also aimed to establish the existing difference between discount and non–discount category, seasonal sales and non–seasonal sales and coupons and non–coupons, sales promotion schemes. The study finding indicated that general characteristics, physical characteristics and location conveniences are primarily considered by the shoppers, however it was found that there exists no significance between the two groups of membership discounts and non–memberships discounts offered by the retailers to the shoppers.

---

[1]S.L. Gupta and Sumitra Pal, Consumer Behaviour–An Indian Perspective, Sultan Chand and Sons, New Delhi, First Edition, 2000.

[2]S.L. Gupta, An Exploratory Research on Promotional Strategies and its Relation with Attributes of Stores as Perceived by Consumers in a ShoPP.ing Mall, PCTE Journal of Business Management, Vol. 3, No. 2, Pp. 8–17, 2006.

Rajaguru and Matanda (2006)[3] research study aimed to study the consumers' perception of store, product attributes in relation with customer loyalty in Indian context. The study found that product attribute and store attributes have positive effects on customer loyalty. Store attributes such as service quality, convenience of store and product attributes such as product quality, price and availability of new products, show significance relation towards customer loyalty.

Sakkthivel. A.M (2007)[4] study aimed to analyse critically the strategic placement of organised retail formats in potential markets. The study covered different retail formats and their locations for reaching the target market. The study found that the majority of the new retail formats are concentrated in tier I cities, the new retail formats are increasingly expanding their operations in tier II and smaller cities also. The result of the study also revealed that categorization of potential markets and mapping of the retail formats are key success factors for the growth of organised retail formats in India.

VenkataRatnam.C.S. (2007)[5] study aimed to study the detail changing consumer behavior in retail trade in India and China The author inferred that sustained and rapid growth of China and India, which together provided home to over a fifth of the humanity, are creating a tremendous surge in consumerism on a scale which is unprecedented. Both the countries are attractive destinations for investment and production as well as sales and marketing. Yet, EIU Survey on corporate priorities for 2007 and beyond suggest that more than a quarter of the CEOs believe that lack of customer insight is a barrier to growth in the emerging economies: The study found that in the developed markets, executives point to high labour costs and saturated markets as the critical challenges, innovation is a priority – respondents primarily look to drive revenue growth by selling new products to existing customers. Also in emerging markets, by contrast, the headaches are quite different such as labour costs are low and markets are largely untapped. Executives are focused instead on managing shortages of local talent and plan to grow mainly by selling existing products to new customers.

---

[3]Rajesh Rajaguru and Margaret J.Matanda, A Study on Consumer Perception of Store and Product Attributes and its Effect on Customer Loyalty within the Indian Retail Sector, Conference, Queensland University of Technology, Pp. 4–6, 2006.

[4]A.M. Sakkthivel, Strategic Placement of Organised Retail Formats in Potential Markets– A Critical Analysis, Indian Retail Review Vol. 1, No. 1, 2007.

[5]C.S. Venkata Ratnam, A study on Changing Consumer Behaviour and Emerging challenges to the Retail Trade In India, Indian Retail Review, Vol. 1, No. 1, 2007.

Mujahid Mohiuddin Babu and Md. Mohiuddin (2008)[6] study aimed to assess the influence of marketing program on customer purchasing behaviour and brand preference. The study found that customer are influenced by the companies' cause related marketing programs while adopting a new brand. During purchase the customers prefer to support generally health and life saving issues.

Pathak. S.V and Aditya (2009)[7] study aimed to find out the factors that affect the buyers decision among modern retail formats and to evaluate the comparative strength of these factors in buying decision of the buyers. The study found that Indian customer are more sensitive to quality, customer service and are still family driven entities. Further the study states that "retailers understanding the customers" is just like climbing the greased pole, so they need to be vigilant.

Tiwari R.K and Abraham.A (2010)[8] research study aimed to evaluate the various shopping dimensional required to offer the targeted consumer in terms of product activity and performance. The study revealed that consumers see malls as a one shop destination for various purpose like dinning, watching movies, hanging out, meeting new/old friends. The shopping aesthetics were valued high by customers in Raipur and item related to aesthetic like interior design, decor and lighting in the malls have received high acceptance from the respondents. The study found that customers in Raipur gave high acceptance to dimensions like exploration and convenience. The young customers in Raipur City were attracted towards mall than their older counterparts.

Baltas. et.al (2010)[9] aimed to study the customer's patronage in multiple stores. The study found the customers who spend heavily and multi-member households tend to disperse supermarket patronage. The heavy grocery spenders and large families adopt shopping patterns which maximizes the value for money. The study also states that the large households shop for heterogeneous product needs of their members. The multi-store patronage may be

---

[6]Mujahid Mohiuddin Babu and Md. Mihiuddin, Cause Related Marketing and Its Impact on the Purchasing Behaviour of the Customers of Bangladesh: An Empirical Study, AIUB Business and Economics Working Paper Series American International University-Bangladesh (AIUB), 2008.

[7]S.V. Pathak and Aditya P. Tripathi, Customer Shopping Behaviors among Modern Retail Formats: A study of Delhi and NCR, Indian Journal of Marketing, Vol. 24, No. 2, 2009.

[8]R.K. Tiwari and A. Abraham, Understanding the consumer behaviour towards shopping malls in Raipur city, International Journal of Management and Strategy, Vol. 1, No. 1, 2010.

[9]Argouslidis Baltas and Skarmeas, The Role of customer Factors in Multiple Store patronage:A Cost Benefit Approach, Journal of Retailing, Vol. 86, No.1, Pp. 37-50, 2010.

suitable for large families and heavy grocery spenders and further retail managers can still try to increase their loyalty.

Shivakumar R. Sharma(2012)[10] study aims to analyze the buying behaviour of Mumbai consumers   in India's retail scenario The study assessed the overall customer satisfaction, response of customers with regard to the availability and quality of products and services offered at shopping malls. The study found that the main factors influencing the customer to shop in the shopping malls are income, frequency of visit, occasion and customer attitude is positive towards shopping in malls.

PandyaAmit and Kameshvari J (2012)[11] aimed to study the consumer behavior, perceptions, motivation and demographic factors of respondents in organised and un organised retail outlets. The study found that majority of the respondents preferred to go to un organised retail outlets for buying staples items like fruits, vegetable etc. They prefer organised retail outlets for packaged food, cosmetics and household cleaning products and spend more for it. In case of food grains and cooking oil respondents preferred both organised and unorganised retail outlets.

Sangeeta Mohanty (2012)[12] study focused on the consumers' attitude towards nearby market, big bazaars and shopping malls in relation to age, education and income. The study explored the reasons for consumers patronizing a store and their preference towards shopping malls. The study found that in order to get a realistic perspective on retailing, it is necessary to comprehend how Indian consumer behaviour is changing; and to understand how retail formats are likely to evolve in a country.

Arun Kumar Singh and Agarwal.P.K (2012)[13] study aimes to explore the changes in Indian traditional retailing structure and consumption behavior of the consumers. The study found that increase in literacy, exposure to media, greater availability and penetration of a

---

[10]Shivakumar R. Sharma, Customer Attitude Towards Shopping Malls in Mumbai, International Journal of Trade and Commerce-IIARTC, Vol. 1, No. 2, Pp. 269-280, 2012.

[11]R. Pandyya Amit and J. Bariya Kameshvari, A Study on Consumer Behaviour of Organised and Unorganised Retail Outlets in Vadodara City, International Journal of Engineering and Management Science, Vol. 3, No.4, Pp. 466-474, 2010.

[12]Sangeeta Mohanty, Drivers of Retail Shopping: An Exploratory Study, International Journal of Scientific and Research Publications, Vol. 2, No. 3, Pp. 1-6, 2012.

[13]Arun Kumar Singh and P.K. Agarwal, A Study on Shifting Consumer Preferences from Un-organised Retailing Vis-aVis to Organised Retailing in Noida, Bookman International Journal of Accounts, Economics and Business Management, Vol. 1, No. 2, Pp. 69-79, 2012.

variety of consumer goods into the interiors of the country, have all resulted in narrowing down the spending differences between the consumers of larger metros and those of smaller towns. The study also stated that the malls must concentrate on attractive offers, fixed prices, customer loyalty program to attract the customers to visit organised retailing including malls.

Mohd.Nadeem Abbas (2012)[14] study aimed to find out the impact of recession on the buying behaviour of consumers during recessionary times. The result of the study revealed that   hypermarkets, supermarkets witness a greater change in shopping behaviour than the Kirana stores. They ascertained that the customers who shop frequently are more likely to respond to discounts vis-à-vis others and that the customers who shop frequently are more likely to spend a higher amount for shopping. The study found that shopping or luxury items faces more fluctuations than regular shopping items, which indicates that customers shopping for luxury items may be postponed in times of recession but they continue to shop for regular items.

Bulakanti and Srinivas (2013)[15] study examined the factors which influence the consumers to buy in organised and unorganised retail stores in Kakinada city. The study revealed that the retail consumers' attitude force them to have diversified patterns of purchase at various buying spots. The study found that situation makes the retailers more vigilant about adopting consumer-friendly marketing strategies in terms of selling the best quality products and services continuously to the consumers.

Girish and Harish (2013)[16] study made an attempt to analyse the customers perception towards service quality variables in organised retail outlets. The study revealed that perception of service quality is influenced by the natures of the customers. The general factors like personal interaction, physical aspects are the dimensions on which influence the consumer perception. The study found that retail outlets have to frame their own strategies in order to attract the customers on a longer basis.

---

[14]Mohd.Nadeem Abbas , Consumer Behaviour in India – Post Recession Scenario, International Journal of Scientific and Engineering Research Vol. 3, No. 12, Pp. 1-7, 2012.

[15]Bulakanti and Romala Vijaya Srinivas, The Most Influential Factors of Consumers Buying Pattern At Organised And Unorganised Retail Stores With Special Reference To Kakinada City, Andhra Pradesh, Indian Journal of Marketing, Vol. 43, No. 1, Pp. 14 -23, 2013.

[16]Girish K Nair and Harish K Nair, An Analysis on Customer Perception towards Service Quality Variables in Selected Organised Retail Outlets, International Journal of Management and Social Sciences Research, Vol. 2, No. 1, Pp. 56-61, 2013.

Dipin Mathur.et.al(2013)[17] research study highlighted the factors that influence consumer buying behaviour in modern retail mall and conventional store The study made a comparative analysis of modern retail format and conventional retail store. The study found that consumer shopping behaviour is influenced by the factors like shopping habits, intention, attitude and perception of the consumers towards modern retail outlet and conventional stores.

Nandhini Devi. G et.al.,(2013)[18] studied the shopping behaviour in Indian context and stated that in the present competitive era, it is imperative for the retailers to understand the behaviour of the consumers which is highly dynamic in nature. The study found that diverse culture and the changing economies of countries are reasons for varying shopping behaviour of consumers in various countries.

Tyagi and Pandey.s (2014)[19] research paper aimed to identify the factors affecting consumer buying behaviour towards FMCG products and finally effecting their decision is making process.The study findings revealed that the consumer behaviour is largely effected by place, product, price, promotion, physiological and pshycological factors. However effect of these factors also differs from product to product.

Vyas and Siddiqui (2015)[20] study aimed to examine the effects of demographic variables on consumer buying behaviour towards household commodities, the study area is Chattisgarh. The study found that consumers in the state are matured buyer but are not exposed to organised retailing. Since strategies to boost up sales in store is directly or indirectly targeting demographic aspects of consumer, investigating its effect will open doors of future strategy planning. Demographics variables such as socio-economic strata, age and decision making criteria and dwelling location of consumer are considered as independent variable and consumer behaviour is considered as dependent variable. The effects of independent variables

---

[17]Dipin Mathur, Apeksha Jain and Manoj Kumar Sharma, Analysis Of Factors Influencing Consumer Buying Behaviour In Modern As Well As Conventional Retail Stores, International Journal of Innovative Research and Development, Vol. 2, No. 6, Pp. 409-415, 2013.

[18]G. Nandhini Devi, S. Sankaranarayana and Deepak Ashokkumar, Consumers' Shopping Behaviour of Convenience Goods in Organised Retail Stores, Asia Pacific Journal of Marketing and Management Review, Vol. 2, No.2, Pp. 87-95, 2013.

[19]Vibhuti, Ajay Kumar Tyagi and Vivek Pandey, A Case Study on Consumer Buying Behaviour towards Selected FMCG Products, InternationalJournal of scientific research and management, Vol. 2, No. 8, Pp. 1168-1182, 2014.

[20]Jay Kumar Dewangan, Dr.J.H. Vyas and Imran Nadeem Siddiqui, Effects of Demographic Variables on Consumer Buying Behaviour: With Reference To Purchase of Household Commodities from Organised Retail Stores in Chhattisgarh, India, Global Journal of Multidisciplinary Studies, Vol. 4, No. 9, 2014.

on dependent variable are calculated using Multivariate linear regression analysis. The results show that age and gender of respondent is insignificant in relationship with consumer behaviour.

2.3. Shoppers Attitude, Preferences and Satisfaction towards Shopping Malls

Shopping in India is usually a family event. Simple observation makes this clear; India is one of the countries least likely to jump on the 'mall culture' bandwagon. The desire to shop with family members seems to outweigh the international trend to social-shop and browse fashion outlets with friends. It's not uncommon to ask for family or friend's recommendations for purchases before making a purchasing decision[21]. Few reviews of yester year studies on shoppers' attitude, preferences and satisfaction towards shopping malls are discussed in this sub-section of the study.

Robert G.V. Barker (2000)[22] study is based on the relationship between trips to shopping mall and planned shopping centre relates the retail trading hour boundaries. The study states that the dynamic aggregate shopping model clearly depicts that the trading time is main constraints for the consumer shopping behaviour and also facilitates that the major innovations in the shopping mall can be the opportunities to view regular consumer behaviour by trading boundaries.

Sherman et al. (2001)[23] study aimed to analyse the factors that influence the shopping practices among new age elders. The study findings revealed that new-age elderly consumers tend to be more optimistic about their financial situations than their traditional elderly counterparts. Further, the study observed that older new-age women (as compared to older men) seem to be more price-conscious and responsive to retail specials and incentives, as well as more adventurous. They also generally possess more market-relevant knowledge in the form of shopping smarts.

---

[21]Differences between American and Indian Shopping Habits, http://www.americanpunjabanpi.com/2014/04/differences -between-american-and-indian.html, 8th April.2014.

[22] Robert G.V. Barker, Towards a dynamic aggregate shopping model and its application to Retail Trading hours and market area analysis, papers in Regional Science, Vol. 79, No. 4, Pp. 413-434, 2004.

[23]Sherman, Elaine, Leon G. Schiffman and Anil Mathur, The Influence of Gender on the New-Age Elderly's Consumption Orientation, Psychology and Marketing, Vol.18, No. 10, Pp. 1073-1089, 2001.

Melody L. Adkins Lehew.et.al., (2002)[24] study investigated the feasibility of the customers loyalty towards enclosed shopping malls and their assessment of mall characteristics to provide a better understanding of those attributes which influence such loyalty. The study found that the attributes such as price, tenants, store, merchandise, mall facilities, atmosphere and location are considered to find out the feasibility of the customers loyalty. The feasible strategy is possible through careful planning of tenant mix with the right assortment of stores, selling products at reasonable price and quality levels are valued by the customer.

Stephen Parket.Ret.al., (2003)[25] in his study compared consumers perception with four critical determinants of the retailers total product offering such as product, physical, price and service. The study included that pertaining to the physical environment outlets stores and regarding the services, there is no significant difference found with regard to the service of department stores compared to outlet stores.

Pancholi.R et.al.,(2004)[26] study aimed to analyse the behaviour of consumer while visiting and purchasing in newly opened malls. The study explored the purpose, motive and value of Indian consumers visiting malls, and their impulse purchase, time and money spend in the mall. The study found that malls should be design in such a way that in future new and innovative aspects can be added to it which will delight the consumer. Successful malls are those that will adjust its mall culture with the consumer sensitiveness and preferences. Managing consumer attitude and innovation are the keys to stay afloat amid competition.

Janson Sit and Bil Mersiley(2005)[27] study aims to understand the shoppers satisfaction with entertainment consumption with five key constructs namely hedonic motives, functional evaluation, affective evaluation, overall satisfaction and behavioural loyalty. The study reported that the primary focus of hedonic consumption is on affective experiences, which are

---

[24] Melody L. Adkins Lehew, Brigetter Burgers and Scarlet Wesley, Expanding The loyalty concept to include preference for a Shopping Mall, The International Review of Retail Distribution and Consumer Research, Vol. 12, No. 3, Pp. 225-236, 2002.

[25] R. Stephen Parket, Charles Pettijohn, linda Petti John and John Kent, Study on An analysis of consumer perception: Factory outlet Malls versus Traditional Departmental Stores, The Marketing Management Journal, Vol. 13, No. 2, Pp. 29-44, 2003.

[26] R. Pancholi, P.K. Sinha, A Banerjee, E.S. Millam and F. Howard, Study on Emergence of Mall Culture in India, International Journal of Retail and Distribution Management, Vol. 32, No 10, Pp. 482-494, 2004.

[27] Janson Sit and BilMersiley, Understanding satisfaction Formation of Shopping Mall Entertainment seekers: A conceptual Model, proceedings of ANZMAC conference: Retailing, Distribution Channels and Supply Chain Management, 2005.

likely to be influenced by functional attributes relative to entertainment consumption. This is consistent with environmental psychology theory. The study found that the impact of hedonic motive on overall satisfaction will be mediated by both functional and affective evaluation. Overall satisfaction of entertainment seekers should result in positive behavioural loyalty.

Tammie-Frost Norton (2005)[28] study revealed that the research turnaround time, client service facilities of the mall and the quality of the service provide better scope for small business. The study observed that the present business will come up with the changing trend in customers as well as marketing environment.

Johan Anselnisson (2006)[29] study explores the factors which are important determinants of consumer satisfaction, investigates the relative effect of the determinants and compare the source of customer satisfaction and visit frequency at shopping malls among the customer segments based on age and gender. The study found that determinants such as atmosphere, convenience, sales people, refreshment, location, promotional activities and merchandising policy governs the customer satisfaction level and the results show that location of the mall is more important than all the other aspects and it has a direct effect towards overall satisfaction for explaining the visit frequency.

Gupta and Kaur (2006)[30] study aimed to study the different promotional frames which attracted shoppers' towards the product which causes the positive buying decision. The study stated that retail location of a store and the distance that the customers must travel to shop are basic criteria in their store choice decisions and the customers consider price discounts as an important promotional tool in the malls. The study found that seasonal sales have a positive effect on the partronage, also the stores using advertising, promotions, seasonal sale and private labels on a particular category of products had caused people to perceive the benefit of buying a product at one store to be higher than it is.

Asif Zameer (2007)[31]study has discussed the need of the malls to differentiate themselves is a sure way of emerging winner and this positioning is ensured through mall management.

---

[28] Tammie - Frost Norton, study on The future of Mall: Current Trends affecting the future of Market Research in Malls, Journal of Consumer Behaviour, Vol. 4, Pp. 229-301, 2005.

[29] Johan Anselnisson, study on Source of Customer Satisfaction with Shopping Malls. A comparative study of different customer segments, The International Review of Retail Distribution and consumer research. Vol. 16, No. I, Pp. 381-403, 2006.

[30]S.L. Gupta and Tripat Kaur, The Framing of Promotional Strategies and its Relation with Attributes of Stores as Perceived by Shoppers in a Shopping Mall, Amity Business Review, Vol. 7, Pp. 24–32, 2006.

[31]Asif Zameer, Study on Management of Events / Promotions at DLF City Center Mall, Gurgaon, Indian Retail Review, Vol. 1, No. 1, 2006.

The study reveals that right from the tenant mix, ensuring the creation of right ambience, cleanliness that creates customer satisfaction, managing various income-streams for the developer, the role of mall-management is complex and dynamic. The study states that the mall management has emerged as the single most differentiating factor in today's scenario where the numbers of malls are multiplying and one of the key functions of mall-management is event management.

Ms. Shelja Jose Kuruvilla (2007)[32] study attempts to understand patterns and reasons for switching shopping habits of the consumers. The study revealed that the size of retail industry in India is about \$350 billion and is expected to grow at 13 per cent per annum. Organised retailing is only 2-3per cent at present, but it is projected to grow at more than 30 per cent p.a. and it is also estimated to reach an astounding INR 1000 billion by 2010. The study stated that rising income level, young population with high disposable income, availability of brands and merchandise, media proliferation, the impact of globalization, saturation in international markets, positive indicators of the economy and the changing mindset of the consumers are the major drivers quoted behind this retail boom.

Gursharan Singh Kainth and Divakar Joshi (2008)[33] research work tried to learn about people's knowledge, beliefs, preferences and satisfaction of customers towards shopping malls in Jaladhar in Punjab. The study found that most of the consumers were satisfied with the prices of products and services. The consumers agreed that professional mall management and wide range of cheaper products have persuaded them to spend more time and money at mall.

Manoj K Trivedi (2008)[34] study discusses the impact of fast approaching retail boom scenario on the Indian traditional retail outlets with positive and negative impact. The study found that the organised sector poses a cut-throat competition for the kiranas the fact still remains that India being a country with diversified social classes there is a scope for both to survive. The emergence of a developed retail sector will pose a competition rather than a threat to the traditional stores which would help these stores change their outlook and ways of working.

---

[32]Shelja Jose Kuruvilla, Study on Malls Vs Kiranas- Challenges and Strategic options, A paper published in Research Conference at Gurukul University, Haridwar, 2007.

[33]Gursharan Singh Kainth and Divakar Joshi, study on The Perception of Customer and Retailers towards Malls in Jaladhar in Punjab, 2008.

[34]Manoj K Trivedi(2008), From Traditional Markets to Shopping Malls- A paradigm shift Published in www.indianmba.com/FC745/fc745.html

Shelja Jose Kuruvilla and J. Ganguli(2008)[35] study attempted to understand the analytical and financial steps for setting up a shopping mall. The study found that the adequate finance, good location, good consumer research and right tenant mix can make the mall management and effective customer service an also paves away for its success in India"

Chung YimYien, et.al (2008)[36] study explores the relationship among shop size (space allocation) tenant type (tenant placement) and location of shop in the shopping mall. The study found that both space allocation and tenant placement strategies have employed in the most non-impulsive trade and the shops were found in upper stores and the shop size significantly affects the profitability of the shops.

Shelja Jose Kuruvilla (2008)[37]study aimed to understand the challenges faced by mall management in fulfilling the HR function when areas as cleaning and security have been contracted out. The study concluded that malls in India literally have a blank sheet of paper on which to create a new HR function. In order to design this new function, it will be important to understand what is critical to the successful operation of a mall and use this information to the mall's approach to HR.,

Amit Singla and Anil Kumar Goyal (2009)[38] research study discussed the growth drivers of retail industry, investment opportunities in different sectors of retailing. After analyzing the retail industry, study found that the organised retail has opportunities to grow in India in spite of the kirana stores. The organised retail is attracting more and more Indian as well as foreign players of the retail industry. The study states that a major portion of the organised retail will be developed in small cities and towns, this opportunity has not been encased by kirana stores and they are unable to meet the requirements of the customers.

Rajagopal(2009)[39] study aimed to examine the impact of growing congestion of shopping malls in urban areas on shopping convenience and it also study the cognitive attributes of the shopper towards attractiveness of the shopping malls and intensity of shopping. The study reveals that long tern customer values are associated with shoppingin malls while customer

[35]Shelja Jose Kuruvilla and J. Ganguli, study on Mall development and operations, an Indian perspective, Journal of Retail and housing property, Vol. 7, No. 3, Pp. 204-215, 2008.

[36]Chung YimYien, Y.S. Sherry and N.G. Hing Cheong, Space Allocation and tenant placement at high rise shoPP.ing malls, Journal of Retail and Leisure Property, Vol. 7, No. 4, Pp. 315-324, 2008.

[37]Ms. Shelja Jose Kuruvilla, study on The River side Mall–A Case Study, Synthesis, Vol. 4, No. 2, 2008.

[38]Amit Singla and Anil Kumar Goyal(2009), study on The Retail Industry: From Myth to Malls published in www.indianmba.com/FC538/fc538.html

[39]Rajagopal, Growing Shopping Malls and Behaviour of Urban Shoppers, Journal of Retail and Leisure property Vol. 18, No. 2, Pp. 99-118, 2009.

may derive short term comparative gains over price and newness of products by shopping in traditional market surrounding large malls. The study concluded that cognitive factors among consumers in brand switching include product, attractiveness, low price, user friendly technology and easy product servicing policies of small retail outlets outside the shopping malls. The ambience of shopping, assortment of stores, sales promotion and comparative economic gains in the malls attract specific higher customer traffic to the mall.

Zairenl N. Mura and Michael Pitt (2009)[40] study revealed the delivering facilities management service to the shopping centers requires particular skills and systems which meets the needs of a public access facility. The study states that maintaining critical service that affect public safety and cost in a volatile retail environment provide a constant success of the shopping enters.

Rajesh Iyer and Jaequeline K. Eastman(2010)[41] study aimed to study the four factors namely price conscious, attitude towards shopping, variety seekers and comparison of shopping by consumers in the shopping malls. The study found that shoppers who are fashion conscious will have a positive attitude towards shopping and they are price conscious too. The study found the mall shopper are variety seekers and also engage in comparison of shopping in different place with shopping malls.

Hardviner Singhet.al.,(2010)[42] study focused on the financial infra-structure of the Indian shopping malls. The study found that the future financial growth of the shopping malls highly depend on the government and more over transparency, accountability and customers orientation and the driving factors for the sustainability of the Indian shopping malls in near future.

Devgan and Kaur (2010)[43] study aimed to analyse six factors, upon whose adaptability the success of any shopping mall would largely depend. The factors are value for money, customer delight, information security, credibility, and store charisma and product excellence. The authors explicated that the modern day customers lay more emphasis on value for money; however, almost equal weightage is given to comfort and enjoyment while shopping from

---

[40]Zairenl N. Mura and Michael Pitt, study on Defining Facilities Management Service Delivery in UK Shopping Centres, Journal of Retail and Leisure Property, Vol. 8, No. 3, Pp. 193-205, 2009.

[41] Rajesh Iyer and Jaequeline K. Eastman, study on The Fashion conscious Mall Shoppers–An Exploratory Study, The Marketing Management Journal, Vol. 20, No. 2, Pp. 42-53, 2010.

[42]Hardviner Singh, Swapna Kumar Bose and Vinia Sahay, Management of Indian Shopping Malls: Impact of the patterns of Financing, Journal of Retail and Leisure Property, Vol. 9, No. 1, Pp. 55-64, 2010.

[43]Deepak Devgan, and Kaur, Mandeep, Shopping Malls in India: Factors affecting Indian Customers' Perceptions, South Asian Journal of Management, Vol. 17, No. 2, Pp. 29–42, 2010.

malls. Also the study stated that customers also care for factors like personal information security and payment security, hence they wish to buy from only that shopping mall which is more reliable from these perspectives.

Swaroop and Prakash (2010)[44] study investigates the consumer decision making styles in mall and it also takes into account the different demographic variables which influence the consumer decision making style. The study states that six factors which influence buying behavior are price, quality, recreation, choice, novelty and variety seeking. The people who are living single are more price conscious than married consumers, Indian consumers aged between 11-20 years prefer recreational aspect in shopping.

Rupesh and Anish 2010)[45] study aimed to investigate the consumer behaviour towards the shopping malls, in Raipur city. The study also tried to facilitate the mall developers, managers, marketers and operators with the perfect blend of necessary acumen in terms of various shopping dimensions required to offer the targeted customers so as to operationalize the mall with utmost productivity and performance. The study found that the mall should have convenience to travel, attractive product merchandises, scores of entertainment bundled with modern, more sophisticated atmospherics and facilities to lure the target customers.

Zhang et.al.,(2011)[46] research paper tried to identify the hedonic shopping values and utilitarian shopping experience and shopping behaviour of shoppers in malls of China. The study found that Chinese consumers are more likely to place greater value on hedonic than on utilitarian experience. The study also indicate that shopping mall atmosphere shapes consumers perception on merchandise, value which in turn influence consumers emotional responses (pleasure and arousal) shopping values (utilitarian and hedonic) and approach behaviour.

Andrew Newmanet.al., (2011)[47] research study examines how consumer buying behaviour in shoppingmalls can be enhanced or improved by exposing shoppers to

---

[44]Swaroop Chandra Sahoo and Prakash Chandra Dash, Consumers decision making style in Shopping Malls – A Empirical study in the Indian Context Indian Journal of Marketing, Vol. 40, Pp. 25-30, 2008.

[45]Rupesh Kumar Tiwari and Anish Abraham, study on Understanding the Consumer Behaviour TowardsShoPP.ing Malls in Raipur City, International Journal of Management and Strategy, Vol. 1, No, 1, Pp. 1-14, 2010.

[46] Zhang, Yan, Chaipoopirutana, Combs Sission and Howard, The influence of the Mall Environment on shoPP.ers value and consumer behaviour in China proceedings of ASBBS Annual Conference:Las Vegas, Vol. 18, No. 1, Pp. 214-224, 2011.

[47]Andrew Newman, Charles Dennis, Len-tiu Wright and Tamira King, study on Shoppers Experience of Digital Signage Cross National Quality Study, International Journal of Digital Content Technology and its Application, Vol. 4, No. 7, Pp. 50-57, 2011.

environmental atmospheric stimuli and draws its inspiration from marketing and environmental psychology. The study found that digital signage screens containing useful information, pleasant scenes and sounds can act as enhances to consumers and also it has taken the form of a wide ranging exploration across types of mall and shoppers.

Mayyer (2012)[48] study aimed to analyse the financial and economic impact of shopping malls on unorganised retail outlet and explore attitude, perception and opinions of customer to identify challenges and threats of retailers. The study found that negative impact of shopping malls on the sample shops can be seen in the form of decline in sales, profit and no of customers. The study advocates the balanced approach to retail and suggest that the government, organised retailer, unorganised retailers should play a constructive role in building a common platform for the co-existence of both organised and unorganised retailer.

Devadas and Manohar(2012)[49] study aimed to study the shopping values and mall attributed in relation to consumer age and gender. The study revealed that consumers across age groups placed entertainment factor as the prime attribute. The hedonism and utilitarianism values have a positive relationship with the various mall attributes. The study found that mall developers can focus on the various hedonistic values such as aesthetics, flow, exploration and utilitarianism values such as value products, safety and convenience as they clearly have an effect on the consumers' attitudes towards shopping.

Ritu Srivastava(2012)[50] study aimed to identified the primary reasons and motivations for Indian customers to visit malls and analyzing the influence of demographic variables of age, education, income and gender on the identified customer motivations to visit malls that could affect mall patronage and segmentation. The study found that people in India visit malls for diversion/browsing, economic reasons, shopping environment, refreshments and snacking, services and social experience, etc. Of the select demographic factors only age shows a significant effect on shopping motivations in malls in India.

Mullick N.H. (2013)[51]research study focused on the implications of mall development and to suggest strategies for better positioning of malls. The study found that the mall developer

---

[48]Sureshramam Mayyer, study on the study on Impact of Shopping Malls on the unorganised retail sector: A case study of Mangalore Region, Indian Journal of Marketing, Vol.42, No. 9, 2012.

[49]AnuradhaDevadas and Hansa Lysander Manohar, Study on A Cross Sectional Study on ShoPP.ing Values and Mall Attributes in Relation to Consumer Age and Gender, European Journal of Social Sciences, Vol. 31, No. 1, Pp. 6-16, 2012.

[50]Ritu Srivastava, study on Mall Motivations in India Aligning Demographics for Segmentations, The International Journal of Social Sciences, Vol. 6, No.1, Pp. 86-102, 2012.

[51]N.H. Mullick, study on The Success of Shopping Malls Lies in the Hands of Mall Developers: A study, Indian Journal of Marketing, Vol. 43, No. 6, Pp. 40-46, 2013.

should select an appropriate location and build a sustainable product, maintain tenant mix to integrate with the community and also enhance its footfalls. Not only this they must also keep the costs and rents competitive, so that it is feasible and productive for their tenants to thrive and earn profit in the future. If the mall developers become more pragmatic, then it is a surety that the future of shopping malls is bright and with the success in metros, it will successfully penetrate into tier-I and tier-II cities of the country.

Yadav and Siraj (2014)[52] study aimed to analyses the patronage behaviour of inter-linkages between shopping motives and shopper demographics The factors like frequency of visits, time spent, and amount spent per visit during shopping is taken into account. The study found that age of respondent, frequency of visit, time spent and amount spent affected their shopping behaviour. The results of the study revealed that high income shoppers were less attached to the mall than the low income shoppers, which reflects the fact that shopping is a hedonic activity for lower income shoppers than for higher income shoppers.

Praveena P. (2015)[53] research study aimed to analyse the factors that influences the consumer buying behaviour in shopping malls in Hyderabad city. The study observed that the consumers are very much influenced by the factors like transportation and parking facilities available in the malls. Consumers were attracted by the ambience features to shop at malls, freshness of goods and credit card usage facilities. The study also found that the occupational status of the consumers greatly influence their shopping behaviour at malls.

2.4.   Role of Outshoppers in a Market Place

Outshopping is defined as the purchase of goods by consumers outside their local trading area. Changing lifestyle of the Indian consumers made it imperative for the retailers to understand the patterns trigger changes in shopping styles of outshoppers. With the increase in the spending capacity, feeling shopping as an entertainment factor have changed the inshoppers into outshoppers. Understanding the outshoppers attitude is important for the retailers to frame the strategies. Now Reviews pertaining to outshopping behaviour are discussed in this final segment of the study.

---

[52]Suman Yadav and Sadaf Siraj, study on Mall Patronage Behaviour: Understanding the Inter-linkages Between Shopping Motives, Shopper Demographics, and Shopping Behaviors, Indian Journal of Marketing , Vol. 44, No. 11, Pp. 36-48, 2014.

[53]P. Lalitha Praveena, A Study on Consumer Buying Behaviour Factors in Shopping Malls In Hyderabad City, International Journal of Engineering and Management Science, Vol. 6, No. 4, Pp. 211-214, 2015.

Sullivan and Savitt (1997)[54] have conducted a study on store patronage (grocery patterns) of rural shoppers. The objective of the study was to determine the proportion of outshopping for groceries and to identify the store patronage and psychographic factors associated with rural grocery shoppers and to determine if such factors correspond with the proportion of grocery expenditures spent elsewhere. Nine store factors were identified such as shopping environment (location, assortment, breadth and services), Price (advertising), leisure activities, convenience, shop around work, family shopping, good shopping, credit and name brands. Results indicate that each group has different store patronage practices, psychographic profiles, and income levels, suggesting that grocery retailers should work with communities to organize retail mix that appeal to different shopping groups. Results of this study also suggest that the community and individual retailers in partnership can provide rural customers with an optimal merchandise mix and shopping experience.

Michael F. Smith, (1999)[55] study aimed to analyse the differences in urban and semi-urban consumers outshopping practices during holiday periods. The study found that urban and suburban shopping environments present unique opportunities and challenges for retailers. Retailers in both urban and suburban locations attempt to attract outshoppers and retain their hold on shoppers in their immediate trade areas. To this end, it is incumbent on retailers to understand the dynamics underlying consumers' decisions to shop in urban versus suburban retailing settings. This is especially important for consumer shopping behaviour during the December holiday selling season which accounts for a disproportionate share of many retailers' yearly revenues and profits. This reports on a three-year study conducted in a major metropolitan area which addresses shopping behaviour, intentions, retail satisfaction and its antecedents between urban resident shoppers and suburban resident shoppers. Implications are presented for retailers who have chosen to emphasize strategically urban or suburban locations as well as for those retailers who have branch stores in both geographic locations.

Denise Jarratt (2000)[56] in his study applied structural equation modeling to the data to confirm relationships previously reported in the literature and relationships established

---

[54]P. Sullivan and S. Ronald, Store patronage and lifestyle factors: implications for rural grocery retailers, Int. J. Retail Distribution Management, Vol. 25, No. 11, Pp. 351–364, 1997.

[55]Michael F. Smith, Urban versus suburban consumers: a contrast in holiday shopping purchase intentions and outshopping behaviour, Journal of Consumer Marketing, Vol. 16, No. 1, Pp. 58–73, 1999.

[56]Denise Jarratt (2000), study on Outshopping behavior: an explanation of behavior by shoPP.er segment using structural equation modeling, The International Review of Retail, distribution and Consumer Research, Volume No. 10, Issue No. 3, PP. 287-304

through causal path method. Anticipated linkages explaining outshopping behaviour by shopper segment are argued from shopper segment descriptors, and separate models of outshopping behaviour presenting different causal explanations are tested for each segment. The study finally concludes the important aspects to specific shopper groups dominate their evaluation of a specific shopping area, and this evaluation contributes directly and, for some shopper segments indirectly, to outshopping through trading area commitment. A segmentation approach to understanding outshopping behaviour provides shopping Centre managers with information to support retail strategy development.

According to Levantis (2001)[57] rural communities have good reason to be extremely concerned about the growth of outshopping as more residents shop and access services in nearby regional centers as it diminishes the viability of providing a full range of products and services that locals require. The author comment that as the range of goods and services available in a particular town decreases residents have greater incentive to shop and access services elsewhere. The author suggest that, the retailers in local regions if not attempt to address these issue, it will result in increase in outshopping, which may be threats for the future viability of smaller rural towns retailers.

Piron (2002)[58] in his research seeks to examine the shopping behaviour and attitudes of Singaporeans in neighboring Malaysia and, specifically, the influence of demographic and retail characteristics on outshopping. The study reveals the importance of various types of secondary costs of outshopping and the impact of consumer ethnocentrism on attitudes toward outshopping are also explored the observance were that frequent outshoppers tended to have lower incomes, lower education levels, and blue collar occupations, differed from most previous out-shopping demographic behavior findings. The study finally concluded that there are different types of international outshoppers and future research might discriminate between utilitarian and touristic out-shopping. Based on the geographical proximity of the two countries in his study, he argued that his respondents exhibited mostly utilitarian behavior.

Kim and Sullivan (2003)[59] study identified four segments of international shoppers and study proposed matrix classification scheme is based upon two dimensions - the degree to

[57]Caroline Levantis, Country Towns: Impact of Farmers' Expenditure on Employment and Population in Australian Towns, Sustaining Regions, Vol. 1, No. 1, Pp. 38-42, 2001.

[58]F. Piron, study on International out-shopping and ethnocentrism, European Journal of Marketing, Vol. 36, No. 1/2, Pp. 189-210, 2002.

[59] E. Kim and P. Sullivan, study on Cross-border tourism and shopping: Consumer segmentation, e-Review of Tourism Research (eRTR), Vol. 1, No. 1, Pp. 14-20, 2003.

which one is a tourist versus the degree that one is a shopper. The study revealed that author have labeled the shoppers into four quadrants of their tourism shopper segmentation matrix as: 1) "Traditional tourists" who are high on tourism and low on shopping, 2) "Traditional out-shoppers" who are low on tourism and high on shopping, 3) "Cross-border tourism shopper" who are high on tourism and high on shopping, and 4) "inactive tourists/shoppers" who are low on tourism and low on shopping. They study finally concluded that retailers who know which segment they are serving can develop more effective strategies to meet the needs of the targeted segment.

Elliott and Edwards (2004)[60] study aimed to investigate the outshopping phenomenon and aimed to address four fundamental issues like (1) individual characteristics i.e., their typical outshoppers possess (2) outshopping reasons and its occurrence (3) nature of products are commonly purchased by outshoppers and the extent of outshopping behaviour exhibited by the outshoppers. The study found that while performing outshopping customers' comparisons of what they expect and what they get, except for the characteristics of any tangible goods involved, each time they make a purchase.

Varshney, S., and Goyal, A. (2005)[61] study segmented the antecedents into demographic variables, psychographic variables, shopping area attributes, product-related factors, and accessibility factors. The study finally concluded that the demographic variables were generally found to be positively associated with outshopping: education, smaller family size, income, and automobile ownership. Likewise, they found the following variables to be negatively associated with outshopping: age, family life cycle state, age of children, number of children, and tenure in the community. Other factors were determined to define variance in outshopping behavior, including gender and cultural backgrounds.

Varshney and Goyal (2006)[62] another study on outshopping behaviour in a small Indian town it was observed that outshopping prevails in most of these countries in the form of rural outshopping, outshopping from small cities or towns to nearby larger cities owing to undeveloped market structures in such places. The study identified strong prevalence of

---

[60]Kevin M. Elliott and Robert R. Edwards, Differentiation Based on Service Quality: A Viable Small Business Strategy for Minimizing the Effects of Outshopping, 2004,

http://citeseerx.ist.psu.edu/viewdoc/download?doi=10.1.1.539.260andrep=rep1andtype=pdf.

[61]S. Varshney and A. Goyal, A review and extension of the out shopping paradigm to the Indian context,Asia Pacific Journal of Marketing and Logistics, Vol. 17, No.4, Pp. 30-63, 2005.

[62]Sanjeey Varshney and Anita Goyal, Outshopping Behaviour in a Small Indian Town: An Exploratory Study, South Asian Journal of Management, Vol.13, No. 2, 2006.

outshopping in India particularly from small to nearby larger cities study was designed to study the phenomenon in the Indian context.

Dmitrovic and Vida (2007)[63] in the study defined economic patriotism as individuals who have higher consumer ethnocentrism, perceive buying local as having a positive impact on one's community, and a favorable perception of the quality of domestic goods. The study revealed that there were no significant differences in affluence between Croatian out and in shoppers. Although they found that Croatian outshopping was primarily economically driven, a lower level of economic patriotism was also found to be a significant predictor of out-shopping behavior. The study finally concluded that both affluence and having more children below the age of 18 in the household as significant predictors of outshopping in Serbia versus Croatia.

Qiu et.al(2008)[64] research paper aimed to identify the factors that influence the frequency of shopping in a neighbourhood food store. The study observed that there are many factors that influences the outshopping practices like: merchandise mix, product freshness, varieties, price etc. the study comment that by and large, outshoppers are not very loyal to local retailers and do not feel obliged to support local establishments.

Guo and Wang (2009)[65] in their study used the framework of tripartite consumer response models to research Mexican national cross-border outshopping determinants in United Sates The study revealed that both quality of merchandise, quality of service, and fashion consciousness were positively related to cross-border shopping frequency, they also found that cross-border shopping frequency is positively related to patriotism. The study founded that quality of merchandise, fashion consciousness, and patriotism are positively and significantly related to cross-border shopping enjoyment, but not quality of service of the retail establishment, terror threats also have no significant relationship on shopping enjoyment.

Bajaj and Bajaj's (2009)[66] research article aimed to determine the consumer's out shopping behaviour in rural and urban markets in India. The study findings clearly disclosed differences in the out shopping behaviour of consumers in the urban and rural area. In

---

[63]T. Dmitrovic and I. Vida, Study on An examination of cross-border shopping behaviour in South-East Europe, European Journal of Marketing, Vol. 41, No.3/4, Pp. 382-395, 2007.

[64]P. Qiu, C. Maksymiuk and E. Bruning, Factors influencing the frequency of shopping in a neighbourhood food store: A social capital theory perspective, Administrative Sciences Association of Canada, Vol. 29, No. 3, 2008.

[65]C. Guo and Y. Wang, A study of cross-border outshopping determinants: Mediating effect of outshopping enjoyment. International Journal of Consumer Studies, Vol. 33, No. 6, Pp. 644-51, 2009.

[66]Chetan Bajaj and Nandini Bajaj, Outshopping Behaviour in Rural and Urban Indian Markets, Global Management Review, Vol. 4, No. 1, 2009

addition, the study findings revealed that out shopper from rural area is functional oriented looking for variety and utility, while the outshopper from urban area is looking for experience and entertainment. Furthermore, it noted that the outshopping behaviour is influenced by demographic variables such as age, income, gender, ownership of vehicles and place of residence.

Sanjeev Varshney (2010)[67] study aimed to analyse the outshopping behaviour among urban and rural people in India. The study findings reveals that outshopping also predominates in India, because of market structures differences across urban and rural areas and needs. The study also found that outshopping establish differences in shopping behaviour for rural and urban customer, later being more habit oriented and second-hand in nature as against value orientation conscious of the urban and rural consumers.

Devadas and Manohar (2011)[68] research article aimed to analyse the shopping behaviour of rural consumer migrated to urban area in the India. The study findings revealed that the migrated consumers consider the following dimensions when shopping in the urban environment: they are shopping conscious, enjoy urban shopping environment, price and quality conscious, and compare different shops when buying. They want shopping to be recreational, price worthy, perfect and buyer oriented. They are unhappy with poor shopping environment, if any. These dimensions describe the factors to which the migrant rural consumers give importance in the urban shopping environment.

Venugopal (2012)[69] research paper aimed to study the outshopping behaviour of rural consumers and identified that the decision of what and where to purchase consumer goods could be inferred by identifying their urban orientation. The study commented that demand for consumer goods in rural markets in the emerging economies is increasing, and these markets are being targeted by multinational companies marketing consumer goods. While all companies are designing distribution strategies to reach the existing rural retail outlets and the periodic markets, a few companies are also developing innovative modes of distribution. Despite the availability of a product in the rural retail formats, some rural consumers were found to make their purchases from a nearby town.

---

[67]Sanjeev Varshney, Outshopping Behaviour, Antecedent, Inter-Relationship Classification, 2010.

https://www.lap-publishing.com/catalog/details/store/ru/book/978-3-8383-7529-8/outshopping-behaviour.

[68]Anuradha Devadas and Hansa Lysander Manohar, Shopping behaviour of rural consumer migrated to urban area in the Indian context- An emerging market, African Journal of Business Management, Vol. 5, No. 6, 2011.

[69]Pingali Venugopal, Urban Orientation of Rural Consumers: Implication for Consumer Goods Distribution, International Journal of Rural Management, Vol. 8, No. 1-2, Pp. 107-119, 2012.

Strydom (2013)[70] study aimed to examine the influence of in shopping and outshopping as special instances of retail patronage in the Soweto Township, South Africa. The study findings establish correlation with the other countries of the world in term of outshopping, but there are also a number of major differences. The study revealed that in South Africa, the situation is unique in that sense that Soweto, outshoppers are forced to do outshopping because of past injustices such as poor planning, the lack of retail facilities and the poor quality of service. The study suggests that the South African retailers should take cognisance of these differences and adapt their retailing strategies accordingly.

Brain A. Zinser and Gray J. Brunswixk (2014)[71] in their study used a cross sectional, retrosive, non-experimental research design to conduct a comparative study using the service model. It developed and validated of service encounters of Canadian cross border shopper versus Canadian in shoppers. The author concluded that the research has contributed to the literature on outshopping, cross–border shopping and international cross border shopping as well as service marketing.

Piyush Sharma and Ting S. Luk (2015)[72] research paper extended the concept of customer perceived value (CPV) to the tourist outshopping context and explores the differences in antecedents and outcomes of CPV between cross-border and international outshoppers. A large-scale field survey in Hong Kong with cross-border outshoppers from main land China and international shoppers from four Western countries (Australia, Canada, UK and USA) revealed that perceived product quality, risk and value-for-money have a stronger effect on CPV for cross-border outshoppers; and employee service quality and lifestyle congruence for international outshoppers. CPV also has a stronger positive effect on satisfaction, word-of-mouth and repeat purchase intentions for cross-border outshoppers; whereas, the study found that satisfaction has a stronger positive impact on word-of-mouth and repeat purchase intentions for international outshoppers.

---

[70]Johan W. Strydom, Retail patronage of Sowetan consumers after 1994, African Journal of Business Management, Vol. 7, No. 29, Pp. 2863-2887, 2013.

[71] Brain A. Zinser and Gray J. Brunswixk, Cross Border Shopping: A Research proposal for a comparison of service encounters of Canadian cross-border shoppers versus Canadian Domestic Inshopper, International Business and Economic Research Journal, Vol.13, No. 5, Pp. 1077-1090, 2014.

[72]Piyush Sharma and Ting S. Luk, Tourist shoppers' evaluation of retail service: a study of Cross-border vs. International outshoppers, Journal of Hospitality and Amp Tourism Research, 2015.

2.5.   Conclusion

The movements of consumers from downtown to retail centers of large cities have been defined as outshopping behavior. There are many studies on this outshopping behavior in the foreign countries and reviews are available in the western countries. The studies on outshopping behavior were also conducted in other parts of the countries. In India there are foreseeing rapid pace of urbanization and growth of suburban shopping centers, lot of consumers are moving out of their home town for shopping. However few studies exist in developing countries like India. There exist a research gap, keeping this in mind and identifying the strong prevalence of outshopping in India particularly from small to nearby larger cities study was designed to study the phenomenon in the Indian context.

CHAPTER III

GROWTH OF RETAILING BUSINESS IN INDIA AND MALL CULTURE AMONG CONSUMERS

This chapter provides a brief theoretical summary and discussion on the retail sector growth in India, retail consumers' preferences towards shopping malls and outshopping practices in India.

3.1. Retail Industries in India

Indian is the worlds' fifth largest global destination in the retail space. The Indian retail industry is fast growing industries in India. It comprises of both organised and unorganised sectors. Traditional retail sector consist of the unorganised sector and with the changing taste and preference of the consumers the industry is becoming an organised sector. The organised retailing refers to trading activities undertaken by licensed retailers, who are registered for sales tax, income tax etc. These include the corporate backed hyper markets and privately owned large retail businesses.

The unorganised retailing refers to the traditional formats of low cost retailing like local kirana shops, general stores, convenience stores, pavement vendors etc. There has been a massive development of new organised retail formats such as malls, hypermarkets, super markets and life style stores. Several new players have entered the industry. The total retail spending is estimated to double in the next five years. Of this, organised retail currently growing at a CAGR at 22 per cent is estimated to be 21 per cent of total expenditure. It accounts for over 10 per cent of the country's Gross Domestic Product (GDP) and around 8 per cent of the employment[1]

The Indian retail sector is projected to reach US$ 1.3 trillion by 2018 and the organised retail market is estimated at compounded annual growth rate of 40per cent.[2] As per the McKinsey Report 'The rise of Indian Consumer Market', by the year 2025, the Indian consumer market is expected to grow four fold. As per the estimates of Indian Retail Report 2011, the modern retail in the next five years is expected to contribute to a minimum of one third of the

---

[1] Media Reports, Press Releases, Deloitte report, Department of Industrial Policy and Promotion website, Union Budget 2015–16

[2] http://business.mapsofindia.com/india-market/retail.html accessed on Sept 29th, 2012.

market of 40 trillion. This report estimates that by the year 2016, the modern retail would have 19.3 percentage share of the total retail market[3].

Table 3.1: Share of Organized Retail Sector in Total Retail Trade

Year	Percentage share of Organised Retail Sector	Source
2005	3.5 Per cent	AT Kearney
2008	5 Per cent	MC- Kinsey & Co
2010	8 Per cent	AT Kearney
2013	10 Per cent	AT Kearney
2014	13 Per cent	Retail Ecommerce Sales in India, 2014
2015-16	14 Per cent	Retail Ecommerce Sales in India ,2014

Source: IRIS Primary Research- India Retail Report 2011 and Ambika Choudhary Mahajan (2015), Retail Ecommerce Sales in India 2014.

According to the tenth report of GRDI (Global Retail Development Index) of AT Kearney, India is having a very favorable retail environment and it is placed at 4th spot in the GRDI. The main reasons behind that is the 9 per cent real GDP (Gross Domestic Product) growth in 2010, forecasted yearly growth of 8.7 per cent through 2016, high saving and investment rate and increased consumer spending. According to report, organised retail accounts for 7 per cent of India's roughly US $435 billion retail market and is expected to reach 20 per cent by 2020. Food accounts for 70 per cent of Indian retail, but it remains under penetrated by organised retail. Organised retail has a 31 per cent share in clothing and apparel and continues to see growth in this sector.

A report by Boston Consulting Group (BCG) has revealed that the country's organised retail is estimated at US $28 billion with around 7 per cent penetration. It is projected to become a US $260 billion business over the next decade with around 21 per cent penetration. The Indian Retail sector is likely to show significant growth of over 9per cent over the next ten years and also see rapid development in organised retail format with proportion likely to reach more respectable 25 per cent by 2018. The BMI (Business Monitor international) India Report for the first quarter of 2012 released forecasts that total retail sales with growth from US $ 422.09 billion in 2011 to US $ 825.46 billion by 2015.The report highlighted strongly underlying economic growth, population expansion, increasing disposable income and rapid emergence of organised retail infrastructure as major factors behind the forecast growth[4].

---

[3] IRIS Primary Research- India Retail Report 2011.

[4] Sunia Sikri and Dipti Wadhwa, Growth and Challenges of Retail Industry in India: An Analysis. Asia Pacific Journal of Marketing and Management Review, Vol.1, No. 1, 2012.

The Indian economy is growing fast with the spending power of the consumers in the retail sector and this development has acquired importance not only in the metropolitan cities but also in the Tier II and Tier III towns. Due to the limited success of these outlets, it is necessary for the retailers to be aware of shoppers' motivations and to understand the ways of attracting the consumers also, due to the limited success of these outlets, it is necessary for retailers to be aware of shopper's motivations and to understand ways of attracting the consumers[5].

3.2. Contribution of Outshoppers to the Growth of Retail Business in India

Indian retail sector has undergone several changes in recent years. Liberalisation policies pursued by Indian government have attracted investment from global retailers. New retail formats that were popular in big cities are increasingly finding their way in smaller towns and cities[6]. Rather, it can be claimed that rural and semi-urban consumers does not hesitate to travel to a long-distance urban market for shopping their life-style products, modern electrical and electronic gazettes and other products. In true senses the Indian consumer is changing and more connected with modern technology and its devices than earlier age customers. Modern day consumers are more techno-savvy and better equipped to benefit themselves from an ever-changing marketplace. While, metros and urban cities will always remain as principal places for marketers and increasing rural and semi-urban consumers shopping in the future. In turn these consumers will be critical for increasing volumes of sales in the urban market in the long run. Moreover, there is a growth opportunity that is vastly under-rated by many marketers today, which could emerge as a key growth engine for the next 10 years. Because, in middle India, its rural pockets and village hamlets region made up of approximately 400 towns each with a population of 1-10 Lakh are home to 100 million Indians and today constitute up to 20 per cent of the country's FMCG consumption and these consumers as outshoppers truly offer an opportunity for growth and expansion of retail business in India.

One of the prominent reasons notified for the growth of outshopping behaviour in India is that still 70 per cent of the Indian population resides in rural areas, poor reach and inadequate infrastructure have made it difficult for marketers to fully tap into the potential of these markets quickly. Most FMCG companies have concentrated their energies on the metro and

---

[5] R. Pancholi, Growth off the Shelf, Hindustan Times, New Delhi, 2006.

[6] Running Head: GAGING THE IMPACT OF ANTECEDENTS ON STORE LOYALTY, Antecedents to Local Store Loyalty: Influence of Cosmopolitanism, Culture and Price,
http://vslir.iimahd.ernet.in:8080/xmlui/bitstream/handle/123456789/11596/CB-PP-322Antecedents_to_Local_Store_Loyalty-89-Pandey_b.pdf?sequence=3

mini-metro regions in the past 10 years. Considering the expected growth of population in this area, rise in incomes and aspirations and the expected influx of people from even smaller towns in India, this market is expected to create huge opportunities for marketers in the coming few years.

Increasing consumers focus on hygiene, health, personal grooming and convenience seems to be driving forces that influence the semi-urban and town consumers to outshop in large cities. Moreover, increased exposure to the media and a gradual improvement in infrastructure have played a substantial role in introducing the outshoppers, to what was earlier only a 'metro' lifestyle, fuelling a desire to improve their standard of living. These factors, combined with an increased spending capacity are rapidly pushing up the demand for a vast consumer product that is now-a-days shopped by the outshoppers across India[7].

3.3.   Importance of Outshopping

Outshopping is important for both local and surrounding retailers. The former want to minimise this behaviour whereas the latter want to maximise it. Outshoppers are often young, members of a large family, and new to the community. Income and education vary by situation. Outshoppers differ in their lifestyles from those who patronise hometown stores. Outshoppers are active and like to travel, enjoy, dine foods, like to change stores, and read out-of-town newspapers. They also downplay hometown stores and compliment out-of-town stores. This is vital data for suburban shopping center. Outshoppers have the same basic reasons for out-of-town shopping whether they reside in small or large communities-easy access, liberal credit, store diversity, product assortments, prices, the presence of large chains, entertainment facilities, customer services and product quality[8]. Moreover, consumer quality perceptions play a vital role in explaining outshopping behaviour. Highly visible products with high unit costs exhibiting fashion characteristics were purchased out-of-town more frequently, the presence of children in the household also influences when consumers do their holiday shopping. The consumer outshopping behaviour is not only product specific, but the product form and the price level of the product.

---

[7] Emerging Consumer Demand: Rise of the Small Town Indian, Report Prepared in Co-ordination of Nielsen (India) Pvt. Ltd and Confederation of Indian Industry (2012).

http://www.nielsen.com/content/dam/corporate/india/reports/2012/Emerging%20Consumer%20Demand%2 0%E2%80%93%20Rise%20of%20the%20Small%20Town%20Indian.pdf.

[8] Barry Berman and Joel R. Evans, Retail Management A strategic Approach, Tenth Edition, Pearson Prentice Hall, Pp 207-208, 2007.

Outshopping is generally accepted as a benefit for urban retailers and it results in a net financial profit to the urban retailers. Generally, outshoppers have high income in comparison to the local shoppers, as outshoppers are dispersed throughout various occupational areas. Therefore, it can be claimed that outshoppers, represents a significant market segment for the retailers to better understand. In modern day marketing outshopping is a significant retailing phenomenon. Outshopping is a complex phenomenon as it is influenced by outbreak of personal, situational and market-dependent factors[9].

3.4. Outshopping Practices in India

Out shopping is also known as market gravitations or market leakage is the practice of shoppers going outside the local community for shopping. This out shopping particularly affects the retailer in the small, rural communities. The main development of this outshopper behavior is due to the better prices, more stores and broader product depth[10].

The changing lifestyle of the Indian consumer made it imperative for the retailers to understand the trigger changes in shopping styles of outshoppers . Nowadays the number of small families has increased as the joint families are split up to nuclear families. The number of children in the family has reduced significantly over the years. More and more women are taking up professions; the average income of the family is increasing. With the increase in their spending capacity, people are looking for more lifestyle products. These opportunities arising in the consumer side are utilized by the retail sector. There is a tremendous growth in the retail sectors such as huge super markets, hyper markets and shopping malls.

The improving job opportunities have made the people to move from the home town and settle in the other places. The cities have become crowded and there is no space left for expansion suburban areas are developing. Improvements in the infrastructure such as roads have shrieked the world. The developments and advancement in the transportation and communication have given an opportunity for the retail sector to attract peoples from far way places. The people have started to move away from their residing area for shopping the products. Thus in shoppers have become outshoppers.

---

[9] Satchidananda Dehuri, Manas Ranjan Patra, Bijan Bihari Misra and Alok Kumar Jagadev, Intelligent Techniques in Recommendation Systems: Contextual Advancements and New methods, Information Science Reference (An Imprint of IGI Global), Pp. 231-233, 2013.

[10] Cathy Ashley, Carol Gaumer and Barry Foltors, The effects of Out shopping on a small rural community the importance of relationships, The Coastal Business Journal Spring, Vol. 8, No. 1, 2009.

3.5.   Reasons for Outshopping

Price is the one of the important factor which attracts the customers towards the product. The shoppers have nowadays become more price conscious and they started to move out of their home for low price goods. They are ready to travel miles to find the less price products. Outshoppers are placing more importance on the quality of the product and service offered. In search of suitable price, best quality product and better service, the shoppers are moving from their local area to the other areas. Customer satisfaction is the important concept nowadays and in todays' world of competition when the marketer fails to meet out the customer satisfaction they will be thrown out of the market. Usually the shoppers when they are not satisfied with the products and services offered by the retail sector in their local area they move on to the other areas for their shopping needs.

Outshoppers are having a high value on enjoyment and entertainment in their shopping decisions. The secondary cost of out shopping may be reduced or offset by the pleasures associated with travel and shopping in more city environment. The outshoppers prefer to shop in the attractive retail facilities. Sometimes the outshoppers shop out to meet the social and recreational needs. Thus the entertainment facility is an important attribute to draw outshoppers into another trading area[11] . Apart from competitive prices and other factors the ample parking space and the easy accessibility are also the major reason for out shopping frequently. Now a day the convenience of the parking is also a deciding factor of the consumer to buy the product from the particular retail sector[12]. Mostly the outshoppers who do shopping outside their local area are young, highly educated, processional consumers with relatively higher process[13].

3.6.   Motives of Outshopping

Utilitarian motivations include convenient shopping, procuring goods, services or specific information, and reduction in the costs that is money, time and effort that may have to be expended in transportation, finding specific products or services and waiting in check outlines[14]. For this type of shoppers, shopping is work where main motivation is to purchase

---

[11]V.L. Blakney and W. Sekely, Retail attributes:influence on shopping mode choice behavior, Journal of Managerial Issues, 1994.

[12] http://dx.doi.org/10.1108/03090560210412755

[13] Coskun Samli. A, Stategic Marketing for success in Retailing, Quorum Books , London

[14] H.S. Kim, Using Hedonic and Utilitarian Shopping Motivations to Profile Inner City Consumers, Journal of Shopping Center Research, Vol. 13, No. 1, Pp. 57-79, 2006.

predetermined goods as quickly as possible. In contrast some consumers enter malls with mainly non utilitarian motives. For them shopping can be hedonic which means fun.

Hedonic motivation refers to the influence of a persons' pleasure and pain receptors on their willingness to move towards a goal or away from a threat. Hedonic motivation is linked to the classical motivational principle that people approach pleasure and avoids pain[15] and is gained from acting on certain behavior that resulted from esthetic and emotional feelings such as love, hate, fear, joy etc[16]. According to the hedonic principle our emotional experience can be thought of as a gauge the ranges from bad to good and our primary motivation is to keep the needle on the gauge as close to goods as possible[17].

Hedonic shopping is viewed as a positive experience of consumers enjoying emotionally the satisfying experience related to the shopping activity regardless of whether or not a purchase was made. It is experiencing fun, amusement, sensory stimulation. These hedonic satisfactions may be derived from ambience, entertainment, browsing and social experience outside the home like meeting friends, watching people[18]

Arnold and Reynolds (2003) developed six hedonic shopping motivations:

- Adventure motivation -shopping is viewed as adventure:

  - Adventure shopping refers to shopping for stimulation, adventure, and the feeling of being in another world. A significant number of respondents reported that they go shopping for the sheer excitement and adventure of the shopping trip. These informants often described the shopping experience in terms of adventure, thrills, stimulation, excitement, and entering a different universe of exciting sights, smells, and sounds

- Social shopping-shoppers see the main purpose of shopping as an opportunity to socialize:

  - Social shopper loves to bring others along for the ride. In a traditional brick and mortar scenario, they would shop with friends or chat with sales people. The

---

[15] Higgins, T.E. (2006) Value from hedonic experience and engagement, American Psychological Association, Volume No. 113, Issue No. 3, PP. 439-460.

[16] Ahtola,O.T. (1985). Hedonic and utilitarian aspects of consumer behavior: An attitudinal perspective

[17] Schacter, D. L., D. T. Gilbert, and D. M. Wegner (2011). Psychology. 2. New York, NY: Worth Publishers, 2011.

[18] Vipul patel and Mahendra Sharma , Consumers' Motivations to shop in Shopping Malls: A Study of Indian Shoppers., Phd Thesis, Institute of Management, Bangalore, India

social shoppers always see for a socializing occasion with family, friends and other people.

- Gratification shopping-shopping is used as reward:
  - Gratification Shoppers shop for gratification purpose are often doing so to improve mood and feel better. They involve in shopping to relieve from stress and to treat themselves fresh

- Idea shopping-this shopping is undertaken to provide the shopper with up-to-date information on products and trends:
  - Idea Shoppers like to be trendsetters. They value staying current and the novelty of new and exciting ideas. They do shopping to keep up with the new trends and fashions. They go for shopping places to see what new products are available in the market and to experience the new things

- Role shopping-shopping motive relates to the shopper's role in society:
  - Roles shoppers gains enjoyment when shopping for others and finding the perfect gift. They feel good when they buy things for the special people in their life. They enjoy shopping for their family members

- Value shopping-the purpose of this activity is to find a bargain:
  - Value shoppers find joy in hunting for bargain. They prefer shopping during the sales offers and hunt for discounts while shopping. Thus they take advantage of the sales offers.

3.7. Shopping Mall and Outshopping Practices

The term "Mall" can mean market for all'. The first mall was constructed in Canada and was known as West Edmonton mall. A mall comprises of Shopping complexes, food courts and retail outlets. Malls usually cater to Shopatainment (Shopping and Entertainment). Today malls are gaining importance as the disposable incomes of consumers are increasing. Both in shoppers and outshoppers visit malls to pass time shop and also to dine at the restaurants located in the malls. There is development of rich in mall segment, which is catering to particular segment of people, they are meant for specific types of products which are called as specialty malls.

3.7.1. History of Malls

Shopping Malls concept was first appeared in 1950's. The first generation of malls was set up in North Gate Mall, US in 1950. The credit towards the invention of modern mall goes to

Australian born architect and American immigrant Victor Green. The Northland Shopping Centre was constructed by Victor Green in US. The first enclosed mall was developed in the suburb of Minneapolis in 1956. The Gulf Gate Mall in Houston was an open air shopping center for customers[19]. In Canda the Norgate shopping centres which was similar to strip mall was started in Saint Laurent, Montreal in the 1949. In British Columbis, Park Royal Shopping centers was started in west Vancourver in the year 1950 and the Nechako Centre was opened in 1954 and the City Centre shopping mall was opened in 1956 to provide shopping to the local shoppers[20].

Southdale Center in Edia, USA is the earliest modern mall; it has the design of updated version of traditional Europan arcades. The mall was surrounded by apartment complexes, schools and other facilities in a huge 463 acres of land. The Southdale was a pioneer for many of the modern malls today.[21] Later as the time passed the malls were shifted from the crowded commercial areas to the residential suburbs. These malls were accessible only through automobiles and therefore gradually became famous destination for retailers across the world. During 1960, in United States, with the growth of shopping centres, the migration of population from cities there were 4500 malls, which accounted for 14 per cent of retail sales. In 1975 there were 16,400 shopping centres which accounted for 3 per cent of retail sales which increased to 30,000 malls in the year 1987 with 50per cent of retail sales.[22]

3.8. Types of Malls

The malls basically are classified on the basis of their Merchandise orientation means types or goods and services sold and their size. The trend towards differentiation and segmentation will continue to add new terminology as the industry matures. Following are the different types of malls.

1) **Regional Malls:** According to International Council of Shopping Centers a regional mall is a Shopping Mall which is designed to service a larger area than a conventional Shopping Mall. It is typically larger than 4,00,000 square feet to 8,00,000 square feet gross leasable area with at least two anchors and offers a wider selection of stores.

---

[19] Emergency of shopping Malls, Chapter Six, 17_Chapter 6.Pdf.

[20] Greg Haseth, Laura Ryser and Shiloh Durkee, Shopping and commuting pattersn in Kitimat, Bc, University of Northern British Columbia, 2005.

[21] http://gizmodo.com/5114869/the-worlds-first-modern-shopping-mall

[22] Richard A. Feinberg and Jennifer Meoli, A Brief History of the Mall , Adances in Consumer Research, Vol. 18, Pp. 429-427, 1991.

2) **Super regional malls:** This is a mall which is almost similar to a regional mall, but it is larger in size than a regional mall. It has more anchor stores, a deeper selection of Merchandise and draws from a larger population base. A super regional mall is according to International Council of Shopping Centers, a Shopping Mall with over 800,000 square feet (74000) of gross leasable area and which serves as the dominant Shopping venue for the region in which it is located.

3) **Outlet Malls:** An outlet mall or outlet center is a type of shopping mall in which manufacturers sell their products directly to the public through their own stores. The other stores in outlet malls are operated by retailers selling returned goods and discontinued products often at heavily reduced price. In India these outlet stores are not shopping malls, they are called generally called as factory outlet shops because they generally call general products directly offered by the company.

4) **Vertical Malls:** Vertical Malls as typically multistory building is common due to the high land price in densely populated and the higher yield on retail property. The concept of the vertical mall departs from the common Western model of the flat shopping mall in which space allocated to retail is configured over a number of stores accessible by escalators linking the different levels of the mall. The challenge of this mall is to overcome the natural tendency of shoppers to move horizontally and encourage shoppers to move upwards and downwards.

5) **Lifestyle Centers:** Lifestyle Center is new designated that has a loose definition. Generally, it's a center that does not have on anchor tenant in the classic sense that is, department store. Lifestyle centers have a cinema as a major tenant.

6) **Dead Malls:** The dead malls are those which have failed to attract new business and often set unused for many years until restored or demolished. This phenomenon of dead and dying malls is examined in detail by the website, deadmills.com which hosts many such photographs as well as historical accounts.

7) **Strip Mall:** Strip mall also called Shopping Plaza or Mini mall. It is an open area shopping center where the stores are arranged in a row with a sidewalk in front. Strip malls are typically developed as a unit and have large parking lots in front. They face major traffic arterials, and tend to be self-contained with few pedestrian connections to surrounding neighborhoods.

8) **Outlet Mall:** Outlet Mall is a type of Shopping Mall in which manufacturers sell their products directly to the public through their own branded stores. Clothing, sporting goods, electrical products, cosmetics and toys are among the types of items sold at

outlet malls. Outlet malls first appeared in the United States as a development of the traditional factory outlet a store attached to a factory or warehouse. An outlet mall places several such outlets under one roof in a convenient location, usually an out of town site. The out of town site minimizes overhead costs.

9) **Luxury Malls**: Luxury Mall is mall which only houses luxury brands. In India luxury malls have been planned to be built soon, most of the tenants are expected to be the best brands in the world such as France's Louis Witton, Greece Dunhill Fendi Mont Benc, Van Clef and Arpels Rolex and Omega.

3.9.   Shopping Mall Agglomeration

Retail and service enterprises seek benefits and synergies from locating their stores within retail agglomerations such as shopping streets and malls. The mall agglomeration influences the consumer perception, the customer satisfaction with the mall, retention proneness at the mall and patronage intention towards the mall. The determinants are of importance for the mall managers to meet their consumers' needs and wants in order to make them stay and to return in the future. Consequently the attractiveness of a mall is related to the share of spending, share of time and share of choice of consumers relative to the competition.

Retail Agglomerations can be characterized by their marketing mix components, which are controllable factors, such as accessibility, parking, product range, merchandise value, sales personnel, Atmosphere, orientation and infrastructural facilities.

1) **Accessibility:** Accessibility is the convenience regarding overcoming the distance between the points of origin and the agglomeration. It encompasses not only special and temporal dimensions concerning how easily and how quickly the destinations can be reached. It also considers perceived obstacles on the way, such as traffic jams, travel frequencies of trains and buses, road work[23].

2) **Parking:** Today cars is the most important means of transportation for consumers, thus the availability of free parking spaces and the type of parking acilities offered at the mall at the time of shopping trip can also be regarded as a major factor enhancing shopping attractiveness[24]

---

[23] C.A. Ingene, Productivity and functional shifting in spatial retailing: private and social perceptiveness, Journal of Retailing and Consumer Service, Vol. 60, No. 3, Pp. 15-26, 1984.

[24] Van der Waerden, P. Borgers and H. Timmermans, The impact of the parking situation In shopping centers on store choice behavior, GeoJournal, Vol. 45, No. 4, Pp 309-315, 1998.

3) **Retail Tenant Mix:** A good tenant mix includes a variety of compatible retail and service providers, an efficient space allocation and proper tenant placement, all of which encourage the interchange of customers and retail activities. The composition, the number and type of retail and non-retail tenants that is bars, eateries, entertainment facilities within agglomerations represent the range of possibilities to satisfy consumers wants and needs, as well as minimize the logistics of the shopping endeavors and influence shopping mall attractiveness[25].

4) **Produce Range, Merchandise Value and Sales Personnel:** Product range offered is the width and breadth of assortment in the shopping mall, while the merchandise value is the overall price level and number of price promotions available. The sales personnel is friendliness, competency and supportiveness. These also show their contribution in meeting the customer' expectations.

5) **Atmosphere:** The Internal atmospheric stimuli including smell, music, decoration, flooring, lighting, air conditions, rest room etc and external atmospheric stimuli like architectural style, layout design and image have an effect on the consumers perception towards the shopping mall attractiveness as well as their shopping behavior which provide enrichment and consequently an extension of the retention period of consumers.

6) **Orientation and Infrastructure facilities:** Orientation accounts for the convenience relates to searching location and accessing stores or other tenants within a mall. It is influenced by the arrangement of tenants as well as the ease of orientation within the retail location. Shopping center management tries to ease this shopping endeavour by providing a clear management of tenants within the premises and setting up directories that enable consumers to easily target and access the tenants they seek. In addition infrastructure services within shopping centers such as cash dispensers and recreational areas to meet the expectations and demand of consumers, support the fulfillment of the defined task.

3.10. Growth of Shopping Malls in India

The India's retail sector has grown enormously from Hat, weekly bazaars to posh, sophisticated and swanky shopping malls. The first shopping mall in India is the Spencer Plaza in Chennai. It was built in 1863-1864, established by Charles Durand and J.W. Spencer in Anna Salai. The property belonged to Spencer & Co Ltd and it opened the first Departmental stores

---

[25] C. Teller and T. Reutterer, The evolving concept of retail attractiveness: what makes retail agglomerations attractive when consumers shop at them?, Journal of Retailing and consumer service, Vol. 15, No. 3, Pp. 127-143, 2008

in the Indian Subcontinent in 1895 and the stores had over 80 individual departments. The present spencer plaza was constructed in 10 acres and operated from 1991[26].

Indians by tradition, see themselves as an integral part of a collective group such as family, friends and colleagues. Malls are a Social phenomenon. The increase in the income level of consumers, influence of consumerism and wide availability of products and services at a single location such as malls has an impact on the buying behavior of Indian consumers. India offers market opportunity because of increased income and changing lifestyle of middle class families. In 2001 there were just three malls in India. The number grew to 343 by 2007 and in May 2013 there are 570 operational malls[27].

Indian malls vary between 35,000 sq ft to 10, 00,000 sq. ft. while U.S. version is between 4,00,000 sq ft to one million sq ft.. The largest malls in Indian metropolitan cities enjoy 25,000 footfalls per day which hikes to an average of 40,000 on weekends[28]. Accordingly the promoters of the malls are focusing to accommodate more shoppers under one roof. The average size of the malls is likely to increase from 4,70,000 sq ft by end of 2015 according to the study by property advisory firm Jones Lang Lasalle. The total shopping malls in top seven cities across India is also expected to grow 25per cent that is from 76 million sq ft in 2013 to 95.7 million sq ft by the end of 2015. Delhi and Mumbai malls together account for 62per cent of the total mall space in India. Banglore and Chennai ranked in second place with combined share of 20per cent. The expected total mall space around India is 107 million sq ft by end of 2017[29]

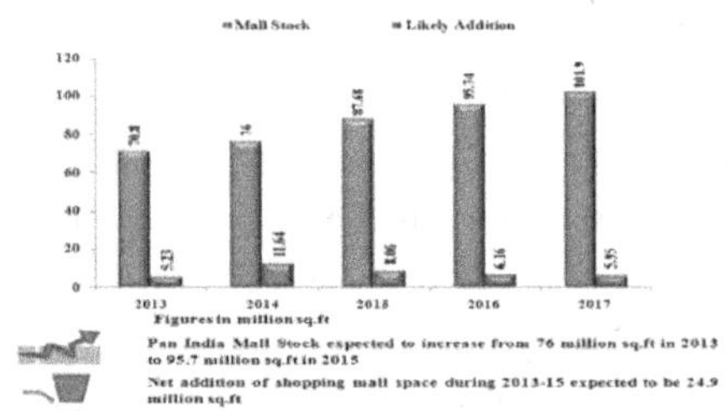

Exhibit 3.1(a): Growth Trend of Shopping Malls in India

Source: Economic Times Report/ Outdoor Mediaplan.Com

---

[26] R. Ravikumar, First mover fails to keep up with times, Business Line (Chennai: THE Hindu), 2011.

[27] http://www.mapsofindia.com/my-india/india/growing-mall-culture-in-india-changing-lifestyles

[28] Basu .B (2006)., India's mall explosion: Sense and direction, Images Retail, PP. 6-9.

[29] Source – Economic Times Report/ OUTDOOR MEDIAPLAN.COM

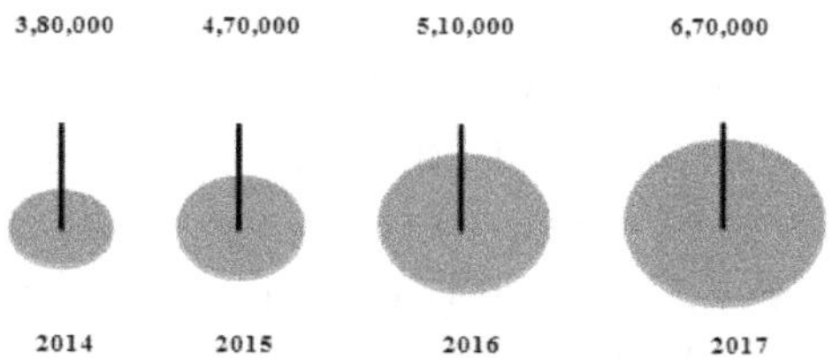

Exhibit 3.2(B): Growth Trend of Shopping Malls in India

Source: Economic Times Report/ Outdoor Mediaplan.Com

With rising income, influence of consumerism and wide availability of products and services at a single location has made a great impact on the shopping activities of Consumers all over the world. Lifestyle of the peoples have changed significantly in the last one decade with both the partners are earning, the time they spend on shopping is reduced significantly. This has given a boost to shopping malls, supermarkets, hypermarkets where such individuals can get everything under one roof. In India the malls have been transformed from shopping area to entertainment area which is spreading to tier I, II and III cities of India. The shopping malls have become place to meet friends, eat, watch movies, browse casually etc. Nowadays shopping malls have become a social phenomenon. Thus the malls apart from shopping have become community centers for social, recreational activities and it has become the place of hang out for different age groups.

The retail sector in India is witnessing a huge revamping exercise as traditional markets wake way for next formats such as departmental stores, hyper markets, supermarkets and specialty stories. Western style malls began to appear in metro cities and tire II cites. The global retail giants wanted to attract the India's middle class towards their new markets. In retail market Shopping mall is ranked in fifth place among most attractive emerging retail market. According to the industry estimate, the industry is set to grow from $ 330 in 2007 to $637 by the end of 2020 The share of modern retail in the total retail market is expected to increase by 22 per cent by 2016[30].

In India population 54 per cent of it is below the age of 25 years of age. As per the Marketing White book (2006) by business world, India has around 192 million households. Of these only a little over six million are affluent i.e with household income in excess of Rs. 2,15,000. Another 75 million household are category of well off immediately below the

---

[30] Satish and Pratysuh, The Growth of organized retailing through shopping malls in India, Current trends in technology and science, Vol. 2, Pp. 146, 147, 2012

affluent, earning between Rs. 45,000 and Rs. 2,15,000. This is a sizable proportion which offers excellent opportunity for organised retailer to serve [31].

Mall development is phenomenal in India. The mall mania is spreading fast and entering the second tire cities in India. The factors such as population densities, city planning, socio-economic parameters, physical space have driven the Indian markets to evolve to Shopping malls. In USA 400,000 to 1 million sq ft in size is termed as shopping malls. In India 80,000 sq ft and 5,00,000 sq ft is the mall areas. Most of the mall developers are concentrating on the small cities like two tire and three tire cities and are expected to see a formidable growth of malls in the near feature [32].

3.11. Elements of Shopping Outshoppers in Malls

Shopping is very distinctive in nature, its more to just purchasing what one wants but it also includes the customer's acceptance of the product, brand or stores as well, using multiple senses like- seeing, smelling, tasting, hearing and even tasting (at times) in total it included a well stated shopping experiences. Shoppers visit to shopping malls can provide an individual/family a very economic means of entertainment, leisure and recreation with a great deal of effortless planning. Moreover, in mall culture, consumers are getting more and more inclined towards a "one stop destination" for their complete shopping desire. The architectural design of the mall was the dimension which contributed the most to the mall excitement, while a mall's interior design had the strong influence on customers" desire to stay longer in the mall. Today's Malls have seen a paradigm shift in the kind of interior which the designers choose for their malls; from a very relaxed environment to architecturally lavish, affluent and sophisticated design. Use of light colours exhibits a sense of spaciousness and calmness whereas bright colours impart a sense of excitement among the minds of the consumers; moreover, even the use of serene music along with warm colours helped the mall by increasing the customers desire to stay for long period inside malls. Operating hours and time taken to reach the outlet are one of the main criteria which the consumers look for while selecting a shopping outlet in malls[33].

---

[31] RBI (2006), Press release 2006-2007/300, www.legalpundits.com/.../rbi-press-release-2006-2007-300-30-aug-06-rbi-releases-annual-report-for-2005-06.htm

[32] AT Kearney, The Global Retail Development Index, 2006.

[33] Rupesh Kumar Tiwari and Anish Abraham, Understanding The Consumer Behavior Towards Shopping Malls in Raipur City, International Journal of Management & Strategy, Vol. 1, No. 1, Pp. 1-14, 2014.

According to a recent customer experience and impact study, sponsored by synchrony financial, there are four key shopping experiment elements. Shopping Experience is closely associated with the customers' loyalty with the retailers, but in case of outshoppers the shoppers shopping experiences may or may turn them loyal, but is also supports in recommending the malls or retail outlet to the future buyers.

- Customers are looking for ways to feel valued and make their lives easier
- Discover which experiences do not matter to customers, in order to focus on areas they value
- Factors determining a positive customer experience varies across retail category
- Finding and implementing the top experiences of customers value has an impact on their buying behavior.

The shopping experience matters and the most compelling experience do drive increased spending and loyalty. Giving customers what they want doesn't have to be expensive, it needs to be relevant. The key is to find out what customers want and give it to them.[34] The migration of youth is significant in metro cities from rural and semi urban areas. This single, young recruited, unmarried youngster reveals the best prospects for retailers because they have high income and very less expenses.

They can spend enough to enjoy a good shopping experience and malls make it happen. In the Western countries malls are located on the outskirts of cities so as to offer entertainment with shopping, whereas malls in India are located in the heart of the cities, making parking a nightmare for shoppers. These malls however are mostly constructed by retail estate property developers and reputed millionaires. Modernistic outlook, ultra-hip architecture, air-conditioned interiors, this is the battleground of the brands and lifestyle fighting for consumer attraction, this is the world of the all new mega mall culture in India, all this are built to enhance the shopping experiences of the shoppers[35].

3.12. Conclusion

The theoretical discussion made in the above sections of the study clearly states that Indian consumers are changing rapidly, shopping today is much more than just buying and become pleasure experience itself. Shoppers are now showing preference for shopping malls. With the growing number of malls shoppers it is essential for the mall managers to know the factors

---

[34]http://www.retailcustomerexperience.com/articles/the-elements-that-matter-most-in-the-retail-customer-shopping-experience.

[35] Ibid., Emergency of shopping Malls, Chapter Six, 17_Chapter 6.Pdf.

which attractive the malls to their shoppers. Due to the limited success of these outlets it is necessary for the retailer to be aware of the shoppers motivations. Understanding these factors can support the mall managers to create the strategies. Outshoppers' concept though popular in foreign countries, not of much research has been carried out in the Indian context. There is clearly a need for research on this issue in India The following chapter IV aims to study the outshoppers shopping expand satisfaction towards the shopping malls in tier II cities in Tamil Nadu namely Coimbatore, Madurai and Trichy.

CHAPTER IV

Analysis and Interpretation

4.1. Introduction

One important feature of shopping behaviour is the extent to which shoppers rely mainly on shops in their own locality or motivated and prepared to travel outside their area to buy the things they want i.e., outshopping. Such movements of shoppers are especially important in terms of competition retailers in a major urban shopping center as they always like to attract shoppers from far distance. Early research work had identified the fact that market characteristics such as superior selections and fashion offerings, and a wide choice and variety of products and brands outside the local area, are primary reasons for outshopping. In addition, it has been found that shopping outside the local trade area can be expensive in terms of transportation, energy; time and money as far as shoppers are concerned. To develop attractive merchandising strategies, retailers need to know more about the "outshopping" who are the ones who are prepared to travel miles. Nevertheless, it seems that some consumers prefer to travel outside their own locality to obtain the items they want. This study aims to analyze shopping experiences and satisfaction levels of outshoppers at shopping malls in Tamil Nadu.

A. *Demographic and Socio Economic Status*

Demographic factors are unique to a person. It involves identification of who is responsible for the decision making or buying and who is the ultimate consumer. Modern day organised retailers have started to focus themselves on respective segments based on factors such as age, income, family, size, gender, occupation, etc. The socio-economic background of the consumer largely determines their lifestyle. Lifestyle is considered to be highly correlated with consumer's values and personality traits. An individual's lifestyles is influenced by the social group to which they belong and his/her income and occupation. It is important for the retailer to consider socio economic change in a geographic region over a period of time as it is indicator of the facilities available at various levels and the quality of life of the population, this would indirectly be related to the spread of organized retail. Socio-cultural differences, coupled with other demographic and psychographic factors, are influencing buying behavior and choice of the store even after the emergence of egalitarian shopping malls. This section of the study provides a detailed discussion on the outshoppers' demographic and socio-economic status.

Gender is an important feature in Indian social situation which is variably affected by any social or economic phenomenon and globalization is not an exception to it. Hence the variable gender was investigated for this study. Data related to gender of the respondent is presented in the Table 4.1.

Table 4.1: Gender Wise Distribution of Outshoppers

Sl. No	Gender	No. of Respondents	Percentage
1.	Male	342	60.53
2.	Female	223	39.47
	Total	565	100

Source: Primary Data

The above table indicates the gender wise distribution of the respondents. Among 565 respondents surveyed, 60.53 per cent of the respondents are male and 39.47 per cent of the respondents are female.

Age of the respondents is one of the most important variables in understanding their views about the particular problem: by and large age indicates level of maturity of individuals in that sense age becomes more important to examine the response. Data related to the age of the respondents are given in Table 4.2.

Table 4.2: Age Wise Dispersion of Outshoppers

Sl. No	Age	No. of Respondents	Percentage
1.	15 - 20 years	155	27.44
2.	21 - 35 years	282	49.91
3.	36-40 years	62	10.97
4.	41 - 55 years	66	11.68
	Total	565	100

Source: Primary Data

The above table gives the description regarding the age of the respondents. It has been inferred that 27.44 per cent of the respondents belong to the age group of 15- 20 years. Followed by 49.91 per cent of respondents are aged between 21-35 years and 10.97 per cent of respondents are aged between 36-40 years. Consequently 11.68 per cent of the sample population belongs to the age group of 41-55 years.

Marriage is one of the most important factors in the social institutions. In a developing country like India, it has undergone many changes. The perception and attitudes of the person can also differ by the marital status of the persons because marriage might make the persons little more responsible and matured in understanding and giving the responses to the questions asked. The details of the marital status of the respondents is presented in Table 4.3

Table 4.3: Marital Status of the Outshoppers

Sl. No	Marital Status	No. of Respondents	Percentage
1.	Married	324	57.35
2.	Unmarried	241	42.65
	Total	565	100

Source: Primary Data

From the above table it has been inferred that, majority i.e., 57.35 per cent of the respondents are married and 42.65 per cent of the respondents are unmarried.

Education in one of the most important characteristic that might affect the person's attitudes and the way of looking and understanding any particular social phenomena. In a way, the response of an individual is likely to be determined by his educational status and therefore it becomes imperative to know the educational background of the respondents. Hence the variable 'Education level' was investigated by the researcher and the data pertaining to education is presented in Table 4.4.

Table 4.4: Educational Qualification of the Outshoppers

Sl. No	Qualification	No. of Respondents	Percentage
1.	SSLC / Matric	18	3.19
2.	HSLC	30	5.30
3.	Under Graduate	156	27.61
4.	Post Graduate	161	28.50
5.	Diploma/Technical Education	43	7.61
6.	Professional Qualification	157	27.79
	Total	565	100

Source: Primary Data

The above table determines the educational qualification of the respondents surveyed. Out of the 565 respondents surveyed, 3.19 per cent of the respondents' have completed SSLC or metric educations, followed by 5.30 per cent of the respondents have completed Higher Secondary Level of Schooling. Further 27.61 per cent of the respondents are under graduates and 28.50 per cent of the respondents are post graduates. Consequently 7.61 per cent of the respondents have completed diploma or technical education and 27.79 per cent of the respondents are professionally qualified.

Person's occupations do have a bearing on his or her personality and so also the ways of looking at the problem before him. The quality of life is also determined by an individual's occupation and the income he derives from it. Occupation of an individual also socialized him or her in a particular fashion which in turn reflects his or her pattern of behaviours and their level of understanding of particular phenomenon. In other words the person's response to a problem is possible, and determined by the type of occupation he is engaged in and hence variable occupation was investigated by the researcher and data pertaining to occupation is presented in Table 4.5.

Table 4.5: Occupational Status of the Outshoppers

Sl. No	Occupation	No. of Respondents	Percentage
1.	Salaried	314	55.60
2.	Business	30	5.30
3.	Professional	101	17.90
4.	Students	114	20.10
5.	Home Maker	6	1.10
	Total	565	100

Source: Primary Data

From the above table it has been observed that majority of 55.60 per cent of the respondents are salaried employees and followed by 5.30 per cent who are running the business on their own. Consequently 17.90 per cent of the respondents are professionals and 20.10 per cent of respondent are students. Similarly 1.10 per cent of the respondents are home makers.

The important factor which determines the buying behavior of a person is monthly earning of a person. The pattern of buying activity is mainly based on the income level of the person monthly income plays an important role in shaping the economic conditions of an individual which in turn is likely to have bearing on the responses about problem posed to him. The researcher, therefore in this study attempted to investigate the income as variable and the data related to income of the respondents is presented in Table 4.6

Table 4.6: Monthly Earning of the Outshoppers

Sl. No	Income	No. of Respondents	Percentage
1.	Below Rs. 10000	96	17.00
2.	Rs.10001 - Rs. 20000	194	34.30
3.	Rs.20001 - Rs. 30000	156	27.60
4.	Rs.30001 – Rs. 40000	54	9.60
5.	Above Rs. 40000	65	11.50
	Total	565	100

Source: Primary Data

From the above table it has been inferred that 17 per cent of the respondents earn below Rs. 10,000 per month. Followed by 34.30 per cent of the respondents monthly income is between Rs.10,001-Rs.20,000. Similarly 27.60 per cent of the respondents' monthly income range between Rs.20,001-Rs.30,000 and 9.60 per cent respondents' monthly income are between Rs.30,001-Rs.40,000. Further the 11.50 per cent of the respondents earn above Rs. 40,000 in a month.

The size of the family in which a person lives and gets socialized has immense importance in deciding his values, beliefs and behavior patterns which are likely to affects his or her buying experience, perception and satisfaction. Hence the family size plays an important role in understanding the buyer behavior and therefore it was thought important to understand the family type of the respondents. Data related to the family type is presented in Table 4.7.

Table 4.7: Family Size of the Outshoppers

Sl. No	Members	No. of Respondents	Percentage
1.	2-4 Members	422	74.69
2.	5-7 Members	115	20.35
3.	More than 7 members	28	4.96
	Total	565	100

Source: Primary Data

From the above table it has been inferred that 74.69 per cent of the respondent's family size consist of 2-4 members. Followed by 20.35 per cent of the respondents' family consist of 5-7 members. Consequently 4.96 per cent of the respondents' family consists of more than 7 members.

The number of earning members in the family plays an important role in determining the buyer behavior activity. The total income of the family is an important factor in decision making process.

The pattern of buying activity is mainly based on the income level of the person therefore it is important to understand the number of earning members in the family. Data related to the number of earning members in the family is presented in a Table 4.8.

Table 4.8: Number of Earning Member in the Family

Sl. No	Members	No. of Respondents	Percentage
1.	One	142	25.13
2.	Two	319	56.46
3.	Three	74	13.10
4.	Four	30	5.31
	Total	565	100

Source: Primary Data

From the above table it has been inferred that 25.13 per cent of the respondents' have only one earning member in the family, followed by 56.46 per cent of the respondents' have two earning members in the family. Further 13.10 per cent of the respondents' have three earning members in the family and remaining 5.31 per cent of the respondents' have four earning members in the family.

The number of dependents in the family is one of the important factors which affect the purchase activity of a person. Usually persons' capacity to spend will mainly depend on the number of dependents in the family. Hence the number of dependents in the family plays an important role and therefore it was thought important to understand the number of dependents in the family. Date related to the number of dependent is presented in a Table 4.9

Table 4.9: Number of Dependents in the Family

Sl. No	Members	No. of Respondents	Percentage
1.	One	111	19.65
2.	Two	276	48.85
3.	Three	115	20.35
4.	Four	63	11.15
	Total	565	100

Source: Primary Data

From the above table it has been inferred that out of 565 respondents 19.65 per cent of the respondents have only one dependent in their family. Similarly 48.85 per cent of the respondents have two dependents in their family followed by 20.35 per cent of the respondents have three dependents in their family. Further 11.15 per cent of the respondents have four dependents in their family.

B. *Level of Awareness about Shopping Malls*

The shopping patterns of the Indian consumer are becoming more effervescent as a result of the vigorous changes taking place in their lifestyle and also due to the impact of global marketing conditions in the retailing industry.

The swing in the consumers, expectations resulted in the competitive environment of the retailing industry.

The consumers around the world are becoming unique as the variety of retailing brands from both National and International delivering shopping entertainment.

Interestingly, consumers are becoming more adaptive to their novel products at the shopping malls without comprehension. This reveals the growing awareness among the consumers to have better accessibility to the shopping malls.

Shoppers' awareness towards malls and its features constitute as an important determinant in their shopping and decision making. This section of the study provided an introspective analysis on outshoppers' level of awareness about malls, its features and shopping elements available there.

Table 4.10: Sources of Awareness about Shopping Malls

Sl. No	Particulars	No. of Respondents (N=565)	Proportionate Percentage
Personal Sources			
1.	Sales Person	42	7.43
2.	Dealers	37	6.55
3.	Advertisements	272	48.14
4.	Friends	307	54.34
5.	Relatives	44	7.79
Non-Personal Sources			
1.	TV	80	14.16
2.	Internet (Social Network)	108	19.12
3.	Newspaper / Magazine	106	18.76
4.	Posters, Banners, Broachers	38	6.73

Source: Primary Data

The empirical data analysis discusses about the source of awareness about the shopping malls through personal and non-personal sources. It has been inferred that 7.43 per cent of the respondents are aware about the shopping mall through sales person. Followed by 6.55 per cent of the respondents were aware about the shopping mall through dealers and 48.14 per cent of the respondents got their awareness about the shopping mall through advertisement. The majority of the respondents 54.34 per cent of the respondents were aware about the shopping mall through friends and 7.79 per cent of the respondents came to know about the shopping malls through their relatives. The above mentioned are the personal source of information. Apart from the above personal sources, the respondents are aware about the shopping malls through non personal sources such as TV, Internet, newspaper, magazine, posters, banners and broachers, 14.16 per cent of the respondents were aware about the shopping malls through Television. Similarly 19.12 per cent of the respondents have identified the shopping malls through internet or social network and 18.76 per cent of the respondents' awareness are through newspaper and magazine. Further 6.73 per cent of the respondents got awareness through posters, banners and broachers.

Table 4.11: Outshoppers Level of Awareness about Various Shopping Malls

Shopping Malls	Very Highly Aware	Highly Aware	Aware	Low Aware	Very Low Aware	Sum	Mean	Rank
Brook Field	379 (67.08)	60 (10.62)	84 (14.87)	24 (4.25)	18 (3.19)	2453	4.34	1
Fun Republic	228 (40.35)	162 (28.67)	127 (22.48)	18 (3.19)	30 (5.31)	2235	3.96	2
Millaneum Mall	67 (11.86)	97 (17.17)	163 (28.85)	103 (18.23)	135 (23.89)	1553	2.75	3
Vishall De Mall	89(15.75)	61(10.80)	137(24.25)	107(18.94)	171(30.27)	1485	2.63	4
Femina Shopping Mall	19(3.36)	88(15.58)	145(25.66)	136(24.07)	177(31.33)	1331	2.36	5

Source: Primary Data

Values in parenthesis are in per cent

It has been inferred that, majority of the respondents are aware about the Brook Field shopping mall and it is ranked first with an average score of 4.34, followed by the Fun Republic shopping mall in second place with mean score of 3.96. Respondents' awareness about the Millaneum mall is ranked in the third place with the score of 2.75. Further it has been inferred that, the respondents awareness about the Vishall De Mall have scored 2.63 and ranked in the fourth place, Femina Shopping Mall is ranked in the fifth place with the mean score of 2.36 regarding the awareness of mall among the respondents.

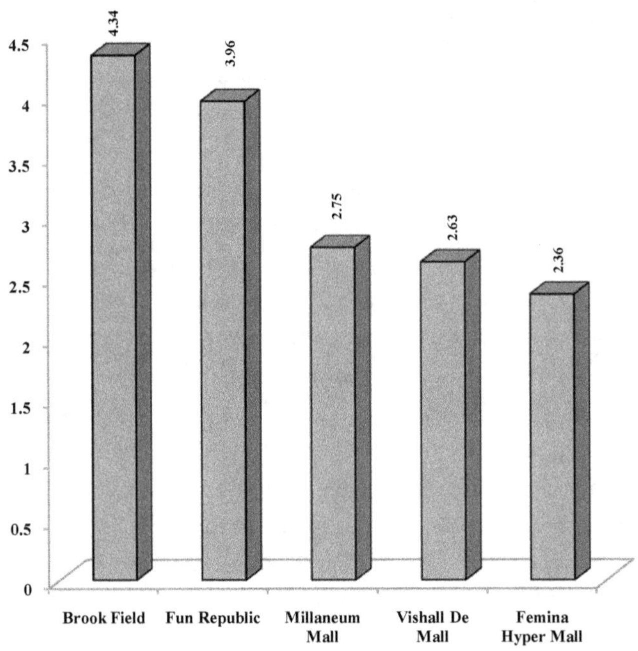

Exhibit 4.1: Outshoppers Level of Awareness About various Shopping Malls

Nowadays, outshoppers have started to believe that the malls are best place to shop or hang out. It is not only a place to shop but also a place for social and recreational activities. The shopping mall is an agglomeration of various retailers and commercial service providers within a well-planned, designed and managed building or group of buildings. Shopping motivation reveals the general predisposition consumers toward the act of shopping. This predisposition may be clearly visible in buyer's decision making process which includes patterns of information search, alternative, evaluation, and product selection. Based on this conceptual understanding following hypothesis is framed and tested with appropriate statistical tool.

H1: There exists close association between outshoppers' level of awareness about a shopping mall and their preference of visit to the malls.

Table 4.12: Result of ANOVA Outshoppers' Level OF Awareness about a Shopping Mall and their Preference of visit to the Malls

Awareness	Source	Sum of Square	DF	Mean square	F	Sig
Brook Field	Between Groups	36.011	4	9.003	8.144	.000
	Within Groups	619.062	560	1.105		
	Total	655.073	564	-		
Fun Republic	Between Groups	7.238	4	1.809	1.471	.209
	Within Groups	688.656	560	1.230		
	Total	695.894	564	-		
Millaneum Mall	Between Groups	13.754	4	3.439	2.009	.092
	Within Groups	958.557	560	1.712		
	Total	972.312	564	-		
Vishall De Mall	Between Groups	27.972	4	6.993	3.554	.007
	Within Groups	1101.975	560	1.968		
	Total	1129.947	564	-		
Femina Shopping Mall	Between Groups	1.618	4	.404	.293	.882
	Within Groups	771.876	560	1.378		
	Total	773.494	564	-		

Level of Significance: 5 per cent

From the above table has been inferred that probability value of ANOVA at 5 per cent level does not establish good relationship between the variables tested. Therefore, the hypothesis framed stands rejected and it has been concluded that there exists no association between outshoppers' level of awareness about a shopping mall and their preference of visit to the malls. However it is exceptional in the case of Brook Field and Vishal De shopping malls.

C. Outshoppers Shopping Experiences at Malls

The reasons for outshopping are varied and have been linked to demographic and psychographic variables and in the case of remote communities improvements in roads and private transportation have also added to the growth in outshopping. Previous studies have identified several reasons for outshopping including the wider range of stores, the perception that larger communities provide cheaper services and products and the fact that many residents from small communities work in nearby larger communities and find shopping there convenient because of the dissatisfaction with the product/shopping options available locally. Another reason for outshopping is that it is a secondary activity on trips to larger centers to access entertainment, social and business services. A successful shopping mall must have an appropriate blend of all these attributes to attract retail outshoppers. At the same time in order to create loyal mall patronage it is important to identify the most important attribute that outweigh all other experience factors, required for the survival and sustainability of the malls in the long run. This section of the analysis and discussion is focused on the outshoppers experiences towards their shopping malls located in the three prime tier II cities of Tamil Nadu i.e., in Coimbatore, Madurai and Trichy.

Table 4.13: Outshoppers' Opinion on their Visits to All Premium Malls Functioning in the Selected Three Cities

Sl. No	Visited	No. of Respondents	Percentage
1.	Have Visited All Five Malls	547	96.81
2.	Not Yet Visited All Five Malls	18	3.19
	Total	565	100

Source: Primary Data

From the above table it has been inferred that majority i.e.,96.81 per cent of respondents have visited all the five malls and remaining 3.19 per cent of the respondents have not yet visited all the five malls.

Table 4.14: Most Preferred and Visited Shopping Malls among the Outshoppers

Sl. No	Leading Shopping Malls	No. of Respondents	Percentage
1.	Brook Field	120	21.24
2.	Fun Republic	119	21.06
3.	Millaneum Mall	110	19.47
4.	Femina Shopping Mall	114	20.18
5.	Vishall De Mall	102	18.05
	Total	565	100

Source: Primary Data

The empirical data analysis indicates that out of 565 respondents surveyed 21.24 per cent of the respondents have stated that among the five shopping malls, Brook field is most preferred and visited shopping mall in Tamil Nadu. Followed by 21.06 per cent respondents have stated that Fun Republic mall is the most preferred and visited shopping mall. Similarly 19.47 per cent of the respondents have stated that most preferred and visited mall is the Millaneum mall. Further 20.18 per cent of the respondents have stated that Femina Shopping Mall is their most preferred and visited mall and remaining 18.05 per cent of the respondents opinion is that the Vishall De Mall is the most preferred and visited mall.

From the above table it is clearly observed that majority of 21.24 per cent of the respondents have stated that Brook Fields is the most preferred and visited mall.

Table 4.15: Outshoppers' Opinion on Elements of Shopping Malls

Sl. No.	Place	No. of Respondents (N=565)	Proportionate Percentage
1.	Means for Shopping	179	31.68
2.	Fun & Entertainment	305	53.98
3.	Place of Outing with Friends	167	29.56
4.	Place for Family Outing	103	18.23
5.	Place for Multi-Cuisine Tasting / Eating's	73	12.92

Source: Primary Data

The above table represents the opinion of the respondents regarding the elements or purpose of visit to the shopping malls. It has been clearly observed that 31.68 per cent of the respondents have stated that they consider shopping malls as means for shopping purpose. Followed by majority of 53.98 per cent of the respondents have visited the shopping malls for fun and entertainment purpose. Consequently 29.56 per cent of the respondents have considered shopping malls as place of outing with friends and further 18.23 per cent of the respondents have considered malls as place of family outing. The remaining 12.92 per cent of the respondents have considered malls as the place for multi-cuisine tasting and eating.

Hence it has been inferred that majority of 53.98 per cent of the respondents have considered shopping malls as place for fun and entertainment.

The study done by Underhill (1999) revealed that, shopping is very distinctive in nature, its more to just purchasing what one wants but it also includes the customer's acceptance of the product, brand or stores as well, using multiple senses like- seeing, smelling, tasting, hearing and even tasting (at times).

Moreover, their demographic and socio-economic status also plays a significant role in defining their shopping behaviour, especially in malls. Based on this conceptual understanding it has been hypothetically believed that outshoppers view about malls does not differ from one demographic and socio-economic segment of populations to others.

To test the feasibility of this statement following hypothesis is framed and tested with appropriate statistical tool.

H2: Outshoppers view about malls does not differ from one demographic and socio-economic segment of populations to others.

Table 4.16: Gender of the Outshoppers and their View about Malls

Motives	Gender		Total
	Male	Female	
Means for Shopping	109(19.29)	70(12.39)	179(31.68)
Fun & Entertainment	207(36.64)	98(17.35)	305(53.98)
Place of Outing with Friends	105(18.58)	62(10.97)	167(29.56)
Place for Family Outing	51(9.03)	52(9.20)	103(18.23)
Place for Multi-Cuisine Tasting / Eating's	62(10.97)	11(1.95)	73(12.92)

Source: Computed from Primary Data

The data presented in the above mentioned cross-table depicts, that male and female outshoppers views about shopping malls varies from one to another.

Table 4.17: Result of Chi-Square Gender of the Outshoppers and their View about Malls

Motives	Chi-square value	DF	Table value	Remark
Means for Shopping	.014	1	3.841	Accepted
Fun & Entertainment	14.938	1	3.841	Rejected
Place of Outing with Friends	.545	1	3.841	Accepted
Place for Family Outing	6.399	1	3.841	Rejected
Place for Multi-Cuisine Tasting / Eating's	20.892	1	3.841	Rejected

Level of Significance: 5 per cent

From the above table it has been inferred that the calculated chi-square values are greater than the table value 3.841 at 5 per cent level of significance. Therefore, the hypothesis framed stands rejected and it has been concluded that the outshoppers view about malls differs according to their gender. However it is exceptional in the case of means for shopping and place of outing with friends.

Table 4.18: Age of the Outshoppers and their View about Malls

Motives	Age				Total
	15 - 20 Years	21 - 35 Years	36-40 Years	41 - 55 Years	
Means for Shopping	48(8.50)	72(12.74)	23(4.07)	36(6.37)	179(31.68)
Fun & Entertainment	107(18.94)	145(25.66)	21(3.72)	32(5.66)	305(53.98)
Place of Outing with Friends	48(8.50)	97(17.17)	12(2.12)	10(1.77)	167(29.56)
Place for Family Outing	12(2.12)	62(10.97)	6(1.06)	23(4.07)	103(18.23)
Place for Multi-Cuisine Tasting/Eating's	30(5.31)	43(7.61)	0(0.00)	0(0.00)	73(12.92)

Source: Computed from Primary Data

The data presented in the above table reveal the outshoppers' view point about various age groups of shoppers. The young shoppers consider malls as a place for entertainments. On the country, the matured adult shopper considers malls as a place for shopping, family outing and place for outing with friends and families.

Table 4.19: Result of Chi-Square Age of the Outshoppers and their View about Malls

Motives	Chi-square value	DF	Table value	Remark
Means for Shopping	21.744	3	7.815	Rejected
Fun & Entertainment	25.777	3	7.815	Rejected
Place of Outing with Friends	12.999	3	7.815	Rejected
Place for Family Outing	29.376	3	7.815	Rejected
Place for Multi-Cuisine Tasting / Eating's	26.054	3	7.815	Rejected

Level of Significance: 5 per cent

From the above table it has been inferred that the calculated chi-square values are greater than the table value 7.815 at 5 per cent level of significance. Therefore, the hypothesis framed stands rejected and it has been concluded that the outshoppers view about malls differs according to their age classification.

Table 4.20: Marital Status of the Outshoppers and their View about Malls

Motives	Marital Status		Total
	Married	Unmarried	
Means for Shopping	120(21.24)	59(10.44)	179(31.68)
Fun & Entertainment	167(29.56)	138(24.42)	305(53.98)
Place of Outing with Friends	51(9.03)	116(20.53)	167(29.56)
Place for Family Outing	85(15.04)	18(3.19)	103(18.23)
Place for Multi-Cuisine Tasting / Eating's	18(3.19)	55(9.73)	73(12.92)

Source: Computed from Primary Data

As stated in the previous table discussion, it has been observed that the unmarried youth consider mall as place for outing with the friends and place for tasting multi-cuisine of various culture and countries or continents. On the contrary, the married couples considers mall as place for shopping.

Table 4.21: Result of Chi-Square Marital Status of the Outshoppers and their View about Malls

Motives	Chi-square value	DF	Table value	Remark
Means for Shopping	10.066	1	3.841	Rejected
Fun & Entertainment	1.819	1	3.841	Accepted
Place of Outing with Friends	69.645	1	3.841	Rejected
Place for Family Outing	32.648	1	3.841	Rejected
Place for Multi-Cuisine Tasting / Eating's	36.619	1	3.841	Rejected

Level of Significance: 5 per cent

From the above table it has been inferred that the calculated chi-square values are greater than the table value 3.841 at 5 per cent level of significance. Therefore, the hypothesis framed stands rejected and it has been concluded that the outshoppers view about malls differs according to their marital status. However it is exceptional in the case of fun & entertainment reasons.

Table 4.22(A): Educational Qualification of the Outshoppers and their View about Malls

Motives	Education			
	SSLC / Matric	HSLC	Under Graduate	Post Graduate
Means for Shopping	6(1.06)	6(1.06)	42(7.43)	74(13.10)
Fun & Entertainment	6(1.06)	24(4.25)	84(14.87)	81(14.34)
Place of Outing with Friends	6(1.06)	0(0.00)	66(11.68)	36(6.37)
Place for Family Outing	0(0.00)	0(0.00)	24(4.25)	26(4.60)
Place for Multi-Cuisine Tasting / Eating's	0(0.00)	12(2.12)	30(5.31)	6(1.06)

Source: Computed from Primary Data

Table 4.22(B): Educational Qualification of the Outshoppers and their View about Malls

Motives	Education		Total
	Diploma/Technical Education	Professional Qualification	
Means for Shopping	13(2.30)	38(6.73)	179(31.68)
Fun & Entertainment	25(4.42)	85(15.04)	305(53.98)
Place of Outing with Friends	19(3.36)	40(7.08)	167(29.56)
Place for Family Outing	6(1.06)	47(8.32)	103(18.23)
Place for Multi-Cuisine Tasting / Eating's	7(1.24)	18(3.19)	73(12.92)

Source: Computed from Primary Data

The data discussion presented in the above table depicts that there exist wide disparity among highly educated and least educated outshoppers view point about malls and its inbuilt features.

Table 4.23: Result of Chi-Square Educational Qualification of the Outshoppers and their View about Malls

Motives	Chi-square value	DF	Table value	Remark
Means for Shopping	22.815	5	11.070	Rejected
Fun & Entertainment	12.440	5	11.070	Rejected
Place of Outing with Friends	34.571	5	11.070	Rejected
Place for Family Outing	26.977	5	11.070	Rejected
Place for Multi-Cuisine Tasting / Eating's	40.567	5	11.070	Rejected

Level of Significance: 5 per cent

From the above table it has been inferred that the calculated chi-square values are greater than the table value 11.070 at 5 per cent level of significance. Therefore, the hypothesis framed stands rejected and it has been concluded that the outshoppers view about malls differs according to their educational qualification.

Table 4.24(A): Occupational Status of the Outshoppers and their View about Malls

Motives	Occupation		
	Salaried	Business	Professional
Means for Shopping	119(21.06)	18(3.19)	18(3.19)
Fun & Entertainment	168(29.73)	0(0.00)	59(10.44)
Place of Outing with Friends	89(15.75)	12(2.12)	6(1.06)
Place for Family Outing	79(13.98)	0(0.00)	12(2.12)
Place for Multi-Cuisine Tasting / Eating's	31(5.49)	0(0.00)	6(1.06)

Source: Computed from Primary Data

Table 4.24(B): Occupational Status of the Outshoppers and their View about Malls

Motives	Occupation		Total
	Students	Home Maker	
Means for Shopping	24(4.25)	0(0.00)	179(31.68)
Fun & Entertainment	72(12.74)	6(1.06)	305(53.98)
Place of Outing with Friends	54(9.56)	6(1.06)	167(29.56)
Place for Family Outing	12(2.12)	0(0.00)	103(18.23)
Place for Multi-Cuisine Tasting / Eating's	36(6.37)	0(0.00)	73(12.92)

Source: Computed from Primary Data

The elaborate data description presented in the above table depicts that shopping intention and view of these shoppers about malls various across various occupational groups surveyed in Coimbatore, Madurai and Trichy.

Table 4.25: Result of Chi-Square Occupational Status of the Outshoppers and their View about Malls

Motives	Chi-square value	DF	Table value	Remark
Means for Shopping	34.418	4	9.488	Rejected
Fun & Entertainment	44.999	4	9.488	Rejected
Place of Outing with Friends	60.518	4	9.488	Rejected
Place for Family Outing	25.409	4	9.488	Rejected
Place for Multi-Cuisine Tasting / Eating's	47.583	4	9.488	Rejected

Level of Significance: 5 per cent

From the above table it has been inferred that the calculated chi-square values are greater than the table value 9.488 at 5 per cent level of significance. Therefore, the hypothesis framed stands rejected and it has been concluded that the outshoppers view about malls differs according to their occupational status.

Table 4.26(A): Monthly Income of the Outshoppers and their View about Malls

Motives	Monthly Income					
	Below Rs. 10000	Rs.10001 – Rs. 20000	Rs.20001 - Rs.30000	Rs. 30001 – Rs.40000	Above Rs.40000	Total
Means for Shopping	18(3.19)	63(11.15)	56(9.91)	6(1.06)	36(6.37)	179(31.68)
Fun & Entertainment	54(9.56)	99(17.52)	91(16.11)	30(5.31)	31(5.49)	305(53.98)
Place of Outing with Friends	30(5.31)	56(9.91)	35(6.19)	18(3.19)	28(4.96)	167(29.56)
Place for Family Outing	12(2.12)	25(4.42)	31(5.49)	12(2.12)	23(4.07)	103(18.23)
Place for Multi-Cuisine Tasting / Eating's	6(1.06)	13(2.30)	36(6.37)	12(2.12)	6(1.06)	73(12.92)

Source: Computed from Primary Data

The cross table descriptions clearly indicated that the higher monthly earning power of outshoppers significantly influences their spending powers at mall, so do their perception or view point about malls also varies from one income class population to other in the study region Coimbatore, Madurai and Trichy.

Table 4.27: Result of Chi-Square Monthly Income of the Outshoppers and their View about Malls

Motives	Chi-square value	DF	Table value	Remark
Means for Shopping	36.184	4	9.488	Rejected
Fun & Entertainment	3.157	4	9.488	Accepted
Place of Outing with Friends	10.052	4	9.488	Rejected
Place for Family Outing	19.522	4	9.488	Rejected
Place for Multi-Cuisine Tasting / Eating's	29.708	4	9.488	Rejected

Level of Significance: 5 per cent

From the above table it has been inferred that the calculated chi-square values are greater than the table value 9.488 at 5 per cent level of significance. Therefore, the hypothesis framed stands rejected and it has been concluded that the outshoppers view about malls differs according to their monthly income. However it is exceptional in the case of fun & entertainment.

Table 4.28: Family size of the Outshoppers and their view about Malls

Motives	Family Size			Total
	2-4 Members	5-7 Members	More than 7 members	
Means for Shopping	141(24.96)	38(6.73)	0(0.00)	179(31.68)
Fun & Entertainment	215(38.05)	72(12.74)	18(3.19)	305(53.98)
Place of Outing with Friends	125(22.12)	26(4.60)	16(2.83)	167(29.56)
Place for Family Outing	65(11.50)	38(6.73)	0(0.00)	103(18.23)
Place for Multi-Cuisine Tasting / Eating's	47(8.32)	26(4.60)	0(0.00)	73(12.92)

Source: Computed from Primary Data

The study tend to reveal that the smaller size of family greatly support the outshoppers to conveniently shop at malls in comparison to the large families in term of its size. Thus, it can be concluded that outshoppers' perception towards malls varies according to their family size.

Table 4.29: Result of Chi-Square Family Size of the Outshoppers and their View about Malls

Motives	Chi-square value	DF	Table value	Remark
Means for Shopping	13.667	2	5.991	Rejected
Fun & Entertainment	6.206	2	5.991	Rejected
Place of Outing with Friends	12.901	2	5.991	Rejected
Place for Family Outing	25.434	2	5.991	Rejected
Place for Multi-Cuisine Tasting / Eating's	14.941	2	5.991	Rejected

Level of Significance: 5 per cent

From the above table it has been inferred that the calculated chi-square values are greater than the table value 5.991 at 5 per cent level of significance. Therefore, the hypothesis framed stands rejected and it has been concluded that the outshoppers view about malls differs according to their family size.

Table 4.30: Number of Earning Members in the Outshoppers Family and their View about Malls

Motives	No. of. Earning Members				Total
	One	Two	Three	Four	
Means for Shopping	18(3.19)	132(23.36)	22(3.89)	7(1.24)	179(31.68)
Fun & Entertainment	75(13.27)	166(29.38)	44(7.79)	20(3.54)	305(53.98)
Place of Outing with Friends	54(9.56)	84(14.87)	12(2.12)	17(3.01)	167(29.56)
Place for Family Outing	20(3.54)	77(13.63)	6(1.06)	0(0.00)	103(18.23)
Place for Multi-Cuisine Tasting / Eating's	24(4.25)	42(7.43)	0(0.00)	7(1.24)	73(12.92)

Source: Computed from Primary Data

The cross data analysis indicated that the dual income families' view about malls and their shopping practices at mall is entirely different from that of the single or multiple income families.

Table 4.31: Result of Chi-Square Number of Earning Members in the Outshoppers Family and their View about Malls

Motives	Chi-square value	DF	Table value	Remark
Means for Shopping	38.655	3	9.837	Rejected
Fun & Entertainment	3.400	3	9.837	Accepted
Place of Outing with Friends	23.402	3	9.837	Rejected
Place for Family Outing	20.881	3	9.837	Rejected
Place for Multi-Cuisine Tasting / Eating's	15.888	3	9.837	Rejected

Level of Significance: 5 per cent

From the above table it has been inferred that the calculated chi-square values are greater than the table value 9.837 at 5 per cent level of significance. Therefore, the hypothesis framed stands rejected and it has been concluded that the outshoppers view about malls differs according to the earning pattern of the family. However it is exceptional in case of Fun and Entertainment.

Table 4.32: Number of Dependents in the Outshoppers Family and their View about Malls

Motives	No. of. Dependents				Total
	One	Two	Three	Four	
Means for Shopping	45(7.96)	91(16.11)	30(5.31)	13(2.30)	179(31.68)
Fun & Entertainment	66(11.68)	143(25.31)	67(11.86)	29(5.13)	305(53.98)
Place of Outing with Friends	28(4.96)	74(13.10)	24(4.25)	41(7.26)	167(29.56)
Place for Family Outing	45(7.96)	33(5.84)	0(0.00)	25(4.42)	103(18.23)
Place for Multi-Cuisine Tasting / Eating's	35(6.19)	19(3.36)	6(1.06)	13(2.30)	73(12.92)

Source: Computed from Primary Data

The study reveals that the dependent size of the small families and their spending power in malls is greater in comparison to those families who have more dependents.

Table 4.33: Result of Chi-Square Number of Dependents in the Outshoppers Family and their View about Malls

Motives	Chi-square value	DF	Table value	Remark
Means for Shopping	9.542	3	9.837	Accepted
Fun & Entertainment	4.315	3	9.837	Accepted
Place of Outing with Friends	44.348	3	9.837	Rejected
Place for Family Outing	89.440	3	9.837	Rejected
Place for Multi-Cuisine Tasting / Eating's	52.509	3	9.837	Rejected

Level of Significance: 5 per cent

From the above table it has been inferred that the calculated chi-square values are greater than the table value 9.837 at 5 per cent level of significance. Therefore, the hypothesis framed stands rejected and it has been concluded that the outshoppers view about malls differs according to the dependents in the family.

From the above Tables: 4.16-4.33 it has been concluded that the calculated chi-square values are greater than the table values at 5 per cent level of significance.

Therefore the hypothesis framed stands rejected and it has been concluded that outshoppers view about malls differs from one demographic and socio-economic segment of populations to others.

Table 4.34: Shopping Behaviour Experienced by the Outshoppers at the Malls

Sl. No	Nature	No. of Respondents	Percentage
1.	Impulsive	174	30.80
2.	Rational	391	69.20
	Total	565	100

Source: Primary Data

The above table indicates that out of the total 565 respondents surveyed, 30.80 per cent of the respondents are impulse buyer at shopping malls and majority of 69.20 per cent of the respondents are rational buyers.

Table 4.35: Outshoppers' Opinion on Frequency of Visit to Shopping Malls in a Year

Sl. No	Frequency	No. of Respondents	Percentage
1.	Very Frequently (Once in a Week)	48	8.50
2.	Frequently (Once in Two Weeks)	77	13.63
3.	Occasionally (Once in month)	221	39.12
4.	Rarely	59	10.44
5.	Based on the Needs	160	28.32
	Total	565	100

Source: Primary Data

The above table infers the frequency of visit of the respondents to the shopping malls in a year. It has been inferred that, 8.50 per cent of the respondents are visiting the malls very frequently i.e., once in a week followed by 13.63 per cent of the respondents visit the shopping malls frequently i.e., once in two weeks. Further, it has been inferred that 39.12 per cent of the respondents visit the malls occasionally i.e., once in a month. Similarly10.44 per cent of the respondents visit the shopping malls rarely and 28.32 per cent of the respondents visit the malls based on their needs.

Table 4.36: Most Preferred Products Shopped by the Outshoppers

Sl. No	Nature of Product	No. of Respondents (N=565)	Proportionate Percentage
1.	Food and Beverage	240	42.48
2.	Life Style	172	30.44
3.	Clothing	349	61.77
4.	Provisions	70	12.39
5.	Watches and Jewelers	89	15.75
6.	Stationeries	55	9.73
7.	Cosmetics and Beauty	119	21.06
8.	Health and Medicine	25	4.42
9.	Foot ware	147	26.02
10.	Household Appliances	145	25.66
11.	Leisure and Personal Goods	78	13.81

Source: Primary Data

The empirical data analysis indicated that out of 565 respondents surveyed, 42.48 per cent of the respondents' preferred to shop in the malls are food and beverage, followed by 30.44 per cent of the respondents' prefer to shop life style products in the malls. Consequently 61.77 per cent of the respondents preferred to buy clothes in the shopping malls and 12.39 per cent prefer to buy provision in shopping malls. Similarly 15.75 of the respondents preferred to shop watches and jewelers, followed by 9.73 per cent of the respondents prefered to buy stationeries. Further 21.06 per cent of the respondents prefer to buy cosmetics and beauty items and 4.42 per cent of the respondents mostly preferred to shop health and medicine products. From the above table it has been observed that 26.02 per cent of the respondents preferred product in the shopping malls is foot ware and 25.66 per cent of the respondents prefer to buy household appliance. Further 13.81 per cent of the respondents preferred product in the shopping malls is leisure and personal goods.

Thus it has been found that majority i.e., 61.77 per cent of the respondents' most preferred products in the shopping malls is clothing.

Shopping malls play a major role in consumers' lifestyles. They have become not only centers for shopping, but also community centers for social and recreational activities across the globe. Modern retail stores, food courts, restaurants, cinemas, children's play areas, interactive entertainment, social use areas, relaxation spaces, are now major components of many shopping mall. The mall features and its in-build elements significantly influence the rational or impulsive buying behaviour among consumers. Similarly, it also influences the nature of products brought by the consumers. To establish the prevailing fact and to draw a cross-diagnostic analysis following hypothesis is framed.

H3: There exists close association between impulsive/rational nature of consumers' and products brought by them in the shopping malls.

Table 4.37: Independent z Test Impulsive/Rational Nature of Outshoppers Purchase on the Shopping Malls

Variables	Impulsive		Rational		Z	Sig	Remark
	Mean	SD	Mean	SD			
Food and Beverage	0.389	0.489	**0.479**	0.500	-1.906	.000	Accepted
Life Style Goods	0.069	0.256	**0.106**	0.308	-0.890	.069	Rejected
Clothing	**0.857**	0.351	0.732	0.444	2.896	.000	Accepted
Provisions	**0.217**	0.415	0.197	0.398	0.419	.410	Rejected
Watches and Jewelers	**0.462**	0.502	0.220	0.415	4.238	.000	Accepted
Stationeries	0.000	0.000	0.240	0.428	-4.949	.000	Accepted
Cosmetics and Beauty	0.308	0.465	**0.448**	0.498	-2.166	.000	Accepted
Health and Medicine	**0.278**	0.456	0.085	0.253	2.852	.000	Accepted
Footwear	1.000	0.000	1.000	0.000	1.821	.000	Accepted
Household Appliances	**0.439**	0.498	0.327	0.470	2.313	.000	Accepted
Leisure and personal goods	**0.247**	**0.433**	0.093	0.291	4.933	.000	Accepted

Level of Significance: 5 per cent

Impulse buying can be defined as unplanned, sudden, and spontaneous impulse buy, which lacks careful evaluation of product and purchase consequences. Where, as planned purchase is characterized by deliberate, thoughtful search and evaluation that normally results in rational, accurate and better decisions. It has been observed from above presented descriptive analysis that consumers mostly buy: clothing, provisions, watches and jewelers, health and medicine, foot ware, household appliances and leisure and personal goods impulsively. Whereas, the sample subjects have exhibited rational buying behaviour while purchase of: food and beverage, cosmetics and beauty stationary and life style goods.

From the above it has been inferred that the probability value of Z is found to be significant at five per cent level. Therefore the hypothesis framed stands accepted and it has been concluded that there exists close association between impulsive/rational nature of consumers' and products brought by them in the shopping malls. However it is exceptional in the case of provisions and life style goods brought by the consumers'.

According to Assael (1987) shopping behavior is the most unique for behavior which the consumers exhibit. Gifts, clothing, groceries, gifts and household items are some of the most common type of shopping which consumers indulge in a highly frequent manner. This study aims to analyse whether demographic and socio-economic status of outshoppers influences the nature of products brought by them. To test these statements rationality following five hypotheses are framed and tested individually.

H4: There exists rational association between the gender of outshoppers and the products shopped at malls.

Table 4.38: Gender of Outshoppers and the Products Shopped by them at Malls

Products	Gender		Total
	Male	**Female**	
Food and Beverage	162 **(18.37)**	78(12.85)	240(16.12)
Life Style	130**(14.74)**	42(6.92)	172(11.55)
Clothing	197(22.34)	152**(25.04)**	349(23.44)
Provisions	27(3.06)	43**(7.08)**	70(4.70)
Watches and Jewelers	36(4.08)	53**(8.73)**	89(5.98)
Stationeries	32(3.63)	23**(3.79)**	55(3.69)
Cosmetics and Beauty	54(6.12)	65**(10.71)**	119(7.99)
Health and Medicine	25**(2.83)**	0(0.00)	25(1.68)
Foot ware	99**(11.22)**	48(7.91)	147(9.87)
Household Appliances	78(8.84)	67(11.04)	145(9.74)
Leisure and Personal Goods	42(4.76)	36(5.93)	78(5.24)

Source: Computed from Primary Data

The table description reveals that there exist differences in products shopped by male and female consumers in the malls.

Table 4.39: Result of Chi-Square Gender of Outshoppers and the Products Shopped by them at Malls

Products	Chi-square value	DF	Table value	Remark
Food and Beverage	8.482	1	3.841	Rejected
Life Style	23.445	1	3.841	Rejected
Clothing	6.373	1	3.841	Rejected
Provisions	16.127	1	3.841	Rejected
Watches and Jewellery	17.832	1	3.841	Rejected
Stationeries	.141	1	3.841	Accepted
Cosmetics and Beauty	14.488	1	3.841	Rejected
Health and Medicine	17.056	1	3.841	Rejected
Foot ware	3.864	1	3.841	Rejected
Household Appliances	3.707	1	3.841	Accepted
Leisure and Personal Goods	1.693	1	3.841	Accepted

Level of Significance: 5 per cent

From the above table it has been inferred that the calculated chi-square values are greater than the table value 3.841 at 5 per cent level of significance. Therefore, the hypothesis framed stands rejected and it has been concluded that there exists no association between the gender of outshoppers and the products shopped at malls. However it is exceptional in the case of stationeries, household appliances and leisure and personal goods.

H5: There exists rational association between the age of outshoppers and the products shopped at malls.

Table 4.40: Age of Outshoppers and the Products Shopped by them at Malls

Products	Age				Total
	15 - 20 Years	21 - 35 Years	36-40 Years	41 - 55 Years	
Food and Beverage	95(19.83)	**114(17.95)**	19(12.26)	12(5.45)	240(16.12)
Life Style	54(11.27)	49(7.72)	26(16.77)	**43(19.55)**	172(11.55)
Clothing	96(20.04)	157(24.72)	**49(31.61)**	47(21.36)	349(23.44)
Provisions	12(2.51)	31(4.88)	**20(12.90)**	7(3.18)	70(4.70)
Watches and jewellery	30(6.26)	41(6.46)	0(0.00)	**18(8.18)**	89(5.98)
Stationeries	18(3.76)	**30(4.72)**	7(4.52)	0(0.00)	55(3.69)
Cosmetics and Beauty	**48(10.02)**	52(8.19)	7(4.52)	12(5.45)	119(7.99)
Health and Medicine	0(0.00)	6(0.94)	7(4.52)	**12(5.45)**	25(1.68)
Foot ware	**66(13.78)**	38(5.98)	13(8.39)	30(13.64)	147(9.87)
Household Appliances	36(7.52)	77(12.13)	0(0.00)	**32(14.55)**	145(9.74)
Leisure and Personal Goods	24(5.01)	**40(6.30)**	7(4.52)	7(3.18)	78(5.24)

Source: Computed from Primary Data

The table description reveals that there exist differences in products shopped by different age group of consumers in the malls.

Table 4.41: Result of Chi-Square Age of Outshoppers and the Products Shopped by them at

Malls

Products	Chi-square value	DF	Table value	Remark
Food and Beverage	42.434	3	7.815	Rejected
Life Style	65.570	3	7.815	Rejected
Clothing	14.755	3	7.815	Rejected
Provisions	26.333	3	7.815	Rejected
Watches and Jewellers	20.022	3	7.815	Rejected
Stationeries	8.173	3	7.815	Rejected
Cosmetics and Beauty	14.204	3	7.815	Rejected
Health and Medicine	47.141	3	7.815	Rejected
Foot ware	58.913	3	7.815	Rejected
Household Appliances	40.303	3	7.815	Rejected
Leisure and Personal Goods	1.298	3	7.815	Accepted

Level of Significance: 5 per cent

From the above table it has been inferred that the calculated chi-square values are greater than the table value 7.815 at 5 per cent level of significance. Therefore, the hypothesis framed stands rejected and it has been concluded that there exists no association between the age of outshoppers and the products shopped at malls. However it is exceptional in the case of leisure and personal goods.

H6: There exists rational association between the educational qualification of outshoppers and the products shopped at malls.

Table 4.42(a): Educational Qualification of Outshoppers and the Products Shopped by them at

Malls

Products	Education			
	SSLC / Metric	HSLC	Under Graduate	Post Graduate
Food and Beverage	**18(33.33)**	12(20.00)	72(15.58)	74(15.55)
Life Style	6(11.11)	12(20.00)	66(14.29)	44(9.24)
Clothing	12(22.22)	24(40.00)	96(20.78)	107(22.48)
Provisions	0(0.00)	0(0.00)	12(2.60)	27(5.67)
Watches and Jewellers	**6(11.11)**	6(10.00)	18(3.90)	48(10.08)
Stationeries	0(0.00)	0(0.00)	18(3.90)	19(3.99)
Cosmetics and Beauty	**6(11.11)**	0(0.00)	48(10.39)	32(6.72)
Health and Medicine	0(0.00)	0(0.00)	6(1.30)	**19(3.99)**
Foot ware	0(0.00)	6(10.00)	60(12.99)	49(10.29)
Household Appliances	6(11.11)	0(0.00)	54(11.69)	38(7.98)
Leisure and Personal Goods	0(0.00)	0(0.00)	12(2.60)	19(3.99)

Source: Computed from Primary Data

Table 4.42(b): Educational Qualification of Outshoppers and the Products Shopped by them at Malls

Products	Education		Total
	Diploma/Technical Education	Professional Qualification	
Food and Beverage	**30(30.30)**	34(10.06)	240(16.12)
Life Style	13(13.13)	31(9.17)	172(11.55)
Clothing	12(12.12)	**98(28.99)**	349(23.44)
Provisions	0(0.00)	**31(9.17)**	70(4.70)
Watches and Jewellers	0(0.00)	11(3.25)	89(5.98)
Stationeries	**7(7.07)**	11(3.25)	55(3.69)
Cosmetics and Beauty	0(0.00)	33(9.76)	119(7.99)
Health and Medicine	0(0.00)	0(0.00)	25(1.68)
Foot ware	**19(19.19)**	13(3.85)	147(9.87)
Household Appliances	**12(12.12)**	35(10.36)	145(9.74)
Leisure and Personal Goods	6(6.06)	**41(12.13)**	78(5.24)

Source: Computed from Primary Data

The table description reveals that there exist differences in products shopped in the mall by the outshoppers possessing different educational qualifications.

Table 4.43: Result of Chi-Square Educational Qualification of Outshoppers and the Products Shopped by them at Malls

Products	Chi-square value	DF	Table value	Remark
Food and Beverage	67.076	5	11.070	Rejected
Life Style	20.959	5	11.070	Rejected
Clothing	26.816	5	11.070	Rejected
Provisions	26.712	5	11.070	Rejected
Watches and Jewellers	47.764	5	11.070	Rejected
Stationeries	9.963	5	11.070	Accepted
Cosmetics and Beauty	30.086	5	11.070	Rejected
Health and Medicine	32.320	5	11.070	Rejected
Foot ware	54.112	5	11.070	Rejected
Household Appliances	18.872	5	11.070	Rejected
Leisure and Personal Goods	33.122	5	11.070	Rejected

Level of Significance: 5 per cent

From the above table it has been inferred that the calculated chi-square values are greater than the table value 11.070 at 5 per cent level of significance. Therefore, the hypothesis framed stands rejected and it has been concluded that there exists no association between the educational qualification of outshoppers and the products shopped at malls. However it is exceptional in the case of stationeries.

H7: There exists rational association between the occupational status of outshoppers and the products shopped at malls.

Table 4.44(a): Occupational Status of Outshoppers and the Products Shopped by them at Malls

Products	Occupation		
	Salaried	Business	Professional
Food and Beverage	138(16.75)	18(16.67)	24(11.16)
Life Style	88(10.68)	**18(16.67)**	24(11.16)
Clothing	198(24.03)	18(16.67)	55(25.58)
Provisions	**51(6.19)**	0(0.00)	13(6.05)
Watches and Jewellers	35(4.25)	12(11.11)	12(5.58)
Stationeries	**37(4.49)**	0(0.00)	6(2.79)
Cosmetics and Beauty	71(8.62)	6(5.56)	12(5.58)
Health and Medicine	19(2.31)	**6(5.56)**	0(0.00)
Foot ware	69(8.37)	12(11.11)	12(5.58)
Household Appliances	79(9.59)	**18(16.67)**	24(11.16)
Leisure and Personal Goods	39(4.73)	0(0.00)	**33(15.35)**

Source: Computed from Primary Data

Table 4.44(b): Occupational Status of Outshoppers and the Products Shopped by them at Malls

Products	Occupation		Total
	Students	Home Maker	
Food and Beverage	**60(18.52)**	0(0.00)	240(16.12)
Life Style	42(12.96)	0(0.00)	172(11.55)
Clothing	72(22.22)	**6(33.33)**	349(23.44)
Provisions	6(1.85)	0(0.00)	70(4.70)
Watches and Jewellery	24(7.41)	**6(33.33)**	89(5.98)
Stationeries	12(3.70)	0(0.00)	55(3.69)
Cosmetics and Beauty	**30(9.26)**	0(0.00)	119(7.99)
Health and Medicine	0(0.00)	0(0.00)	25(1.68)
Foot ware	48(14.81)	6(33.33)	147(9.87)
Household Appliances	24(7.41)	0(0.00)	145(9.74)
Leisure and Personal Goods	6(1.85)	0(0.00)	78(5.24)

Source: Computed from Primary Data

The table description reveals that there exist differences in products shopped and the occupational status of outshoppers in the malls.

Table 4.45: Result of Chi-Square Occupational Status of Outshoppers and the Products Shopped by them at Malls

Products	Chi-square value	DF	Table value	Remark
Food and Beverage	27.767	4	9.488	Rejected
Life Style	20.203	4	9.488	Rejected
Clothing	6.335	4	9.488	Accepted
Provisions	14.740	4	9.488	Rejected
Watches and Jewellery	53.954	4	9.488	Rejected
Stationeries	7.118	4	9.488	Accepted
Cosmetics and Beauty	9.088	4	9.488	Accepted
Health and Medicine	29.404	4	9.488	Rejected
Foot ware	48.589	4	9.488	Rejected
Household Appliances	22.115	4	9.488	Rejected
Leisure and Personal Goods	43.479	4	9.488	Rejected

Level of Significance: 5 per cent

From the above table it has been inferred that the calculated chi-square values are greater than the table value 9.488 at 5 per cent level of significance. Therefore, the hypothesis framed stands rejected and it has been concluded that there exists no association between the occupational status of outshoppers and the products shopped at malls. However it is exceptional in the case of clothing, stationeries, cosmetics and beauty products.

Consumer's buyer behavior is greatly influenced by the spending power. In India spending power of the household are usually linked with their monthly income to assess the significance of this statement following hypothesis is framed and tested.

H8: There exists rational association between the monthly income of outshoppers and the products shopped at malls.

Table 4.46(a): Monthly Income of Outshoppers and the Products Shopped by them at Malls

Products	Monthly Income		
	Below Rs. 10000	Rs. 10001 – Rs. 20000	Rs. 20001 – Rs. 30000
Food and Beverage	60(21.74)	64(18.44)	68(13.60)
Life Style	42(15.22)	12(3.46)	57(11.40)
Clothing	66(23.91)	94(27.09)	89(17.80)
Provisions	6(2.17)	14(4.03)	38(7.60)
Watches and Jewellery	18(6.52)	30(8.65)	17(3.40)
Stationeries	6(2.17)	0(0.00)	31(6.20)
Cosmetics and Beauty	12(4.35)	35(10.09)	54(10.80)
Health and Medicine	0(0.00)	6(1.73)	13(2.60)
Foot ware	30(10.87)	24(6.92)	51(10.20)
Household Appliances	30(10.87)	22(6.34)	56(11.20)
Leisure and Personal Goods	6(2.17)	46(13.26)	26(5.20)

Source: Computed from Primary Data

Table 4.46(b): Monthly Income of Outshoppers and the Products Shopped by them at Malls

Products	Monthly Income		Total
	Rs.30001 – Rs. 40000	Above Rs. 40000	
Food and Beverage	30(17.86)	18(9.09)	240(16.12)
Life Style	**30(17.86)**	31(15.66)	172(11.55)
Clothing	**48(28.57)**	52(26.26)	349(23.44)
Provisions	12(7.14)	0(0.00)	70(4.70)
Watches and Jewellers	6(3.57)	18(9.09)	89(5.98)
Stationeries	12(7.14)	6(3.03)	55(3.69)
Cosmetics and Beauty	6(3.57)	12(6.06)	119(7.99)
Health and Medicine	0(0.00)	6(3.03)	25(1.68)
Foot ware	18(10.71)	**24(12.12)**	147(9.87)
Household Appliances	6(3.57)	**31(15.66)**	145(9.74)
Leisure and Personal Goods	0(0.00)	0(0.00)	78(5.24)

Source: Computed from Primary Data

The elaborate data discussion presented in the above table clearly depicts the existence of disparities in the spending pattern of outshoppers and the products brought by them in shopping malls according to their monthly income Status.

Table 4.47: Result of Chi-Square Monthly Income of Outshoppers and the Products Shopped by them at Malls

Products	Chi-square value	DF	Table value	Remark
Food and Beverage	32.572	4	9.488	Rejected
Life Style	89.891	4	9.488	Rejected
Clothing	43.984	4	9.488	Rejected
Provisions	42.709	4	9.488	Rejected
Watches and Jewellers	11.292	4	9.488	Rejected
Stationeries	50.095	4	9.488	Rejected
Cosmetics and Beauty	26.014	4	9.488	Rejected
Health and Medicine	16.944	4	9.488	Rejected
Foot ware	29.263	4	9.488	Rejected
Household Appliances	53.525	4	9.488	Rejected
Leisure and Personal Goods	40.736	4	9.488	Rejected

Level of Significance: 5 per cent

From the above table it has been inferred that the calculated chi-square values are greater than the table value 9.488 at 5 per cent level of significance. Therefore, the hypothesis framed stands rejected and it has been concluded that there exists no association between the monthly income of outshoppers and the products shopped at malls.

From the above Tables: 4.38 to 4.47 it has been concluded that there exists no association between the demographic and socio-economic status of outshoppers and the products shopped at malls.

Table 4.48: Outshoppers Opinion on Shopping in Shopping Malls and other Retail Shops

Sl. No	Opinion	No. of Respondents	Percentage
1.	Comparatively Better in Mall	346	61.24
2.	No Differences	219	38.76
	Total	565	100

Source: Primary Data

From the above table it has observed that out of the 565 respondents surveyed 61.24 per cent of the respondents' opine that is shopping in malls are comparatively better than in other retail shops and 38.76 per cent of the respondents have opinion that shopping in malls and other retail shops have no difference.

Table 4.49: Primary Reasons Stated by the Outshoppers for Shopping at Malls

Reasons	Sum	Mean	Rank
Availability all Under One Roof	7056	12.49	1
Accessibility (Distance of Travel)	4551	8.05	8
Retail Tenant Mix	4469	7.91	9
Product Range, Merchandise Value	4925	8.72	4
Orientation and Infrastructure facilities	4666	8.26	6
Better Sales Service	3959	7.01	12
Parking Facilities	4980	8.81	3
External Atmospheric Clues (Architectural Style, Layout Design and Image)	4196	7.43	11
Internal Atmospheric Clues (E.g: Flooring, Lighting, Air Condition, Music Rest Rooms etc.,)	4621	8.18	7
Hospitality (Food courts & Resting Places)	4201	7.44	10
Entertainment (Multiplex Screening the Latest Blockbusters)	5671	10.04	2
Lifestyle Outlets (Health and Beauty)	3620	6.41	13
Offers and Discounts	4700	8.32	5
Competitive Price	3604	6.38	14
Status Symbol	3203	5.67	15

Source: Primary Data

The above tables states the primary reasons stated by the respondents for shopping at malls. The reason availability of all products under one roof is ranked first by the respondents with the highest mean score of 12.49. The entertainment facilities such as multiplex screening the latest blockbusters are ranked by the respondents in the place of two with the higher average score of 10.04 and parking facilities available in the malls scored a high mean score of 8.81 with third rank. Similarly product range and merchandise value is ranked in fourth place, with a mean score of 8.72 and Offers and discounts is ranked in fifth place with mean score of 8.32. The orientation and infra-structure facilities and the internal atmospheric clues such as flooring, lighting, air condition, music, rest room etc are ranked in sixth and seventh place with the mean score of 8.26 and 8.18.

The accessibility factor i.e distance of travel has mean score of 8.05 with the eighth rank. Further the reasons like retail tenant mix, hospitality factor such as food courts and restrooms and external atmospheric clues such as Architectural Style, Layout Design and Image of the shopping malls are ranked in ninth, tenth and eleventh place respectively with average score of 7.91, 7.44 and 7.43 accordingly. The factors like better sales service, life style outlets like health and beauty, competitive price and status symbol are ranked in twelfth, thirteenth, fourteenth and fifteenth place with the mean score of 7.01, 6.41, 6.38 and 5.67.

Thus from the above table, it can be inferred that the primary reason for outshopper to visit shopping mall is availability of all products under one roof it has been ranked in the first place with the mean score of 12.49.

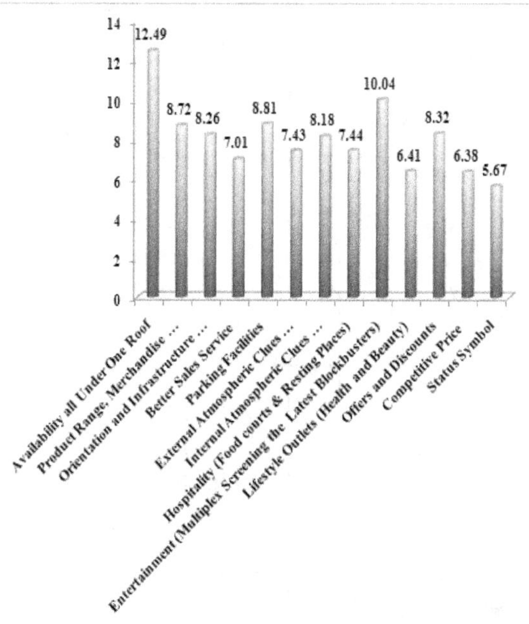

Exhibit 4.2: Primary Reasons Stated by the Outshoppers for Shopping at Malls

Table 4.50: Comparative Score of Primary Reasons Stated by the Outshoppers for Shopping at Various Malls

Particulars	Leading Shopping Malls														
	Brook Field (N:120)			Fun Republic (N:119)			Millaneum Mall (N:110)			Vishall De Mall (N:114)			Femina Shopping Mall (N:102)		
	Sum	Mean	Rank	Sum	Mean	Rank	Sum	Mean	Rank	Sum	Mean	Rank	Sum	Mean	Rank
Availability all Under One Roof	1551	12.93	1	1434	12.05	5	1352	12.29	4	1428	12.53	3	1291	12.66	2
Accessibility (Distance of Travel)	1016	8.47	2	940	7.90	3	853	7.75	4	877	7.69	5	865	8.48	1
Retail Tenant Mix	951	7.93	3	970	8.15	1	876	7.96	2	894	7.84	4	778	7.63	5
Product Range, Merchandise Value	1048	8.73	3	1032	8.67	4	985	8.95	1	908	7.96	5	952	9.33	2
Orientation and Infrastructure facilities	1017	8.48	1	978	8.22	4	910	8.27	3	959	8.41	2	802	7.86	5
Better Sales Service	851	7.09	2	828	6.96	3	764	6.95	4	829	7.27	1	687	6.74	5
Parking Facilities	1058	8.82	2	1024	8.61	5	950	8.64	4	1049	9.20	1	899	8.81	3
External Atmospheric Clues (Architectural Style, Layout Design and Image)	886	7.38	3	853	7.17	5	843	7.66	1	838	7.35	4	776	7.61	2
Internal Atmospheric Clues (E.g: Flooring, Lighting, Air Condition, Music Rest Rooms etc.,)	913	7.61	5	966	8.12	4	931	8.46	2	972	8.53	1	839	8.23	3
Hospitality (Food courts & Resting Places)	834	6.95	5	926	7.78	2	858	7.80	1	839	7.36	3	744	7.29	4
Entertainment (Multiplex Screening the Latest Blockbusters)	1153	9.61	5	1209	10.16	2	1103	10.03	3	1188	10.42	1	1018	9.98	4
Lifestyle Outlets (Health and Beauty)	792	6.60	2	736	6.18	4	670	6.09	5	786	6.89	1	636	6.24	3
Offers and Discounts	967	8.06	4	1051	8.83	1	934	8.49	2	899	7.89	5	849	8.32	3
Competitive Price	759	6.33	3	815	6.85	1	690	6.27	4	692	6.07	5	648	6.35	2
Status Symbol	679	5.66	3	719	6.04	1	575	5.23	5	632	5.54	4	598	5.86	2

Source: Computed Data

The above table portrays the comparative score of primary reasons stated by the outshoppers for shopping at leading five malls namely Brook Field mall, Fun Republic, Millaneum Mall, Vishall De Mall and Femina Shopping Mall.

The respondents have stated the reason that availability of all product under one roof and excellent orientation and infrastructure facilities are the main reason for them to visit the Brook Field Mall.

The outshoppers are stated that the retail tenant mix, offers and discounts, competitive price and status symbol are reason why they visit the Fun Republic Mall. Millaneum Mall have attracted the outshoppers with regard to Product Range, Merchandise Value, External Atmospheric Clues and Hospitality like food court and rest rooms.

The main reasons of the respondents visiting the Vishal De Mall was Better Sales Service, Parking Facilities, Internal Atmospheric Clue Entertainments, Lifestyle Outlet.

The outshoppers has stated the reason that accessibility, that is the distance of travel was convenient for them to reach the Femina Shopping Mall.

Modern day consumers have started accepting shopping malls due to its features and service elements like:

- good music
- efficient use of space
- window-shopping opportunities
- a one-stop shopping destination
- fine-dining restaurants

Fast-food eateries are also attractive to many Indian consumers. In short, consumers are visiting malls for various motivational factors.

Various motivational factors are aesthetic appreciation, diversion, social relationship, browsing, and convenience. Drawing theoretical evidences from the above statement following hypothesis is framed.

H9: There exists rational association between demographic and socio-economic status of the outshoppers and the primary reasons stated by them for visiting shopping malls.

Table 4.51: Result of ANOVA Gender of the Outshoppers and Primary Reasons Stated by them for Visiting Shopping Malls

Variables	Source	Sum of Square	DF	Mean square	F	Sig
Availability all Under One Roof	Between Groups	409.350	1	409.350	33.489	.000
	Within Groups	6881.825	563	12.223		
	Total	7291.175	564	-		
Accessibility (Distance of Travel)	Between Groups	52.566	1	52.566	3.206	.074
	Within Groups	9230.733	563	16.396		
	Total	9283.299	564	-		
Retail Tenant Mix	Between Groups	54.956	1	54.956	2.863	.091
	Within Groups	10805.440	563	19.193		
	Total	10860.396	564	-		
Product Range, Merchandise Value	Between Groups	326.237	1	326.237	16.984	.000
	Within Groups	10814.453	563	19.209		
	Total	11140.690	564	-		
Orientation and Infrastructure facilities	Between Groups	93.553	1	93.553	6.233	.013
	Within Groups	8450.719	563	15.010		
	Total	8544.273	564	-		
Better Sales Service	Between Groups	257.894	1	257.894	16.012	.000
	Within Groups	9068.077	563	16.107		
	Total	9325.972	564	-		
Parking Facilities	Between Groups	549.879	1	549.879	38.156	.000
	Within Groups	8113.608	563	14.411		
	Total	8663.487	564	-		
External Atmospheric Clues (Architectural Style, Layout Design and Image)	Between Groups	430.710	1	430.710	39.254	.000
	Within Groups	6177.492	563	10.972		
	Total	6608.202	564	-		
Internal Atmospheric Clues (E.g: Flooring, Lighting, Air Condition, Music Rest Rooms etc.,)	Between Groups	2.437	1	2.437	.193	.660
	Within Groups	7098.508	563	12.608		
	Total	7100.945	564	-		
Hospitality (Food courts & Resting Places)	Between Groups	6.271	1	6.271	.390	.533
	Within Groups	9050.621	563	16.076		
	Total	9056.892	564	-		
Entertainment (Multiplex Screening the Latest Blockbusters)	Between Groups	161.639	1	161.639	9.947	.002
	Within Groups	9148.580	563	16.250		
	Total	9310.219	564	-		
Lifestyle Outlets (Health and Beauty)	Between Groups	56.359	1	56.359	3.969	.047
	Within Groups	7994.013	563	14.199		
	Total	8050.372	564	-		
Offers and Discounts	Between Groups	164.569	1	164.569	9.819	.002
	Within Groups	9436.086	563	16.760		
	Total	9600.655	564	-		
Competitive Price	Between Groups	114.763	1	114.763	6.935	.009
	Within Groups	9316.182	563	16.547		
	Total	9430.945	564	-		
Status Symbol	Between Groups	11.739	1	11.739	.507	.477
	Within Groups	13029.369	563	23.143		
	Total	13041.108	564	-		

Level of Significance: 5 per cent

The data presented in the above table indicates that the probability value of ANOVA at 5 per cent level establishes good relationship between the variables tested. Majority of the variables tested were rated below the probability mark of five per cent. Therefore, the hypothesis framed stands accepted and it has been concluded that there exists rational

association between gender of the outshoppers and the primary reasons stated by them for visiting shopping malls. However it is exceptional in the case of accessibility (distance of travel), retail tenant mix, internal atmospheric clues (e.g. flooring, lighting, air condition, music rest rooms etc.,), hospitality (food courts & resting places) and status symbol.

Table 4.52: Result of ANOVA Age of the Outshoppers and Primary Reasons Stated by them for Visiting Shopping Malls

Variables	Source	Sum of Square	DF	Mean square	F	Sig
Availability all Under One Roof	Between Groups	236.120	3	78.707	6.259	.000
	Within Groups	7055.055	561	12.576		
	Total	7291.175	564	-		
Accessibility (Distance of Travel)	Between Groups	525.654	3	175.218	11.224	.000
	Within Groups	8757.645	561	15.611		
	Total	9283.299	564	-		
Retail Tenant Mix	Between Groups	464.982	3	154.994	8.364	.000
	Within Groups	10395.414	561	18.530		
	Total	10860.396	564	-		
Product Range, Merchandise Value	Between Groups	616.795	3	205.598	10.960	.000
	Within Groups	10523.895	561	18.759		
	Total	11140.690	564	-		
Orientation and Infrastructure facilities	Between Groups	697.700	3	232.567	16.628	.000
	Within Groups	7846.573	561	13.987		
	Total	8544.273	564	-		
Better Sales Service	Between Groups	605.349	3	201.783	12.981	.000
	Within Groups	8720.622	561	15.545		
	Total	9325.972	564	-		
Parking Facilities	Between Groups	126.702	3	42.234	2.775	.041
	Within Groups	8536.784	561	15.217		
	Total	8663.487	564	-		
External Atmospheric Clues (Architectural Style, Layout Design and Image)	Between Groups	352.122	3	117.374	10.525	.000
	Within Groups	6256.080	561	11.152		
	Total	6608.202	564	-		
Internal Atmospheric Clues (E.g: Flooring, Lighting, Air Condition, Music Rest Rooms etc.,)	Between Groups	144.541	3	48.180	3.886	.009
	Within Groups	6956.404	561	12.400		
	Total	7100.945	564	-		
Hospitality (Food courts & Resting Places)	Between Groups	900.351	3	300.117	20.642	.000
	Within Groups	8156.541	561	14.539		
	Total	9056.892	564	-		
Entertainment (Multiplex Screening the Latest Blockbusters)	Between Groups	130.400	3	43.467	2.656	.048
	Within Groups	9179.819	561	16.363		
	Total	9310.219	564	-		
Lifestyle Outlets (Health and Beauty)	Between Groups	71.670	3	23.890	1.680	.170
	Within Groups	7978.702	561	14.222		
	Total	8050.372	564	-		
Offers and Discounts	Between Groups	74.355	3	24.785	1.460	.225
	Within Groups	9526.300	561	16.981		
	Total	9600.655	564	-		
Competitive Price	Between Groups	312.860	3	104.287	6.416	.000
	Within Groups	9118.085	561	16.253		
	Total	9430.945	564	-		
Status Symbol	Between Groups	703.226	3	234.409	10.658	.000
	Within Groups	12337.882	561	21.993		
	Total	13041.108	564	-		

Level of Significance: 5 per cent

The data presented in the above table indicates that the probability value of ANOVA at 5 per cent level establishes good relationship between the variables tested. Majority of the variables tested were rated below the probability mark of five per cent. Therefore, the hypothesis framed stands accepted and it has been concluded that there exists rational association between age of the outshoppers and the primary reasons stated by them for visiting shopping malls. However it is exceptional in the case of lifestyle outlets (health and beauty), offers and discounts.

Table 4.53: Result of ANOVA Marital Status of the Outshoppers and Primary Reasons Stated by them for Visiting Shopping Malls

Variables	Source	Sum of Square	DF	Mean square	F	Sig
Availability all Under One Roof	Between Groups	2.274	1	2.274	.176	.675
	Within Groups	7288.901	563	12.947		
	Total	7291.175	564	-		
Accessibility (Distance of Travel)	Between Groups	753.861	1	753.861	49.760	.000
	Within Groups	8529.438	563	15.150		
	Total	9283.299	564	-		
Retail Tenant Mix	Between Groups	69.842	1	69.842	3.644	.057
	Within Groups	10790.555	563	19.166		
	Total	10860.396	564	-		
Product Range, Merchandise Value	Between Groups	13.225	1	13.225	.669	.414
	Within Groups	11127.465	563	19.765		
	Total	11140.690	564	-		
Orientation and Infrastructure facilities	Between Groups	25.424	1	25.424	1.680	.195
	Within Groups	8518.848	563	15.131		
	Total	8544.273	564	-		
Better Sales Service	Between Groups	419.238	1	419.238	26.500	.000
	Within Groups	8906.733	563	15.820		
	Total	9325.972	564	-		
Parking Facilities	Between Groups	2.956	1	2.956	.192	.661
	Within Groups	8660.531	563	15.383		
	Total	8663.487	564	-		
External Atmospheric Clues (Architectural Style, Layout Design and Image)	Between Groups	1.585	1	1.585	.135	.713
	Within Groups	6606.617	563	11.735		
	Total	6608.202	564	-		
Internal Atmospheric Clues (E.g: Flooring, Lighting, Air Condition, Music Rest Rooms etc.,)	Between Groups	29.562	1	29.562	2.354	.126
	Within Groups	7071.383	563	12.560		
	Total	7100.945	564	-		
Hospitality (Food courts & Resting Places)	Between Groups	162.955	1	162.955	10.315	.001
	Within Groups	8893.937	563	15.797		
	Total	9056.892	564	-		
Entertainment (Multiplex Screening the Latest Blockbusters)	Between Groups	.882	1	.882	.053	.817
	Within Groups	9309.337	563	16.535		
	Total	9310.219	564	-		
Lifestyle Outlets (Health and Beauty)	Between Groups	11.066	1	11.066	.775	.379
	Within Groups	8039.306	563	14.279		
	Total	8050.372	564	-		
Offers and Discounts	Between Groups	5.189	1	5.189	.304	.581
	Within Groups	9595.466	563	17.043		
	Total	9600.655	564	-		
Competitive Price	Between Groups	.078	1	.078	.005	.946
	Within Groups	9430.867	563	16.751		
	Total	9430.945	564	-		
Status Symbol	Between Groups	3.577	1	3.577	.154	.694
	Within Groups	13037.530	563	23.157		
	Total	13041.108	564	-		

Level of Significance: 5 per cent

The data presented in the above table indicates that the probability value of ANOVA at 5 per cent level does not establish good relationship between the variables tested. Majority of the variables tested were rated above the probability mark of five per cent. Therefore, the hypothesis framed stands rejected and it has been concluded that there exists no association between marital status of the outshoppers and the primary reasons stated by them for visiting shopping malls. However it is exceptional in the case of accessibility (distance of travel), better sales service and hospitality (food courts & resting places).

Table 4.54: Result of ANOVA Educational Qualification of the Outshoppers& Primary Reasons Stated by them for Visiting Shopping Malls

Variables	Source	Sum of Square	DF	Mean square	F	Sig
Availability all Under One Roof	Between Groups	448.482	5	89.696	7.328	.000
	Within Groups	6842.693	559	12.241		
	Total	7291.175	564	-		
Accessibility (Distance of Travel)	Between Groups	542.050	5	108.410	6.933	.000
	Within Groups	8741.249	559	15.637		
	Total	9283.299	564	-		
Retail Tenant Mix	Between Groups	732.560	5	146.512	8.087	.000
	Within Groups	10127.837	559	18.118		
	Total	10860.396	564	-		
Product Range, Merchandise Value	Between Groups	252.862	5	50.572	2.596	.025
	Within Groups	10887.828	559	19.477		
	Total	11140.690	564	-		
Orientation and Infrastructure facilities	Between Groups	330.188	5	66.038	4.494	.001
	Within Groups	8214.085	559	14.694		
	Total	8544.273	564	-		
Better Sales Service	Between Groups	888.396	5	177.679	11.771	.000
	Within Groups	8437.576	559	15.094		
	Total	9325.972	564	-		
Parking Facilities	Between Groups	214.701	5	42.940	2.841	.015
	Within Groups	8448.786	559	15.114		
	Total	8663.487	564	-		
External Atmospheric Clues (Architectural Style, Layout Design and Image)	Between Groups	314.574	5	62.915	5.588	.000
	Within Groups	6293.628	559	11.259		
	Total	6608.202	564	-		
Internal Atmospheric Clues (E.g: Flooring, Lighting, Air Condition, Music Rest Rooms etc.,)	Between Groups	533.320	5	106.664	9.079	.000
	Within Groups	6567.626	559	11.749		
	Total	7100.945	564	-		
Hospitality (Food courts & Resting Places)	Between Groups	695.033	5	139.007	9.293	.000
	Within Groups	8361.859	559	14.959		
	Total	9056.892	564	-		
Entertainment (Multiplex Screening the Latest Blockbusters)	Between Groups	138.732	5	27.746	1.691	.135
	Within Groups	9171.488	559	16.407		
	Total	9310.219	564	-		
Lifestyle Outlets (Health and Beauty)	Between Groups	441.480	5	88.296	6.487	.000
	Within Groups	7608.892	559	13.612		
	Total	8050.372	564	-		
Offers and Discounts	Between Groups	523.200	5	104.640	6.444	.000
	Within Groups	9077.455	559	16.239		
	Total	9600.655	564	-		
Competitive Price	Between Groups	466.039	5	93.208	5.812	.000
	Within Groups	8964.906	559	16.037		
	Total	9430.945	564	-		
Status Symbol	Between Groups	219.983	5	43.997	1.918	.090
	Within Groups	12821.125	559	22.936		
	Total	13041.108	564	-		

Level of Significance: 5 per cent

The data presented in the above table indicates that the probability value of ANOVA at 5 per cent level establishes good relationship between the variables tested. Majority of the variables tested were rated below the probability mark of five per cent. Therefore, the hypothesis framed stands accepted and it has been concluded that there exists rational

association between educational qualification of the outshoppers and the primary reasons stated by them for visiting shopping malls. However it is exceptional in the case of entertainment (multiplex screening the latest blockbusters) and status symbol.

Table 4.55: Result of ANOVA Occupational Status of the Outshoppers& Primary Reasons Stated by them for Visiting Shopping Malls

Variables	Source	Sum of Square	DF	Mean square	F	Sig
Availability all Under One Roof	Between Groups	129.533	4	32.383	2.532	.039
	Within Groups	7161.642	560	12.789		
	Total	7291.175	564	-		
Accessibility (Distance of Travel)	Between Groups	514.391	4	128.598	8.213	.000
	Within Groups	8768.909	560	15.659		
	Total	9283.299	564	-		
Retail Tenant Mix	Between Groups	950.411	4	237.603	13.427	.000
	Within Groups	9909.985	560	17.696		
	Total	10860.396	564	-		
Product Range, Merchandise Value	Between Groups	369.320	4	92.330	4.800	.001
	Within Groups	10771.371	560	19.235		
	Total	11140.690	564	-		
Orientation and Infrastructure facilities	Between Groups	522.053	4	130.513	9.111	.000
	Within Groups	8022.220	560	14.325		
	Total	8544.273	564	-		
Better Sales Service	Between Groups	961.850	4	240.462	16.100	.000
	Within Groups	8364.122	560	14.936		
	Total	9325.972	564	-		
Parking Facilities	Between Groups	450.815	4	112.704	7.685	.000
	Within Groups	8212.671	560	14.665		
	Total	8663.487	564	-		
External Atmospheric Clues (Architectural Style, Layout Design and Image)	Between Groups	374.210	4	93.552	8.404	.000
	Within Groups	6233.992	560	11.132		
	Total	6608.202	564	-		
Internal Atmospheric Clues (E.g: Flooring, Lighting, Air Condition, Music Rest Rooms etc.,)	Between Groups	569.057	4	142.264	12.197	.000
	Within Groups	6531.888	560	11.664		
	Total	7100.945	564	-		
Hospitality (Food courts & Resting Places)	Between Groups	546.748	4	136.687	8.995	.000
	Within Groups	8510.144	560	15.197		
	Total	9056.892	564	-		
Entertainment (Multiplex Screening the Latest Blockbusters)	Between Groups	449.685	4	112.421	7.105	.000
	Within Groups	8860.534	560	15.822		
	Total	9310.219	564	-		
Lifestyle Outlets (Health and Beauty)	Between Groups	374.105	4	93.526	6.823	.000
	Within Groups	7676.267	560	13.708		
	Total	8050.372	564	-		
Offers and Discounts	Between Groups	84.029	4	21.007	1.236	.294
	Within Groups	9516.626	560	16.994		
	Total	9600.655	564	-		
Competitive Price	Between Groups	144.927	4	36.232	2.185	.069
	Within Groups	9286.018	560	16.582		
	Total	9430.945	564	-		
Status Symbol	Between Groups	564.636	4	141.159	6.336	.000
	Within Groups	12476.471	560	22.279		
	Total	13041.108	564	-		

Level of Significance: 5 per cent

The data presented in the above table indicates that the probability value of ANOVA at 5 per cent level establishes good relationship between the variables tested. Majority of the variables tested were rated below the probability mark of five per cent. Therefore, the hypothesis framed stands accepted and it has been concluded that there exists rational association between occupational status of the outshoppers and the primary reasons stated by them for visiting shopping malls. However it is exceptional in the case of offers, discounts and competitive price.

Table 4.56: Result of ANOVA Monthly Income of the Outshoppers& Primary Reasons Stated by them for Visiting Shopping Malls

Variables	Source	Sum of Square	DF	Mean square	F	Sig
Availability all Under One Roof	Between Groups	417.056	4	104.264	8.494	.000
	Within Groups	6874.119	560	12.275		
	Total	7291.175	564	-		
Accessibility (Distance of Travel)	Between Groups	583.184	4	145.796	9.384	.000
	Within Groups	8700.116	560	15.536		
	Total	9283.299	564	-		
Retail Tenant Mix	Between Groups	162.358	4	40.590	2.125	.076
	Within Groups	10698.038	560	19.104		
	Total	10860.396	564	-		
Product Range, Merchandise Value	Between Groups	820.859	4	205.215	11.136	.000
	Within Groups	10319.831	560	18.428		
	Total	11140.690	564	-		
Orientation and Infrastructure facilities	Between Groups	613.706	4	153.427	10.834	.000
	Within Groups	7930.566	560	14.162		
	Total	8544.273	564	-		
Better Sales Service	Between Groups	465.385	4	116.346	7.353	.000
	Within Groups	8860.587	560	15.822		
	Total	9325.972	564	-		
Parking Facilities	Between Groups	156.564	4	39.141	2.577	.037
	Within Groups	8506.923	560	15.191		
	Total	8663.487	564	-		
External Atmospheric Clues (Architectural Style, Layout Design and Image)	Between Groups	40.569	4	10.142	.865	.485
	Within Groups	6567.633	560	11.728		
	Total	6608.202	564	-		
Internal Atmospheric Clues (E.g: Flooring, Lighting, Air Condition, Music Rest Rooms etc.,)	Between Groups	362.933	4	90.733	7.541	.000
	Within Groups	6738.012	560	12.032		
	Total	7100.945	564	-		
Hospitality (Food courts & Resting Places)	Between Groups	1354.760	4	338.690	24.625	.000
	Within Groups	7702.132	560	13.754		
	Total	9056.892	564	-		
Entertainment (Multiplex Screening the Latest Blockbusters)	Between Groups	175.148	4	43.787	2.684	.031
	Within Groups	9135.071	560	16.313		
	Total	9310.219	564	-		
Lifestyle Outlets (Health and Beauty)	Between Groups	166.301	4	41.575	2.953	.020
	Within Groups	7884.071	560	14.079		
	Total	8050.372	564	-		
Offers and Discounts	Between Groups	61.521	4	15.380	.903	.462
	Within Groups	9539.134	560	17.034		
	Total	9600.655	564	-		
Competitive Price	Between Groups	329.858	4	82.464	5.074	.001
	Within Groups	9101.087	560	16.252		
	Total	9430.945	564	-		
Status Symbol	Between Groups	527.622	4	131.905	5.903	.000
	Within Groups	12513.486	560	22.346		
	Total	13041.108	564	-		

Level of Significance: 5 per cent

The data presented in the above table indicates that the probability value of ANOVA at 5 per cent level establishes good relationship between the variables tested. Majority of the variables tested were rated below the probability mark of five per cent. Therefore, the hypothesis framed stands accepted and it has been concluded that there exists rational association between monthly income of the outshoppers and the primary reasons stated by them for visiting shopping malls. However it is exceptional in the case of retail tenant mix, external atmospheric clues (architectural style, layout design and image), offers and discounts.

Table 4.57: Result of ANOVA Family Size of the Outshoppers& Primary Reasons Stated by them for Visiting Shopping Malls

Variables	Source	Sum of Square	DF	Mean square	F	Sig
Availability all Under One Roof	Between Groups	227.134	2	113.567	9.035	.000
	Within Groups	7064.041	562	12.569		
	Total	7291.175	564	-		
Accessibility (Distance of Travel)	Between Groups	337.689	2	168.844	10.607	.000
	Within Groups	8945.610	562	15.917		
	Total	9283.299	564	-		
Retail Tenant Mix	Between Groups	297.279	2	148.639	7.908	.000
	Within Groups	10563.117	562	18.796		
	Total	10860.396	564	-		
Product Range, Merchandise Value	Between Groups	164.107	2	82.054	4.201	.015
	Within Groups	10976.583	562	19.531		
	Total	11140.690	564	-		
Orientation and Infrastructure facilities	Between Groups	422.207	2	211.104	14.607	.000
	Within Groups	8122.065	562	14.452		
	Total	8544.273	564	-		
Better Sales Service	Between Groups	374.942	2	187.471	11.771	.000
	Within Groups	8951.029	562	15.927		
	Total	9325.972	564	-		
Parking Facilities	Between Groups	203.547	2	101.774	6.761	.001
	Within Groups	8459.940	562	15.053		
	Total	8663.487	564	-		
External Atmospheric Clues (Architectural Style, Layout Design and Image)	Between Groups	879.142	2	439.571	43.120	.000
	Within Groups	5729.060	562	10.194		
	Total	6608.202	564	-		
Internal Atmospheric Clues (E.g: Flooring, Lighting, Air Condition, Music Rest Rooms etc.,)	Between Groups	416.065	2	208.033	17.489	.000
	Within Groups	6684.880	562	11.895		
	Total	7100.945	564	-		
Hospitality (Food courts & Resting Places)	Between Groups	334.958	2	167.479	10.792	.000
	Within Groups	8721.934	562	15.519		
	Total	9056.892	564	-		
Entertainment (Multiplex Screening the Latest Blockbusters)	Between Groups	376.433	2	188.217	11.840	.000
	Within Groups	8933.786	562	15.896		
	Total	9310.219	564	-		
Lifestyle Outlets (Health and Beauty)	Between Groups	90.791	2	45.396	3.205	.041
	Within Groups	7959.580	562	14.163		
	Total	8050.372	564	-		
Offers and Discounts	Between Groups	41.841	2	20.921	1.230	.293
	Within Groups	9558.814	562	17.009		
	Total	9600.655	564	-		
Competitive Price	Between Groups	112.724	2	56.362	3.399	.034
	Within Groups	9318.221	562	16.580		
	Total	9430.945	564	-		
Status Symbol	Between Groups	68.887	2	34.444	1.492	.226
	Within Groups	12972.220	562	23.082		
	Total	13041.108	564	-		

Level of Significance: 5 per cent

The data presented in the above table indicates that the probability value of ANOVA at 5 per cent level establishes good relationship between the variables tested. Majority of the variables tested were rated below the probability mark of five per cent. Therefore, the hypothesis framed stands accepted and it has been concluded that there exists rational association between family size of the outshoppers and the primary reasons stated by them for visiting shopping malls. However it is exceptional in the case of offers, discounts and status symbol.

Table 4.58: Result of ANOVA Earning Pattern of the Outshoppers Family & Primary Reasons Stated by them for Visiting Shopping Malls

Variables	Source	Sum of Square	DF	Mean square	F	Sig
Availability all Under One Roof	Between Groups	202.477	3	67.492	5.341	.001
	Within Groups	7088.698	561	12.636		
	Total	7291.175	564	-		
Accessibility (Distance of Travel)	Between Groups	106.727	3	35.576	2.175	.090
	Within Groups	9176.573	561	16.358		
	Total	9283.299	564	-		
Retail Tenant Mix	Between Groups	1294.624	3	431.541	25.308	.000
	Within Groups	9565.772	561	17.051		
	Total	10860.396	564	-		
Product Range, Merchandise Value	Between Groups	277.672	3	92.557	4.780	.003
	Within Groups	10863.018	561	19.364		
	Total	11140.690	564	-		
Orientation and Infrastructure facilities	Between Groups	764.593	3	254.864	18.379	.000
	Within Groups	7779.679	561	13.868		
	Total	8544.273	564	-		
Better Sales Service	Between Groups	233.361	3	77.787	4.799	.003
	Within Groups	9092.611	561	16.208		
	Total	9325.972	564	-		
Parking Facilities	Between Groups	124.489	3	41.496	2.726	.043
	Within Groups	8538.998	561	15.221		
	Total	8663.487	564	-		
External Atmospheric Clues (Architectural Style, Layout Design and Image)	Between Groups	179.439	3	59.813	5.220	.001
	Within Groups	6428.762	561	11.459		
	Total	6608.202	564	-		
Internal Atmospheric Clues (E.g: Flooring, Lighting, Air Condition, Music Rest Rooms etc.,)	Between Groups	189.377	3	63.126	5.124	.002
	Within Groups	6911.568	561	12.320		
	Total	7100.945	564	-		
Hospitality (Food courts & Resting Places)	Between Groups	258.960	3	86.320	5.504	.001
	Within Groups	8797.932	561	15.683		
	Total	9056.892	564	-		
Entertainment (Multiplex Screening the Latest Blockbusters)	Between Groups	79.012	3	26.337	1.601	.188
	Within Groups	9231.208	561	16.455		
	Total	9310.219	564	-		
Lifestyle Outlets (Health and Beauty)	Between Groups	171.394	3	57.131	4.068	.007
	Within Groups	7878.978	561	14.045		
	Total	8050.372	564	-		
Offers and Discounts	Between Groups	378.685	3	126.228	7.679	.000
	Within Groups	9221.970	561	16.438		
	Total	9600.655	564	-		
Competitive Price	Between Groups	228.927	3	76.309	4.652	.003
	Within Groups	9202.019	561	16.403		
	Total	9430.945	564	-		
Status Symbol	Between Groups	612.404	3	204.135	9.214	.000
	Within Groups	12428.704	561	22.155		
	Total	13041.108	564	-		

Level of Significance: 5 per cent

The data presented in the above table indicates that the probability value of ANOVA at 5 per cent level establishes good relationship between the variables tested. Majority of the variables tested were rated below the probability mark of five per cent. Therefore, the hypothesis framed stands accepted and it has been concluded that there exists rational association between earning pattern of the outshoppers family and the primary reasons stated by them for visiting shopping malls. However it is exceptional in the case of accessibility (distance of travel) and entertainment (multiplex screening the latest blockbusters).

Table 4.59: Result of ANOVA Number of Dependents in the Outshoppers Family & Primary Reasons Stated by them for Visiting Shopping Malls

Variables	Source	Sum of Square	DF	Mean square	F	Sig
Availability all Under One Roof	Between Groups	94.085	3	31.362	2.445	.063
	Within Groups	7197.091	561	12.829		
	Total	7291.175	564	-		
Accessibility (Distance of Travel)	Between Groups	832.234	3	277.411	18.415	.000
	Within Groups	8451.065	561	15.064		
	Total	9283.299	564	-		
Retail Tenant Mix	Between Groups	813.428	3	271.143	15.140	.000
	Within Groups	10046.968	561	17.909		
	Total	10860.396	564	-		
Product Range, Merchandise Value	Between Groups	887.466	3	295.822	16.186	.000
	Within Groups	10253.224	561	18.277		
	Total	11140.690	564	-		
Orientation and Infrastructure facilities	Between Groups	41.558	3	13.853	.914	.434
	Within Groups	8502.715	561	15.156		
	Total	8544.273	564	-		
Better Sales Service	Between Groups	415.689	3	138.563	8.724	.000
	Within Groups	8910.283	561	15.883		
	Total	9325.972	564	-		
Parking Facilities	Between Groups	201.289	3	67.096	4.448	.004
	Within Groups	8462.197	561	15.084		
	Total	8663.487	564	-		
External Atmospheric Clues (Architectural Style, Layout Design and Image)	Between Groups	452.855	3	150.952	13.758	.000
	Within Groups	6155.347	561	10.972		
	Total	6608.202	564	-		
Internal Atmospheric Clues (E.g: Flooring, Lighting, Air Condition, Music Rest Rooms etc.,)	Between Groups	524.510	3	174.837	14.914	.000
	Within Groups	6576.435	561	11.723		
	Total	7100.945	564	-		
Hospitality (Food courts & Resting Places)	Between Groups	31.161	3	10.387	.646	.586
	Within Groups	9025.731	561	16.089		
	Total	9056.892	564	-		
Entertainment (Multiplex Screening the Latest Blockbusters)	Between Groups	933.722	3	311.241	20.845	.000
	Within Groups	8376.498	561	14.931		
	Total	9310.219	564	-		
Lifestyle Outlets (Health and Beauty)	Between Groups	78.745	3	26.248	1.847	.137
	Within Groups	7971.627	561	14.210		
	Total	8050.372	564	-		
Offers and Discounts	Between Groups	726.894	3	242.298	15.318	.000
	Within Groups	8873.761	561	15.818		
	Total	9600.655	564	-		
Competitive Price	Between Groups	420.894	3	140.298	8.735	.000
	Within Groups	9010.051	561	16.061		
	Total	9430.945	564	-		
Status Symbol	Between Groups	392.849	3	130.950	5.808	.001
	Within Groups	12648.259	561	22.546		
	Total	13041.108	564	-		

Level of Significance: 5 per cent

The data presented in the above table indicates that the probability value of ANOVA at 5 per cent level establishes good relationship between the variables tested. Majority of the variables tested were rated below the probability mark of five per cent. Therefore, the hypothesis framed stands accepted and it has been concluded that there exists rational

association between number of dependents in the outshoppers family and the primary reasons stated by them for visiting shopping malls.

However it is exceptional in the case of availability all under one roof, orientation and infrastructure facilities, hospitality (food courts & resting places) and lifestyle outlets (health and beauty). From the above Tables: 4.51-4.59 it has been inferred that the probability value of ANOVA at 5 per cent level establishes good relationship between the variables tested. Majority of the variables tested were rated below the probability mark of five per cent.

Therefore, the hypothesis framed stands accepted and it has been concluded that there exists rational association between demographic and socio-economic status of the outshoppers and the primary reasons stated by them for visiting shopping malls. However it is exceptional in the case of marital status of the outshoppers.

Table 4.60: Outshoppers Opinion on Influence of Cultural & Religious Festival Sales on their Shopping Behaviour

Sl. No	Opinion	No. of Respondents	Percentage
1.	Do Influence	349	**61.77**
2.	Does Not Influence	216	38.23
	Total	565	100

Source: Primary Data

The above table indicates the respondents' opinion on influence of culture and religious festivals sales periods on shopping behavior. It has inferred that the majority of 61.77 per cent of the respondents have stated that cultural and religious festivals sales periods do influence their shopping behavior in shopping malls. Further 38.23 per cent of the respondents have an opinion that the cultural and religious festivals sales periods do not influence their shopping behavior in shopping malls.

Table 4.61: Outshoppers Opinion on Level of Influence of Cultural & Religious Festivals Sales Periods on Shopping Behaviour

Festivals	Very High	High	Moderate	Low	Very Low	Sum	Mean	Rank
Religious Festivals:(Diwali, Christmas, Ramzan etc.,)	198 (56.73)	91 (26.07)	60 (17.19)	0 (0.00)	0 (0.00)	1534	4.40	1
Social Festivals(Republic Day, Independence day)	44 (12.61)	80 (22.92)	67 (19.20)	97 (27.79)	61 (17.48)	996	2.85	3
Personal Festivals:(Birthday, Wedding, Anniversary)	157 (44.99)	107 (30.66)	67 (19.20)	0 (0.00)	18 (5.16)	1432	4.10	2

Source: Primary Data

Values in parenthesis are in per cent

From the above table it has been inferred that the level of influene of the religious festivals like diwali, christmas, ramzan is very high on their shopping behavior and this variable is ranked in the first place with the mean score of 4.40. The personal festivals like birthdays, wedding anniversary of the respondents have also influenced their buyer behavior and is ranked in the second place with the mean score of 4.10. The respondents have stated that the social festivals like Republic day, Independence Day influence their buying activity and are ranked in third place with the mean score of 2.85.

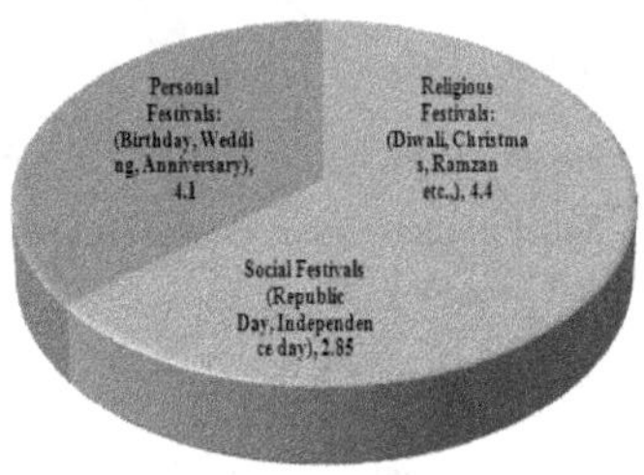

Exhibit 4.3: Outshoppers Opinion on Level of Influence of Cultural & Religious Festivals Sales Periods on Shopping Behaviour

Table 4.62: Outshoppers Opinion on their Influencing Person to Buy at Shopping Malls

Sl. No	Influencing Person	No. of Respondents(N=565)	Proportionate Percentage
1.	Self	197	34.87
2.	Spouse	71	12.57
3.	Children	97	17.17
4.	Parents & Elders	12	2.12
5.	Friends	282	49.91
6.	Colleagues	46	8.14

Source: Primary Data

From the above table it has been inferred that out of the 565 respondents surveyed 34.87 per cent of the respondents have stated that their buyer behavior in shopping mall is influenced by themselves. Consequently 12.57 per cent of the respondents have stated that their spouse have influenced their buyer behavior in the shopping mall. Similarly 17.17 per cent of the respondent have opinioned that their children have influenced their buying activity and 2.12 per cent respondents are influenced by their parents and elders during their buying activity. Further majority of the respondents of 49.91 per cent have stated that their buyer behaviour is influenced by their friends and 8.14 per cent of the respondents are influenced by their colleagues during buying activity in the shopping malls. Hence majority of the outshoppers' i.e 49.91 per cent are influenced by their friends to shop at shopping mall.

D. *Outshoppers' Level of Perception towards Shopping Malls*

Shopping malls play an important part in modern consumer lifestyle. Consumers' views of shopping malls have changed from seeing them as merely a place for shopping to seeing them as a centre where different activities, such as entertainment and eating, could be exercised. Due to the intense competition between malls, shoppers can be more selective and are more likely to patronize those shopping malls with which they perceive as good and derive more satisfaction. This section of the study draws empirical analysis on outshoppers' level of perception towards shopping malls.

Table 4.63: Outshoppers Level of Perception towards Shopping at Malls

Statements	Strongly Agree	Agree	Neither Agree nor Disagree	Disagree	Strongly Disagree	Sum	Mean	Rank
Shopping Malls provides better quality of goods and services	152 (26.90)	294 (52.04)	119 (21.06)	0 (0.00)	0 (0.00)	2293	4.06	3
Shopping Malls provides better customer care service	149 (26.37)	259 (45.84)	116 (20.53)	41 (7.26)	0 (0.00)	2211	3.91	5
Information system provided is adequate in Shopping Malls	132 (23.36)	324 (57.35)	91 (16.11)	12 (2.12)	6 (1.06)	2259	4.00	4
Shopping Malls are Adequately Modernized	250 (44.25)	254 (44.96)	61 (10.80)	0 (0.00)	0 (0.00)	2449	**4.33**	1
Parking facility is Adequate in Malls	239 (42.30)	229 (40.53)	49 (8.67)	48 (8.50)	0 (0.00)	2354	4.17	2
Promotional offers are provided in the Shops at Shopping Malls	138 (24.42)	254 (44.96)	120 (21.24)	47 (8.32)	6 (1.06)	2166	3.83	6
Billing method is convenient	145 (25.66)	239 (42.30)	109 (19.29)	54 (9.56)	18 (3.19)	2134	3.78	8
Shopping at Shopping Malls is better than other shops	156 (27.61)	199 (35.22)	114 (20.18)	90 (15.93)	6 (1.06)	2104	3.72	9
It helps customers to save time	115 (20.35)	311 (55.04)	74 (13.10)	53 (9.38)	12 (2.12)	2159	3.82	7
Purchasing at shopping Malls is status Symbol to Customers	147 (26.02)	223 (39.47)	89 (15.75)	76 (13.45)	30 (5.31)	2076	3.67	10

Source: Primary Data

Values in parenthesis are in per cent

The above table portrays the outshoppers' level of perception towards shopping malls. It has been inferred that, majority of the respondents have said that shopping malls are adequately modernized, it is ranked in the first place with the highest mean score of 4.33. Highest mean score of 4.17 have been scored by the respondents who felt that parking facility is adequate in malls, it is ranked in the second place. Subsequently the factors like shopping malls provided better quality of goods and services, information system provided is adequate in shopping malls and Shopping Malls provides better customer care service are ranked in third, fourth and fifth place respectively with the high mean score of 4.06, 4.0 and 3.91. Simultaneously Promotional offers are provided in the Shops at Shopping Malls, Shopping Malls helps customers to save time and convenient billing method are ranked in the sixth, seventh and eighth place respectively with the mean score of 3.83, 3.82 and 3.78 respectively. Further the factors like Shopping at Shopping Malls is better than other shops, Purchasing at shopping Malls is status Symbol to Customers are ranked in ninth and tenth place respectively with the mean score of 3.72 and 3.67.

Thus it is concluded that, majority of the respondents' perceive shopping malls as good because it is adequately modernized and hence it is in the first position with the highest mean score of 4.33.

Exhibit 4.4: Outshoppers Level of Perception in Leading Shopping at Malls

Table 4.64: Comparative Score of Outshoppers Perception Towards Shopping Malls

Particulars	Leading Shopping Malls														
	Brook Field (N:120)			Fun Republic (N:119)			Millaneum Mall (N:110)			Vishall De Mall (N:114)			Femina Shopping Mall (N:102)		
	Sum	Mean	Rank	Sum	Mean	Rank	Sum	Mean	Rank	Sum	Mean	Rank	Sum	Mean	Rank
Shopping Malls provides better quality of goods and services	502	4.18	1	470	3.95	5	439	3.99	4	473	4.15	2	409	4.01	3
Shopping Malls provides better customer care service	477	3.98	2	459	3.86	4	430	3.91	3	456	4.00	1	389	3.81	5
Information system provided is adequate in Shopping Malls	493	4.11	2	455	3.82	5	432	3.93	4	474	4.16	1	405	3.97	3
Shopping Malls are Adequately Modernized	521	4.34	3	504	4.24	5	483	4.39	2	505	4.43	1	436	4.27	4
Parking facility is Adequate in Malls	517	4.31	1	471	3.96	5	462	4.20	3	490	4.30	2	414	4.06	4
Promotional offers are provided in the Shops at Shopping Malls	484	4.03	1	431	3.62	5	419	3.81	3	447	3.92	2	385	3.77	4
Billing method is convenient	467	3.89	1	436	3.66	5	416	3.78	3	433	3.80	2	382	3.75	4
Shopping at Shopping Malls is better than other shops	479	3.99	1	418	3.51	5	401	3.65	3	434	3.81	2	372	3.65	3
It helps customers to save time	459	3.83	3	443	3.72	5	428	3.89	1	435	3.82	4	394	3.86	2
Purchasing at shopping Malls is status Symbol to Customers	435	3.63	5	436	3.66	4	408	3.71	1	420	3.68	3	377	3.70	2

Source: Computed from Primary Data

The above table portrays the comparative score of outshoppers' level of perception towards the leading five premium malls namely Brook Filed mall, Fun Republic, Millaneum Mall, Vishall De Mall and Femina Shopping Mall.

The respondent have perceived Brook Field shopping mall as good and ranked in the first place in comparison with other malls for the following reasons. The outshoppers have stated that Brook Filed is best mall for better quality of goods and services, parking is adequate, promotional offers are excellent, billing method is convenient and it is the better place to shop when compared to other shops. Millaneum Mall is ranked in the first place for saving the customers time during shopping and providing status symbol for the customers who purchase at the mall. The outshoppers have ranked the Vishall De Mall in the first place for providing better customer care service, adequate information system and they state that the shopping mall is adequately modernized.

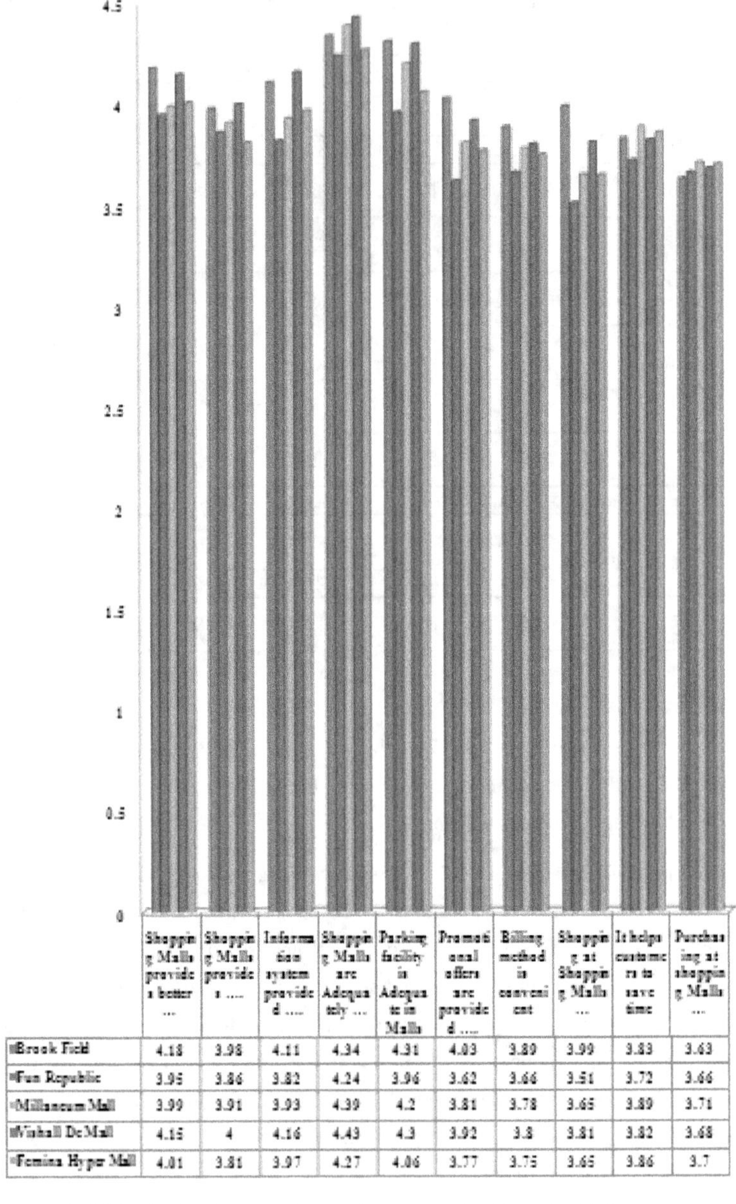

	Shopping Malls provide a better ...	Shopping Malls provide s	Information system provided	Shopping Malls are Adequately ...	Parking facility is Adequate in Malls	Promotional offers are provided	Billing method is convenient	Shopping at Shopping Malls ...	It helps customers to save time	Purchasing at shopping Malls ...
Brook Field	4.18	3.98	4.11	4.34	4.31	4.03	3.89	3.99	3.83	3.63
Fun Republic	3.95	3.86	3.82	4.24	3.96	3.62	3.66	3.51	3.72	3.66
Millaneum Mall	3.99	3.91	3.93	4.39	4.2	3.81	3.78	3.65	3.89	3.71
Vishall De Mall	4.15	4	4.16	4.43	4.3	3.92	3.8	3.81	3.82	3.68
Femina Hyper Mall	4.01	3.81	3.97	4.27	4.06	3.77	3.75	3.65	3.86	3.7

Exhibit 4.5: Outshoppers Perception in Leading Shopping Malls

Modern day consumers have started accepting shopping malls due to its features and service elements like: good music, efficient use of space, window-shopping opportunities, a one-stop shopping destination, fine-dining restaurants, and fast-food eateries are also attractive to many Indian consumers. In short, consumers are visiting malls for various motivational factors. Various motivational factors are aesthetic appreciation, diversion, social relationship, browsing, and convenience. Drawing theoretical evidences from the above statement following hypothesis is framed.

H10: Primary reasons stated by the outshoppers' for visiting shopping mall greatly influence their perception towards it.

The multiple regression analysis was performed to evaluate whether the primary reasons stated by the outshoppers' for shopping at mall greatly influence their perception towards it.

The dependent variable considered was reasons stated by outshoppers' for shopping at malls and the independent variables are (perceived values) : X1= Shopping Malls provides better quality of goods and services, X2= Shopping Malls provides better customer care service, X3= Information system provided is adequate in Shopping Malls, X4= Shopping Malls are Adequately Modernized, X5= Parking facility is Adequate in Malls, X6= Promotional offers are provided in the Shops at Shopping Malls, X7= Billing method is convenient, X8= Shopping at Shopping Malls is better than other shops, X9= It helps customers to save time, X10= Purchasing at shopping Malls is status Symbol to Customers.

Reasons stated by outshoppers' for shopping at malls= f (Shopping Malls provides better quality of goods and services, Shopping Malls provides better customer care service, Information system provided is adequate in Shopping Malls, Shopping Malls are Adequately Modernized, Parking facility is Adequate in Malls, Promotional offers are provided in the Shops at Shopping Malls, Billing method is convenient, Shopping at Shopping Malls is better than other shops, It helps customers to save time and Purchasing at shopping Malls is status Symbol to Customers).

Measured reasons stated by outshoppers' for shopping at malls was considered as dummy variable and run the following regression model to identify whether the primary reasons stated by the outshoppers' for shopping at mall greatly influence their perception towards it. Specifically,

Reasons stated by outshoppers' for shopping at malls(Y1) = $\beta 0 + \beta 1X1 + \beta 2X2 + \beta 3X3 + \beta 4X4 + \beta 5X5 + \beta 6X6 + \beta 7X7 + \beta 8X8 + \beta 9X9 + \beta 10X10 + e$

Where,

Y1= Reasons stated by outshoppers' for shopping at malls

$\beta 0$ = Intercept

$\beta 1 - \beta 10$= Slopes (estimates of coefficients)

X_1=Shopping Malls provides better quality of goods

X_2= Shopping Malls provides better customer care service

X_3= Information system provided is adequate in Shopping Malls

X_4= Shopping Malls are Adequately Modernized

X_5= Parking facility is Adequate in Malls

X_6= Promotional offers are provided in the Shops at Shopping Mall

X_7= Billing method is convenient

X_8=Shopping at Shopping Malls is better than other shops

X_9=It helps customers to save time

X_{10}= Purchasing at shopping Malls is status Symbol to Customers and

e = Random error, which the authors assumed as NID for this research

Table 4.65: Multiple Regression Model Summary Association Between Outshoppers' Perceived Value about Shopping Malls and the Primary Reasons Stated by them for Shopping at Malls

R	R²	Adjusted R²	SE	F Value	Sig
.337	.114	.098	.30415	7.117	.000

Level of Significance: 5 per cent

$$Y_1=8.031+.059X_1-.072X_2+.022X_3+.064X_4-.061X_5-.016X_6+.032_7-.069X_8+.015X_9-.008X_{10}$$

It has been revealed from the above econometric analysis that F ratio (7.117) is statistically insignificant at 5 per cent level.

This indicates the entire regression is significant, it establishes 33.70 per cent relationship between the variables tested.

From the above table it seen that the coefficient of correlation (R) value .337 and the coefficient of determinant (R^2) 0.114 describe good relationship between the variables tested.

Therefore the hypothesis framed stands accepted and it has been concluded that primary reasons stated by the outshoppers' for shopping at mall greatly influence their perception towards it.

The following table shows the value of constant and coefficient value of each attributes to analyse the reasons stated by outshoppers' for shopping at malls.

Table 4.66: Association between Outshoppers' Perceived Value about Shopping Malls and the Primary Reasons Stated by them for Shopping at Malls

Variables	Un standardized Coefficients		Standardized Coefficients	t	Sig.	Collinearity Statistics	
	B	SE	Beta			Tolerance	VIF
Constant	8.031	.051		157.097	.000	-	-
Shopping Malls provides better quality of goods and services	.059	.024	.128	2.467	.014	.595	1.680
Shopping Malls provides better customer care service	-.072	.019	-.196	-3.806	.000	.605	1.653
Information system provided is adequate in Shopping Malls	.022	.021	.053	1.052	.293	.633	1.580
Shopping Malls are Adequately Modernized	.064	.025	.133	2.579	.010	.605	1.653
Parking facility is Adequate in Malls	-.061	.020	-.173	-3.063	.002	.502	1.994
Promotional offers are provided in the Shops at Shopping Malls	-.016	.020	-.047	-.790	.430	.456	2.194
Billing method is convenient	.032	.017	.104	1.897	.058	.536	1.867
Shopping at Shopping Malls is better than other shops	-.069	.015	-.230	4.483	.000	.606	1.650
It helps customers to save time	.015	.018	.042	.819	.413	.596	1.678
Purchasing at shopping Malls is status Symbol to Customers	-.008	.014	-.029	-.576	.565	.614	1.629

Level of Significance: 5 per cent

To determine of one or more of the independent variables are significant predictors to identify the association between outshoppers' perceived value about shopping malls and the primary reasons for shopping at malls with the information provided in the co-efficient table is examined. Out of 10 parameter statements considered five parameter statements are statistically significant. The standardized co-efficient beta column reveals that reasons stated by outshoppers' for shopping at malls met have beta standard co-efficient 4.299 which is statistically significantly at 0.007. To assess multi-collinearity one looks at the size of tolerance and VIF (Variance Inflated Factor). For the tolerance small indicate the absence of collinearity. The VIF is the inverse (opposite) of tolerance, one looks for large values. If the tolerance value is smaller than .10, it is concluded that multi-collinearity is a problem. Similarly, if the VIF is 5 or larger, then multi-collinearity is a problem. Since the tolerance value is substantially above .10 and the VIF is smaller than 5 it is concluded that multi-collinearity among the independent variable is statistically significant.

Predicated Value of

Reasons stated by outshoppers' for shopping at malls=

    +8.031 (Constant)

    +0.59 (Shopping malls provides better quality of goods and services)

    ± 0.072 (Shopping malls provides better customer care service)

    +0.064 (Shopping malls are Adequately Modernized)

    ± 0.061 (Parking facility is Adequate in Malls)

    ±0.069 (Shopping at Shopping malls is better than other shops)

To assess the reasons stated by outshoppers' for shopping at malls multiple regression modeling was performed and to the relative importance of the individual dimension of the generated scale, Multiple Regression Analysis indicated out of 10 variables tested variables tested it was observed that five variables were observed to the statistically significant. However, it was observed that two variables depict positive perception of outshopper like: Shopping malls provides better quality of goods and services and Shopping malls are Adequately Modernized, whereas, three variables reveals negative perception of the outshoppers on: Shopping malls does not provides better customer care service, inadequate parking facility in malls and shopping at shopping malls is no where better than other shops.

E. *Shopping Motives and Buying Behaviour among Outshoppers*

Arnold and Reynolds (2003) developed six hedonic shopping motivations:

1) Adventure motivation -shopping is viewed as adventure.
2) Value shopping-shopping is to find a offers and discount and to bargain.
3) Role shopping-shopping motive relates to the shopper's role in society.
4) Idea shopping- shopping is undertaken to provide the shopper with up-to-date information on products and trends.
5) Social shopping-shoppers see the main purpose of shopping as an opportunity to socialize.
6) Gratification shopping-shopping is used as reward.

According to Assael (1987), shopping behavior is the most unique for behavior which the consumers exhibit. Gifts, clothing, groceries, gifts and household items are some of the most common type of shopping which consumers indulge in a highly frequent manner. But according to Dholakia (1999), occasion and motives are also some crucial points which influence the consumers shopping behavior. For example, for some consumers, shopping is all about getting the best deal out of bargaining, forsome (especially teenagers or the young crowd) shopping is a means of getting acquainted and interact more with others in a social context and for some it is a way of breaking out from the regular monotonous professional and personal routine (Reid and Brown, 1996).

Drawing theoretical evidences from the above discussion this section of analysis and interpretation are focused on understanding the influences of shopping motives and buying behaviour among outshoppers.

Table 4.67(A): Outshoppers Shopping Motives at Malls

Variables	Strongly Agree	Agree	Neither Agree nor disagree	Disagree	Strongly disagree	Sum	Mean	Rank
Adventure Shopping								
I Find shopping stimulating	200 (35.40)	219 (38.76)	86 (15.22)	48 (8.50)	12 (2.12)	2242	3.97	1
Shopping is a thrill to me	141 (24.96)	156 (27.61)	178 (31.50)	84 (14.87)	6 (1.06)	2037	3.61	3
Shopping makes me feel like I am in my own universe	135 (23.89)	223 (39.47)	115 (20.35)	67 (11.86)	25 (4.42)	2071	3.67	2
Value Shopping								
For the most part, I go shopping when there are sales offers	208 (36.81)	247 (43.72)	74 (13.10)	30 (5.31)	6 (1.06)	2316	4.10	1
I enjoy looking and hunting for discount when shopping	155 (27.43)	294 (52.04)	98 (17.35)	12 (2.12)	6 (1.06)	2275	4.03	2
I go shopping to take advantage of sales offers	149 (26.37)	225 (39.82)	137 (24.25)	42 (7.43)	12 (2.12)	2152	3.81	3
Role Shopping								
I feel good when I buy things for the special people in my life	255 (45.13)	221 (39.12)	56 (9.91)	33 (5.84)	0 (0.00)	2393	4.24	1
I enjoy shopping for my family members	281 (49.73)	202 (35.75)	65 (11.50)	17 (3.01)	0 (0.00)	2442	4.32	2
I enjoy shopping for around to find the perfect gift for friends	175 (30.97)	270 (47.79)	79 (13.98)	29 (5.13)	12 (2.12)	2262	4.00	3

Source: Primary Data

Values in parenthesis are in per cent

Table 4.67(B): Outshoppers Shopping Motives at Malls

Variables	Strongly Agree	Agree	Neither Agree nor disagree	Disagree	Strongly disagree	Sum	Mean	Rank
Idea Shopping								
I go shopping to keep up with the new trends and fashions	222 (39.29)	252 (44.60)	56 (9.91)	24 (4.25)	11 (1.95)	2345	4.15	1
I go shopping to see what new products available in the market	156 (27.61)	288 (50.97)	68 (12.04)	36 (6.37)	17 (3.01)	2225	3.94	2
I go shopping to experience new things	168 (29.73)	251 (44.42)	99 (17.52)	30 (5.30)	17 (3.01)	2218	3.93	3
Social Shopping								
I go shopping with my family to socialize	207 (36.64)	173 (30.62)	131 (23.19)	42 (7.43)	12 (2.12)	2216	3.92	2
I enjoy socializing with others when shopping	150 (26.55)	236 (41.77)	125 (22.12)	30 (5.31)	24 (4.25)	2153	3.81	3
To me, shopping with friends is a social occasion	204 (36.11)	204 (36.11)	81 (14.34)	64 (11.33)	12 (2.12)	2219	3.93	1
Gratification Shopping								
When I am in down mood, I go shopping to make me feel better	193 (34.16)	179 (31.68)	99 (17.52)	58 (10.27)	36 (6.37)	2130	3.77	1
To me, shopping is a way to relieve stress	153 (27.08)	234 (41.42)	94 (16.64)	66 (11.68)	18 (3.19)	2133	3.78	3
To me, shopping is a way to treat myself fresh	180 (31.86)	206 (36.46)	91 (16.11)	45 (7.96)	43 (7.61)	2130	3.77	1

Source: Primary Data

Values in parenthesis are in per cent

The data presented in the above table indicates the outshoppers shopping motives at malls.

The majority of the adventure shoppers have found shopping as stimulating and most of the value shoppers have done shopping during the sales offers.

Most of the role shoppers have felt good when they purchased goods for their special people in their life.

The majority of the idea shoppers have done shopping to keep up with new trends and fashion products available in the market.

Most of the social shoppers have felt that shopping as a social occasion, when they shop with their friends.

The gratification shoppers have preferred shopping during their down mood to make them feel better and to treat themselves fresh.

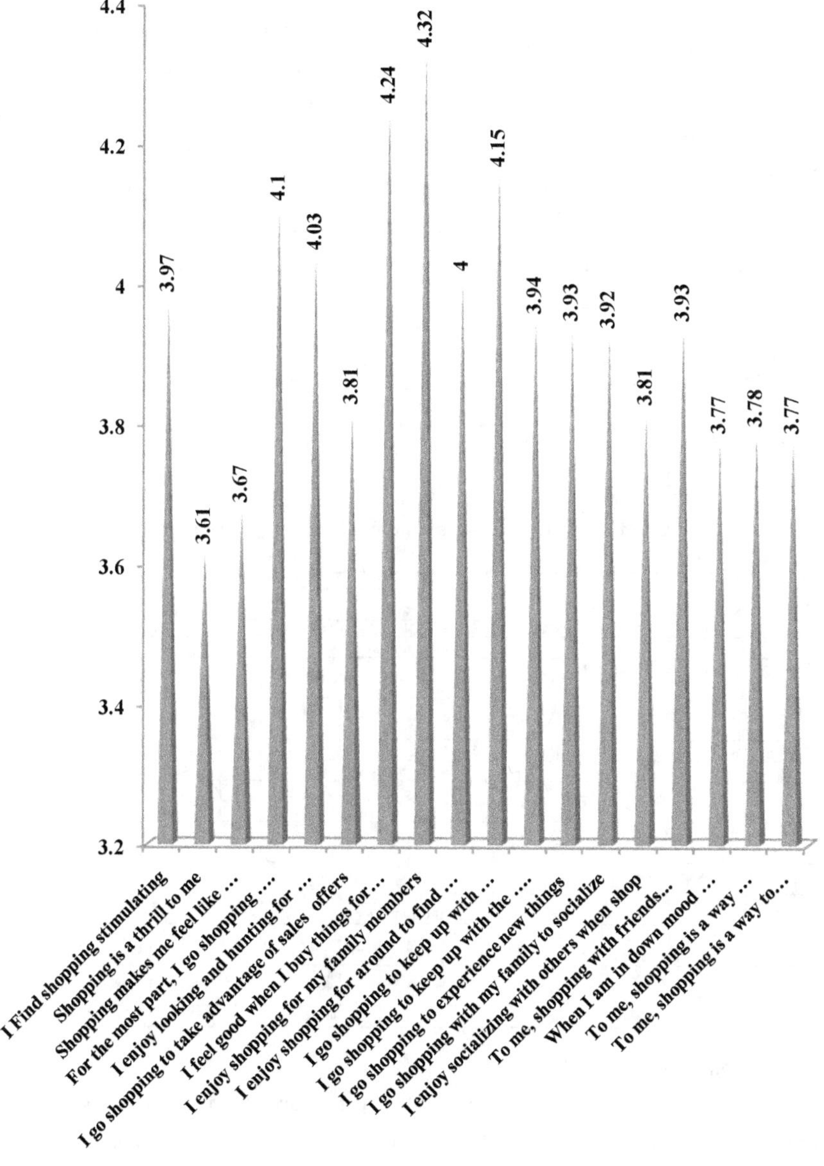

Exhibit 4.6: Outshoppers Shopping Motives at Malls

Table 4.68(A): Comparative Score of Outshoppers Shopping Motives at Various Malls

Particulars	Leading Shops														
	Brook Field (N:120)			Fun Republic (N:119)			Millaneum Mall (N:110)			Vishall De Mall (N:114)			Femina Shopping Mall (N:102)		
	Sum	Mean	Rank	Sum	Mean	Rank	Sum	Mean	Rank	Sum	Mean	Rank	Sum	Mean	Rank
Adventure Shopping															
I find shopping stimulating	473	3.94	4	472	3.97	2	433	3.94	4	459	**4.03**	**1**	405	3.97	2
Shopping is a thrill to me	428	3.57	5	426	3.58	3	396	3.60	2	422	**3.70**	**1**	365	3.58	3
Shopping makes me feel like I am in my own universe	443	3.69	2	434	3.65	3	400	3.64	4	426	**3.74**	**1**	368	3.61	5
Value Shopping															
For the most part, I go shopping when there are sales offers	483	4.03	4	493	4.14	2	461	**4.19**	**1**	468	4.11	3	411	4.03	4
I enjoy looking and hunting for discount when shop	474	3.95	5	474	3.98	3	455	**4.14**	**1**	468	4.11	2	404	3.96	4
I go shopping to take advantage of sales offers	454	3.78	4	456	3.83	3	425	**3.86**	**1**	424	3.72	5	393	3.85	2
Role Shopping															
I feel good when I buy things for the special people in my life	506	4.22	4	504	4.24	2	473	**4.30**	**1**	479	4.20	5	431	4.23	3
I enjoy shopping for my family members	521	4.34	3	504	4.24	5	478	4.35	2	498	**4.36**	**1**	441	4.32	4
I enjoy shopping for around to find the perfect gift for friends	476	3.97	4	476	4.00	2	439	3.99	3	452	3.96	5	419	**4.11**	**1**

Source: Computed Data

Table 4.68(B): Outshoppers Shopping Motives at Various Malls

Particulars	Leading Shops														
	Brook Field (N:120)			Fun Republic (N:119)			Millaneum Mall (N:110)			Vishall De Mall (N:114)			Femina Shopping Mall (N:102)		
	Sum	Mean	Rank	Sum	Mean	Rank	Sum	Mean	Rank	Sum	Mean	Rank	Sum	Mean	Rank
Idea Shopping															
I go shopping to keep up with the new trends and fashions	502	**4.18**	**1**	485	4.08	5	459	4.17	2	474	4.16	4	425	4.17	2
I go shopping to see what new products available in the market	481	**4.01**	**1**	450	3.78	5	438	3.98	2	454	3.98	2	402	3.94	4
I go shopping to experience new things	457	3.81	5	468	3.93	3	440	**4.00**	**1**	448	3.92	4	405	3.97	2
Social Shopping															
I go shopping with my family to socialise	479	3.99	2	453	3.81	5	433	3.94	3	456	**4.00**	**1**	395	3.87	4
I enjoy socializing with others when shopping	463	3.86	2	445	3.74	5	418	3.80	3	432	3.79	4	395	**3.87**	**1**
To me, shopping with friends is a social occasion	456	3.80	5	472	3.97	2	446	**4.05**	**1**	450	3.95	3	395	3.87	4
Gratification Shopping															
When I am in down mood, I go shopping to make me feel better	448	3.73	4	451	3.79	2	415	3.77	3	438	**3.84**	**1**	378	3.71	5
To me, shopping is a way to relieve stress	458	3.82	2	437	3.67	5	408	3.71	4	448	**3.93**	**1**	382	3.75	3
To me, shopping is a way to treat	452	3.77	2	446	3.75	3	413	3.75	3	441	**3.87**	**1**	378	3.71	5

Source: Computed Data

The above table states the respondents shopping motive at five shopping malls namely Brook Field, Fun Republic, Millaneum Mall, Vishall De Mall and Femina Shopping Mall.

The adventure shoppers have found the shopping more stimulating in the Vishall De Mall among the five shopping malls. They have also found that shopping as a thrill to them and make them felt they were in their own universe. Thus all the three factors are ranked in the first place in the VIshall De Mall. The Value shoppes have preferred the Fun Republic mall in the first place. They have done shopping during the sales offers and enjoyed while hunting for discounts and have taken advantage of sales offers. The role shoppers have enjoyed shopping with their family members in the Vishall De mall, they have enjoyed shopping while finding the perfect gift for their friends in the Femina Shopping Mall. The roler shoppers have enjoyed during buying things for the special people in their life in the Millaneum Mall.

The Idea shoppers have found new trends and fashion goods in the Brook Field mall and also have shopped in the mall to discover the new products available in the market. The shoppers preferred the Millaneum mall to experience the new things. The social shoppers have enjoyed shopping with their family in the Vishall De mall. They have socialized with others during shopping in the Femina Shopping Mall. Social shoppers have felt that shopping with their friends as a social occasion in the Millaneum Mall. The gratification shoppers have preferred the Vishall De Mall for shopping during their down mood to make them feel better, to relieve from stress and to treat themselves fresh.

Table 4.69: Comparative Status of Outshoppers Shopping Motives at Various Malls

Category of Shoppers	Brook Field (N:120)	Fun Republic (N:119)	Millaneum Mall (N:110)	Vishall De Mall (N:114)	Femina Shopping Mall (N:102)
Adventure Shopping	3.74	3.73	3.72	3.82	3.72
Value Shopping	3.92	3.98	4.06	3.98	3.95
Role Shopping	4.18	4.16	4.21	4.17	4.22
Idea Shopping	4.00.	3.93	4.05	4.02	4.03
Social Shopping	3.88	3.84	3.93	3.91	3.87
Gratification Shopping	3.77	3.74	3.74	3.88	3.72

The above table indicates the comparative status of outshoppers shopping motives at various malls namely Brook Field, Fun Republic, Millaneum Mall, Vishall De Mall and Femina Shopping Mall. The majority of the adventure shoppers have scored the highest mean score of 3.82 in the Vishall Mall.

In the Millaneum Mall the means score of the value shoppers are 4.06. The role shopping motive has been the higher means scores in all the five malls and the role shoppers in Millaneum Mall scored the highest mean value of 4.21. The idea shopper have scored the great mean score in the Millaneum Mall. Also the social shoppers have scored the maximum of 3.93 means score in the Millaneum Mall. The most of the gratification shoppers are found in the Vishall De Mall with the highest means score of 3.88.

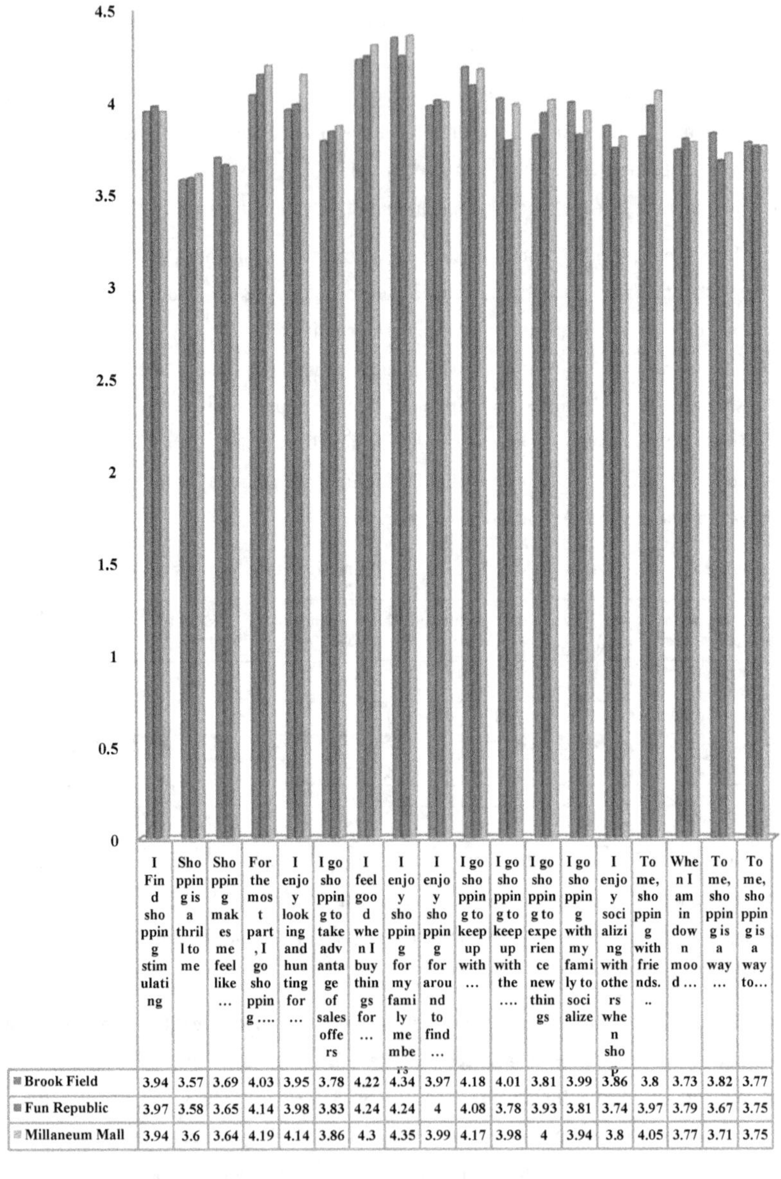

	I Find shopping stimulating	Shopping is a thrill to me	Shopping makes me feel like ...	For the most part, I go shopping	I enjoy looking and hunting for ...	I go shopping to take advantage of sales offers	I feel good when I buy things for ...	I enjoy shopping for my family membe rs	I enjoy shopping for around to find ...	I go shopping to keep up with ...	I go shopping to keep up with the	I go shopping to experience new things	I go shopping with my family to socialize	I enjoy socializing with others when shop p	To me, shopping with friends. ..	When I am in down moo d ...	To me, shopping is a way ...	To me, shopping is a way to...
Brook Field	3.94	3.57	3.69	4.03	3.95	3.78	4.22	4.34	3.97	4.18	4.01	3.81	3.99	3.86	3.8	3.73	3.82	3.77
Fun Republic	3.97	3.58	3.65	4.14	3.98	3.83	4.24	4.24	4	4.08	3.78	3.93	3.81	3.74	3.97	3.79	3.67	3.75
Millaneum Mall	3.94	3.6	3.64	4.19	4.14	3.86	4.3	4.35	3.99	4.17	3.98	4	3.94	3.8	4.05	3.77	3.71	3.75

Exhibit 4.7(A): Outshoppers Shopping Motives at Various Malls

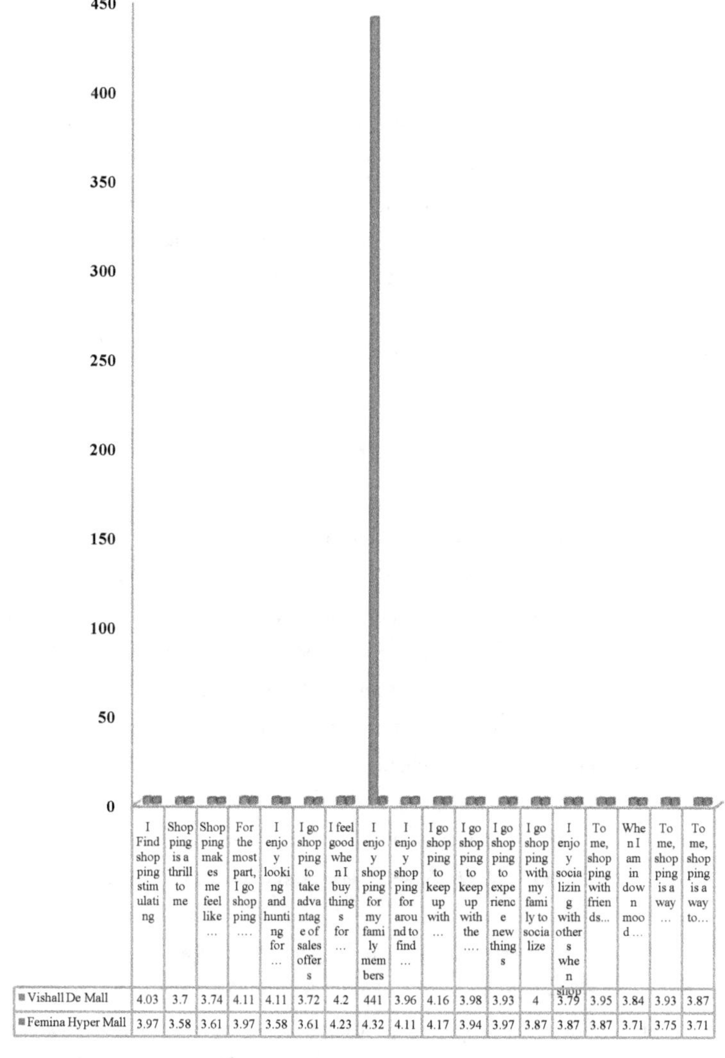

	I Find shopping stimulating	Shopping is a thrill to me	Shopping makes me feel like …	For the most part, I go shopping ….	I enjoy looking and hunting for …	I go shopping to take advantage of sales offers	I feel good when I buy things for …	I enjoy shopping for my family members	I enjoy shopping for around to find …	I go shopping to keep up with …	I go shopping to keep up with the ….	I go shopping to experience new things	I go shopping with my family to socialize	I enjoy socializing with others when shop	To me, shopping with friends…	When I am in down mood …	To me, shopping is a way …	To me, shopping is a way to…
Vishall De Mall	4.03	3.7	3.74	4.11	4.11	3.72	4.2	441	3.96	4.16	3.98	3.93	4	3.79	3.95	3.84	3.93	3.87
Femina Hyper Mall	3.97	3.58	3.61	3.97	3.58	3.61	4.23	4.32	4.11	4.17	3.94	3.97	3.87	3.87	3.87	3.71	3.75	3.71

Exhibit 4.7(b): Outshoppers Shopping Motives at Various Malls

Moreover, shopping malls, because of their exciting, lavish and sophisticated environments proffer a sense of relief and break to the customers from the same monotonous and routine rituals of job and personal works. The theoretical understanding gained from above discussion provided scope of framing following hypothesis which aims to analysis the association between shopping motives among consumers and their revealed perception about modern shopping malls.

H11:   There exist a great influence of Shopping motives on the perception of outshoppers towards shopping malls.

The multiple regression model was performed to evaluate influence of shopping motives of outshoppers greatly influence their perception towards shopping malls.

The dependent variable considered was influence of shopping motives on outshoppers and the independent variables are (outshoppers perception towards malls): X_1= Shopping Malls provides better quality of goods and services, X_2= Shopping Malls provides better customer care service, X_3= Information system provided is adequate in Shopping Malls, X_4= Shopping Malls are Adequately Modernized, X_5= Parking facility is Adequate in Malls, X_6= Promotional offers are provided in the Shops at Shopping Malls, X_7= Billing method is convenient, X_8= Shopping at Shopping Malls is better than other shops, X_9= It helps customers to save time, X_{10}= Purchasing at shopping Malls is status Symbol to Customers.

Influence of shopping motives on outshoppers = f (Shopping Malls provides better quality of goods and services, Shopping Malls provides better customer care service, Information system provided is adequate in Shopping Malls, Shopping Malls are Adequately Modernized, Parking facility is Adequate in Malls, Promotional offers are provided in the Shops at Shopping Malls, Billing method is convenient, Shopping at Shopping Malls is better than other shops, It helps customers to save time, Purchasing at shopping Malls is status Symbol to Customers).

Measured influence of shopping motives on outshoppers as a dummy variable and run the following regression model to identify whether the shopping motives of outshoppers greatly influence their perception towards shopping malls. Specifically,

(i) Influence of adventurers shopping motives on outshoppers perception towards shopping malls (Y1)= $\beta 0 + \beta 1X1 + \beta 2X2 + \beta 3X3 + \beta 4X4 + \beta 5X5 + \beta 6X6 + \beta 7X7 + \beta 8X8 + \beta 9X9 + \beta 10X10 + \beta 10X11 + \beta 10X12 + e.$

(ii) Influence of value shopping motives on outshoppers perception towards shopping malls (Y2) = $\beta 0 + \beta 1X1 + \beta 2X2 + \beta 3X3 + \beta 4X4 + \beta 5X5 + \beta 6X6 + \beta 7X7 + \beta 8X8 + \beta 9X9 + \beta 10X10 + e.$

(iii) Influence of role shopping motives on outshoppers perception towards shopping malls (Y3)= $\beta 0 + \beta 1X1 + \beta 2X2 + \beta 3X3 + \beta 4X4 + \beta 5X5 + \beta 6X6 + \beta 7X7 + \beta 8X8 + \beta 9X9 + \beta 10X10 + e.$

(iv) Influence of idea shopping motives on outshoppers perception towards shopping malls (Y4) = $\beta 0 + \beta 1X1 + \beta 2X2 + \beta 3X3 + \beta 4X4 + \beta 5X5 + \beta 6X6 + \beta 7X7 + \beta 8X8 + \beta 9X9 + \beta 10X10 + e.$

(v) Influence of social shopping motives on outshoppers perception towards shopping malls (Y5) = $\beta 0 + \beta 1X1 + \beta 2X2 + \beta 3X3 + \beta 4X4 + \beta 5X5 + \beta 6X6 + \beta 7X7 + \beta 8X8 + \beta 9X9 + \beta 10X10 + e.$

(vi) Influence of gratification offers are provided in the Shops at Shopping Malls on their Buyer Behaviour (Y6)= β0 + β1X1 + β2X2 +β3X3 + β4X4 + β5X5 + β6X6 + β7X7+ β8X8+ β9X9+ β10X10 + e.

Where independent variables are:

Y =Influence of shopping motives on outshoppers.

β0 = Intercept.

β1-β10= Slopes (estimates of coefficients).

X_1= Shopping Malls provides better quality of goods and services.

X_2= Shopping Malls provides better customer care service.

X_3= Information system provided is adequate in Shopping Malls.

X_4= Shopping Malls are Adequately Modernized.

X_5= Parking facility is Adequate in Malls.

X_6= Promotional offers are provided in the Shops at Shopping Malls

X_7= Billing method is convenient.

X_8= Shopping at Shopping Malls is better than other shops.

X_9= It helps customers to save time.

X_{10}= Purchasing at shopping Malls is status Symbol to Customers.

e = Random error, which the authors assumed as NID for this research.

Table 4.70: Influence of Shopping Motives on Outshoppers Perception Towards Shopping Malls

Shopping Malls Vs Buyer Behaviour	Adventure Shopper			Value Shopper			Role Shopper			Idea Shopper			Social Shopper			Gratification Shopper		
	β	t	sig	β	t	sig	β	t	sig	β	t	sig	β	t	sig	β	t	sig
Constant	-	8.458	.000	-	13.520	.000	-	7.802	.000	-	5.536	.000	-	3.784	.000	-	9.604	.000
Shopping Malls provides better quality of goods and services	.321	6.563	.000	-.037	-.711	.477	-.003	-.074	.941	.119	2.721	.007	-.037	-.815	.415	.195	3.929	.000
Shopping Malls provides better customer care service	.074	1.534	.126	.130	2.548	.011	.009	.199	.843	-.006	-.148	.882	.193	4.288	.000	.107	2.176	.030
Information system provided is adequate in Shopping Malls	-.054	-1.143	.253	-.179	-3.578	.000	-.193	-4.264	.000	-.079	-1.853	.064	.056	1.263	.207	-.198	-4.103	.000
Shopping Malls are Adequately Modernized	-.108	-2.221	.027	-.047	-.924	.356	.370	8.002	.000	.156	3.606	.000	.220	4.889	.000	-.015	-.312	.755
Parking facility is Adequate in Malls	-.064	-1.200	.231	.022	.393	.694	-.065	-1.288	.198	-.063	-1.331	.184	.034	.685	.494	-.217	-4.013	.000
Promotional offers are provided in the Shops at Shopping Malls	-.149	-2.658	.008	.130	2.210	.028	.147	2.752	.006	.144	2.878	.004	-.037	-.717	.474	.116	2.049	.041
Billing method is convenient	.287	5.571	.000	.122	2.248	.025	.054	1.093	.275	.196	4.261	.000	.149	3.121	.002	.239	4.550	.000
Shopping at Shopping Malls is better than other shops	-.029	-.594	.553	.045	.889	.374	.003	.054	.957	-.078	-1.804	.072	-.022	-.492	.623	-.053	-1.071	.285
It helps customers to save time	.055	1.132	.258	.152	2.952	.003	.286	6.137	.000	.376	8.614	.000	.322	7.107	.000	.136	2.737	.006
Purchasing at shopping Malls is status Symbol to Customers	.155	3.228	.001	-.032	-.641	.522	-.019	-.418	.676	-.029	-.679	.498	-.108	-2.414	.016	-.036	-.745	.457
R		.459			.357			.532			.608			.568			.429	
R2		.211			.127			.283			.369			.322			.184	
F		14.828			8.074			21.839			32.449			26.336			12.498	
sig		.000			.000			.000			.000			.000			.000	

Level of Significance: 5 per cent

To determine whether one or more of the independent variables are significant predictors of influence of personality of shopping malls on their buyer behavior the information provided in the co-efficient table is examined. Out of six parameter statements considered, all six variables were observed to be statistically significant. The standardized co-efficient beta column reveals that the association between influences of personality of shopping malls on their buyer behavior met have beta standard co-efficient which is statistically significant at 0.000.

To assess multi-collinearity one looks at the size of tolerance and VIF (Variance Inflated Factor). For the tolerance small indicate the absence of collinearity. The VIF is the inverse (opposite) of tolerance, one looks for large values. If the tolerance value is smaller than .10, it is concluded that multi-collinearity is a problem. Similarly, if the VIF is 5 or larger, then multi-collinearity is a problem. Since the tolerance value is substantially above .10 and the VIF is smaller than 5 it is concluded that multi-collinearity among the independent variable is statistical significant.

From the detailed data analysis it has been observed that the adventures shoppers were observed to positively correlate with the stimulation like: better quality of products & services, billing conveniences and feel of status symbol. These categories of shoppers were observed to express negatively perception on: Information system provided is adequate in shopping malls, adequately modernized and promotional offers are provided. It has been observed that the value shoppers were observed to positively correlate with the stimulation like:better customer care service, bill conveniences and time saving features. Value shoppers were observed to express negatively perception on inadequate information system provided at shopping malls. Further it has been observed that the role shoppers have expressed negative perception towards all 10 variables constructed for the effective conduct of study. Therefore it has been concluded that shopping motives of outshoppers' greatly influence their perception towards shopping malls. Factor analysis technique has been applied to find the underlying dimension (factors) that exists among 18 variables relating to the shopping motives of outshoppers' and their preference towards shopping malls.

Table 4.71: KMO and BARTLETT'S Test Shopping Motives of Outshoppers and their Preferred Shopping Malls

Kaiser-Meyer-Olkin Measure of Sampling Adequacy	.808
Bartlett's Test of Sphericity Approx. Chi-Square	248.514
DF	120
Sig	.000

Table 4.72: Cumulative Shopping Motives of Outshoppers and their Preferred Shopping Malls

Variables	Initial	Extraction
Adventure Shopping		
I Find shopping stimulating	1.000	.717
Shopping is a thrill to me	1.000	.799
Shopping makes me feel like I am in my own universe	1.000	.759
Value Shopper		
For the most part, I go shopping when there are sales offers	1.000	.735
I enjoy looking and hunting for discount when shopping	1.000	.766
I go shopping to take advantage of sales offers	1.000	.753
Role Shopper		
I feel good when I buy things for the special people in my life	1.000	.524
I enjoy shopping for my family members	1.000	.788
I enjoy shopping for around to find the perfect gift for friends	1.000	.725
Idea Shopper		
I go shopping to keep up with the new trends and fashions	1.000	.644
I go shopping to keep up with the new products available in the market	1.000	.605
I go shopping to experience new things	1.000	.656
Social Shopper		
I go shopping with my family to socialize	1.000	.687
I enjoy socializing with others when shopping	1.000	.838
To me, shopping with friends is a social occasion	1.000	.835
Gratification Shopper		
When I am in down mood, I go shopping to make me feel better	1.000	.782
To me, shopping is a way to relieve stress	1.000	.736
To me, shopping is a way to treat myself fresh	1.000	.721

In order to provide a more parsimonious interpretation of the results, 18-item scale was then Factor analyzed using the Principal Component method with Equamax rotation. Factor analysis attempts to identify underlying variables, or factors, that explain the pattern of correlations within a set of observed variables.

Factor analysis is often used in data reduction to identify a small number of factors that explain most of the variance observed in a much larger number of manifest variables.

In the current study rotation factor analysis is performed to measure the shopping motives of outshoppers' and their preference towards shopping malls.

The significance of relationship between the variables is depicted in the following table.

Table 4.73: Rotated Component Matrix Shopping Motives of Outshoppers and their Preferred Shopping Malls

Factors	Leading shopping Malls				
	Brook Field	Fun Republic	Millaneum Mall	Vishall De Mall	Femina Shopping Mall
Adventure Shopping					
X_1- I Find shopping stimulating	-	-	-	.756	-
X_2- Shopping is a thrill to me	-	-	-	.733	-
X_3- Shopping makes me feel like I am in my own universe	-	-	-	.791	-
Value Shopper					
X_4- For the most part, I go shopping when there are sales offers	-	-	.716	-	-
X_5- I enjoy looking and hunting for discount when shopping	-	-	.844	-	-
X_6- I go shopping to take advantage of sales offers	-	-	.801	-	-
Role Shopper					
X_7- I feel good when I buy things for the special people in my life	-	.576		-	-
X_8- I enjoy shopping for my family members	-	-	-	-	.850
X_9- I enjoy shopping for around to find the perfect gift for friends	-	-	-	-	.768
Idea Shopper					
X_{10}- I go shopping to keep up with the new trends and fashions	-	-	-	-	-
X_{11}- I go shopping to keep up with the new products available in the market	.531	-	-	-	-
X_{12}- I go shopping to experience new things	-	-	-	-	.515
Social Shopper					
X_{13}- I go shopping with my family to socialize	-	.597	-	-	-
X_{14}- I enjoy socializing with others when shopping	-	.868	-	-	-
X_{15}- To me, shopping with friends or friends is a social occasion	-	.843	-	-	-
Gratification Shopper					
X_{16}- When I am in down mood, I go shopping to make me feel better	.822	-	-	-	-
X_{17}- To me, shopping is a way to relieve stress	.789	-	-	-	-
X_{18}-To me, shopping is a way to treat myself fresh	.734	-	-	-	-
Eigen value	**4.248**	**3.733**	**3.643**	**3.619**	**3.347**
% of Variance	**17.698**	**15.556**	**15.178**	**15.078**	**13.946**
Cumulative%	**17.698**	**33.254**	**48.432**	**63.510**	**77.456**

Level of Significance: 5 per cent

Five factors extracted together account for 77.456 per cent of the total variance (information contained in the original 18 variables). This is good, because the researcher are able to economize on the number of variables (from 18 researcher have reduced them to five underlying factors), while the data lost only about 22.54 per cent of the information content

(77.456 per cent is retained by the five factors extracted out of the 18 original variables). Since the idea of factor analysis is to identify the factors that meaningfully summarize the sets of closely related variables, the rotation phase of the factor analysis attempts to transfer initial matrix into one that is easier to interpret. Equamax rotation method is used to extract meaningful factors.

Five factors were identified as being maximum Percentage variance accounted. The variables X_{11}, X_{16}, X_{17} and X_{18} constitute the factor I and it accounts for 17.698 per cent of the total variance. The variables X_7, X_{13}, X_{14} and X_{15}a re grouped as factor II and it accounts for 15.586 per cent of the total variance. Three variables X_4, X_5 and X_6 constitute the factor III and it accounts for 15.178 per cent of the total variance. Again three variables X_1, X_2 and X_3 are grouped as factor IV and it accounts for 15.078 per cent of the total variance. Next three variables X_8, X_9 and X_{12} are grouped as factor V and it accounts for 13.946 per cent of the total variance.

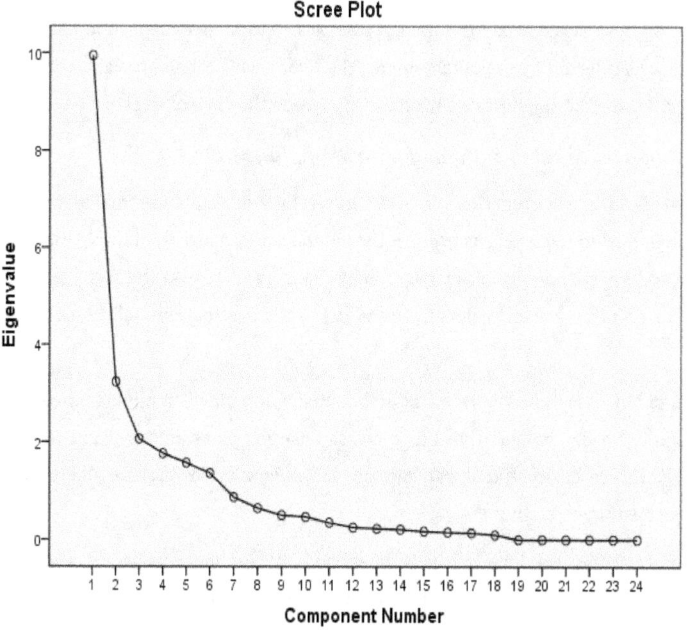

Exhibit 4.8: Scree Plot Shopping Motives of Outshoppers and their Preferred Shopping Malls

Table 4.74: Summary of Rotation Factor Analysis & Cronbach's Alpha Shopping Motives of Outshoppers and their Preferred Shopping Malls

Factors	Factor Interpretation	Variables included in the factors	Cronbach's Alpha
F_1	Brook Field	I go shopping to keep up with the new products available in the market, When I am in down mood, I go shopping to make me feel better, To me, shopping is a way to relieve stress and -To me, shopping is a way to treat myself fresh.	.865
F_2	Fun Republic	I feel good when I buy things for the special people in my life, I go shopping with my family to socialize, I enjoy socializing with others when shop, To me, shopping with friends is a social occasion.	.732
F_3	Millennium Mall	For the most part, I go shopping when there are sales offers, I enjoy looking and hunting for discount when shopping, I go shopping to take advantage of sales offers.	.711
F_4	Vishall De Mall	I Find shopping stimulating, Shopping is a thrill to me, Shopping makes me feel like I am in my own universe.	.698
F_5	Femina Shopping Mall	I enjoy shopping for my family members,I enjoy shopping for around to find the perfect gift for friends, I go shopping to experience new things.	.684

Source: Computed From Primary Data

Factor analysis was used to find out the association between shopping motives and shopping malls selected by the outshoppers. The Cronbach's reliability values (.865, .732, 711, .698, and .684) indicate significant correlation between the variables tested.

F. Outshoppers Level of Satisfaction to Shopping Malls

In today's largely competitive market environment, shopping malls are increasingly realizing the need to focus on customer satisfaction as a measure to improve their competitive position. Modern shopping mall managers have started to realise the fact that shoppers are reluctant to visit the weaker malls and are going to the destination malls which have the best stores.

Hence, it can be rightly said that customer satisfaction plays an important role in retailers' success and to be stay competitive. Customer satisfaction plays an important role in retaining the customers. Hence, customer satisfaction and customer loyalty are the most important elements of customer retention.

Various activities are done by the retailers to have a sufficient base of retained and loyal customers. A customer is satisfied only when his/her expectations are met. This section of the study focuses its analysis and interpretation on outshoppers level of satisfaction derived at various shopping malls.

Table 4.75: Outshoppers Level of Satisfaction to Shopping Malls

Reasons	Highly Satisfied	Satisfied	Neither satisfied nor dissatisfied	Dissatisfied	Highly Dissatisfied	Sum	Mean	Rank
Availability all under one roof	294 (52.04)	228 (40.35)	31 (5.49)	6 (1.06)	6 (1.06)	2493	4.41	1
Accessibility (Distance of Travel)	89 (15.75)	353 (62.48)	93 (16.46)	30 (5.31)	0 (0.00)	2196	3.89	11
Retail Tenant Mix	97 (17.17)	265 (46.90)	172 (30.44)	25 (4.42)	6 (1.06)	2117	3.75	13
Product Range, Merchandise Value	106 (18.76)	372 (65.84)	39 (6.90)	48 (8.50)	0 (0.00)	2231	3.95	8
Orientation and Infrastructure facilities	167 (29.56)	291 (51.50)	95 (16.81)	0 (0.00)	12 (2.12)	2296	4.06	6
Better Sales service	142 (25.13)	255 (45.13)	125 (22.12)	37 (6.55)	6 (1.06)	2185	3.87	12
Parking Facilities	212 (37.52)	237 (41.95)	75 (13.27)	29 (5.13)	12 (2.12)	2303	4.08	4
External Atmospheric Clues (architectural style, Layout design and image)	163 (28.85)	295 (52.21)	96 (16.99)	11 (1.95)	0 (0.00)	2305	4.08	4
Internal Atmospheric Clues (eg flooring, lighting, air condition, music rest rooms etc)	205 (36.28)	235 (41.59)	102 (18.05)	17 (3.01)	6 (1.06)	2311	4.09	3
Hospitality (Food courts & Resting Places)	170 (30.09)	288 (50.97)	83 (14.69)	7 (1.24)	17 (3.01)	2282	4.04	7
Entertainment (Multiplex Screening the latest blockbusters)	308 (54.51)	190 (33.63)	42 (7.43)	7 (1.24)	18 (3.19)	2458	4.35	2
Lifestyle Outlets (Health and Beauty)	140 (24.78)	290 (51.33)	99 (17.52)	19 (3.36)	17 (3.01)	2212	3.92	9
Offers anddiscounts	135 (23.89)	279 (49.38)	115 (20.35)	36 (6.37)	0 (0.00)	2208	3.91	10
Competitive price	104 (18.41)	231 (40.88)	158 (27.96)	66 (11.68)	6 (1.06)	2056	3.64	15
Status Symbol	105 (18.58)	249 (44.07)	133 (23.54)	66 (11.68)	12 (2.12)	2064	3.65	14

Source: Primary Data

Values in parenthesis are in per cent

The above table exemplifies the outshoppers' opinion on level of satisfaction towards the selected shopping malls.

It has been inferred that, majority of the respondents opine good level of satisfaction towards availability all under one roof with the mean score of 4.41. Followed by, the sample populations are satisfied with the entertainment factors like multiplex screening the latest block blusters and Internal Atmospheric Clues like flooring, lighting, air condition, music rest rooms etc these variable are rated in second place and third place with the mean score of 4.35 and 4.09. Consequently the respondents are satisfied with parking facilities and External Atmospheric Clues like architectural style, Layout design and image with a mean score of 4.08 and both are ranked in the fourth place.

The respondents are moderately satisfied with orientation and infra structure facilities, hospitality like food courts and resting place and product range, merchandise value in the sixth, seventh and eighth place with the mean score of 4.06, 4.04 and 3.95. Further, opine modest level of satisfaction towards lifestyle outlets like health and beauty, offers and discounts offered in malls are ranked in the ninth and tenth place with the mean score of 3.92 and 3.91.It has been inferred that the respondents opine low level of satisfaction towards accessibility i.e distance of travel, better sales service and retail tenant mix with the mean score of 3.89, 3.87 and 3.75 in the place of eleven, twelve and thirteen.

Further the respondents have low level of satisfaction towards status symbol and competitive price which are ranked in fourteenth and fifteenth place with the mean score of 3.65 and 3.64. Thus it can be finally concluded that the majority of the respondents are satisfied with the availability of all product under one roof.

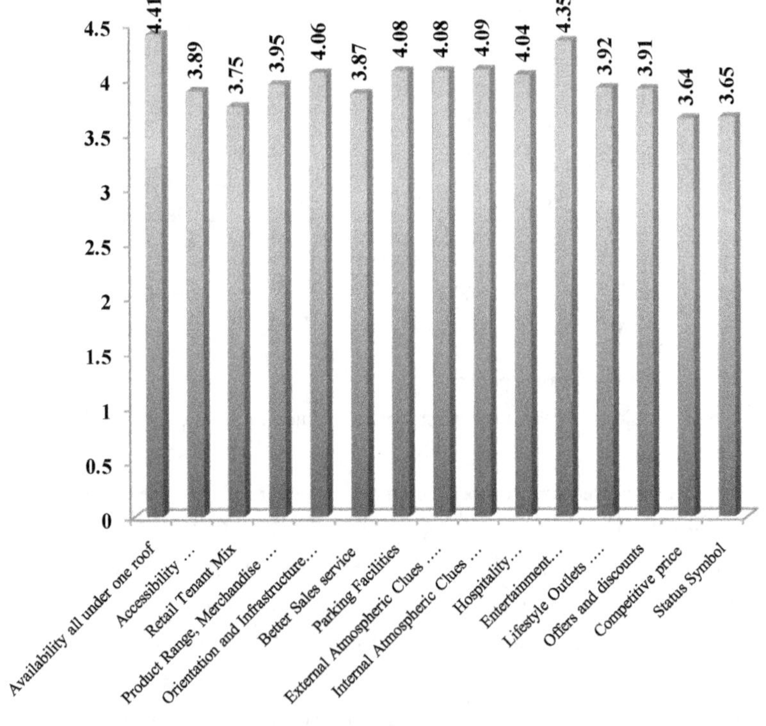

Exhibit 4.9: Outshoppers Level of Satisfaction towards Shopping Malls

Table 4.76: Comparative Status of Outshoppers Level of Satisfaction at Various Shopping Malls

Particulars	Leading Shops														
	Brook Field (N:120)			Fun Republic (N:119)			Millaneum Mall (N:110)			Vishall De Mall (N:114)			Femina Shopping Mall (N:102)		
	Sum	Mean	Rank	Sum	Mean	Rank	Sum	Mean	Rank	Sum	Mean	Rank	Sum	Mean	Rank
Availability all under one roof	538	4.48	1	518	4.35	4	478	4.35	5	502	4.40	3	457	4.48	2
Accessibility (Distance of Travel)	478	3.98	2	442	3.71	5	426	3.87	3	456	4.00	1	394	3.86	4
Retail Tenant Mix	453	3.78	2	439	3.69	4	406	3.69	5	436	3.82	1	383	3.75	3
Product Range, Merchandise Value	471	3.93	4	466	3.92	5	438	3.98	1	450	3.95	3	406	3.98	1
Orientation and Infrastructure facilities	491	4.09	2	479	4.03	5	445	4.05	3	461	4.04	4	420	4.12	1
Better Sales service	470	3.92	3	449	3.77	5	432	3.93	2	448	3.93	1	386	3.78	4
Parking Facilities	501	4.18	1	466	3.92	5	451	4.10	3	474	4.16	2	411	4.03	4
External Atmospheric Clues (architectural style, Layout design and image)	492	4.10	2	484	4.07	3	455	4.14	1	459	4.03	5	415	4.07	4
Internal Atmospheric Clues (eg flooring, lighting, air condition, music restrooms etc)	490	4.08	4	479	4.03	5	454	4.13	1	469	4.11	2	419	4.11	3
Hospitality (Food courts & Resting Places)	489	4.08	2	472	3.97	5	444	4.04	3	469	4.11	1	408	4.00	4
Entertainment (Multiplex Screening the latest blockbusters)	528	4.40	1	510	4.29	5	482	4.38	2	497	4.36	3	441	4.32	4
Lifestyle Outlets (Health and Beauty)	475	3.96	2	455	3.82	5	425	3.86	4	441	3.87	3	416	4.08	1
Offers and discounts	475	3.96	1	464	3.90	4	430	3.91	3	438	3.84	5	401	3.93	2
Competitive price	442	3.68	1	434	3.65	3	399	3.63	4	408	3.58	5	373	3.66	2
Status Symbol	453	3.78	1	433	3.64	4	403	3.66	2	403	3.54	15	372	3.65	3

Source: Computed Data

The above table reveals the comparative status of the respondents level of satisfaction towards various factors involved in various shopping malls namely Brook Fields, Fun Republic, Millaneum Mall, Vishal De Mall and Femina Shopping Mall.

Among the five premium malls which is selected for our study the respondents have felt that they are very much satisfied with Brook Field Mall regarding the factors like availability of all products under one roof, parking facilities, Entertainment facilities, offers and discounts, competitive price and status symbol. The outshoppers prefer Millaneum Mall and are satisfied with the product range, merchandise value, external atmospheric clues and internal atmospheric clues.

The otushoppers ranked the Vishall De mall first for accessibility, retail tenant mix, better sales services and hospitality. Femina Shopping mall is ranked first for orientation and infrastructure facilities when compared to other shopping malls.

Table 4.77: Comparative Score of Outshoppers Overall Level of Satisfaction to Shopping Malls

Reasons	Brook Field (N:120)	Fun Republic (N:119)	Millaneum Mall (N:110)	Vishall De Mall (N:114)	Femina Shopping Mall (N:102)
Availability all under one roof	4.48	4.35	4.35	4.40	4.48
Accessibility (Distance of Travel)	3.98	3.71	3.87	4.00	3.86
Retail Tenant Mix	3.78	3.68	3.69	3.82	3.75
Product Range, Merchandise Value	3.93	3.92	3.98	3.95	3.98
Orientation and Infrastructure facilities	4.09	4.03	4.05	4.04	4.12
Better Sales service	3.92	3.77	3.93	3.93	3.78
Parking Facilities	4.18	3.92	4.10	4.16	4.03
External Atmospheric Clues (architectural style, Layout design and image)	4.10	4.07	4.14	4.03	4.07
Internal Atmospheric Clues (eg flooring, lighting, air condition, music rest rooms etc)	4.08	4.03	4.13	4.11	4.10
Hospitality (Food courts & Resting Places)	4.08	3.97	4.04	4.11	4.00
Entertainment (Multiplex Screening the latest blockbusters)	4.40	4.29	4.38	4.36	4.32
Lifestyle Outlets (Health and Beauty)	3.96	3.82	3.86	3.87	4.08
Offers and discounts	3.96	3.90	3.91	3.84	3.93
Competitive price	3.68	3.65	3.63	3.58	3.66
Status Symbol	3.78	3.64	3.66	3.54	3.65
Total Mean	**60.40**	**58.75**	**59.71**	**59.74**	**59.81**
Average Mean	**4.02**	**3.91**	**3.98**	**3.98**	**3.99**
Rank	**1**	**5**	**3**	**3**	**2**

Source: Computed data

The above tables exemplify the overall satisfaction level of the outshoppers surveyed in the five famous malls in Tamil nadu namely Brook Field, Fun Republic, Millaneum Mall, Vishall De Mall and Femina Shopping Mall. The overall mean score opined by the outshoppers in the Brook Field mall is 60.40. Out of the 120 respondents surveyed they have given the average mean score of 4.02 which stands in the first place and Brook Field is ranked in the first place. The second have been given to Femina Shopping Mall by the 102 outshoppers surveyed in the mall. They have scored the total mean of 59.81 and average mean of 3.99. The third place has been shared by Vishall De Mall and Millaneum Malls with the total score of 59.74 and 59.72 and average mean of 3.98. Out of the 110 outshoppers surveyed in the Fun Republic the respondents have opted total mean of 58.76 and average mean of 3.91 and ranked in the fifth place regarding the level of satisfaction.

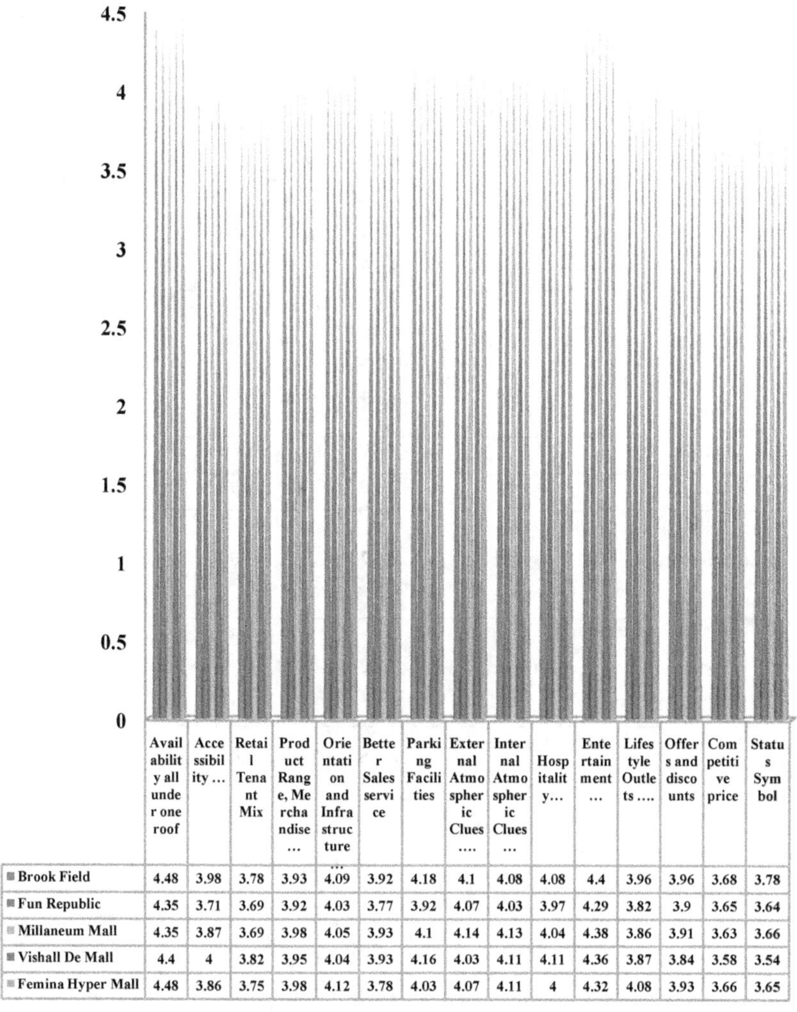

	Availability all under one roof	Accessibility …	Retail Tenant Mix	Product Range, Merchandise …	Orientation and Infrastructure	Better Sales service	Parking Facilties	External Atmospheric Clues ….	Internal Atmospheric Clues …	Hospitality…	Entertainment …	Lifestyle Outlets ….	Offers and discounts	Competitive price	Status Symbol
Brook Field	4.48	3.98	3.78	3.93	4.09	3.92	4.18	4.1	4.08	4.08	4.4	3.96	3.96	3.68	3.78
Fun Republic	4.35	3.71	3.69	3.92	4.03	3.77	3.92	4.07	4.03	3.97	4.29	3.82	3.9	3.65	3.64
Millaneum Mall	4.35	3.87	3.69	3.98	4.05	3.93	4.1	4.14	4.13	4.04	4.38	3.86	3.91	3.63	3.66
Vishall De Mall	4.4	4	3.82	3.95	4.04	3.93	4.16	4.03	4.11	4.11	4.36	3.87	3.84	3.58	3.54
Femina Hyper Mall	4.48	3.86	3.75	3.98	4.12	3.78	4.03	4.07	4.11	4	4.32	4.08	3.93	3.66	3.65

Exhibit 4.10: Outshoppers Level of Satisfaction at Various Shopping Malls

It is now widely accepted that exceeding customer expectations is key to customer satisfaction, delight, and loyalty. Accordingly, it is critical for marketers to try to find out in advance what their customers' expectations are, because a failure to meet or exceed those expectations could lead to dissatisfaction and defection. Based on this literature understanding following hypothesis is framed.

125

H12: There exists wide gap between the reasons stated by the outshoppers' for visiting the shopping malls and the level of satisfaction derived by

Table 4.78: Measures of Dispersion Primary Reasons Stated by Outshoppers for Shopping at Malls and Level of Satisfaction Derived by them

Particulars	Reasons		Satisfaction		Correlation
	Mean	SD	Mean	SD	
Availability all Under One Roof	3.51	3.595	1.59	.738	.355
Accessibility (Distance of Travel)	7.95	4.057	2.11	.723	-.089
Retail Tenant Mix	8.09	4.388	2.25	.828	-.152
Product Range, Merchandise Value	7.28	4.444	2.05	.771	.026
Orientation and Infrastructure facilities	7.74	3.892	1.94	.807	.020
Better Sales Service	8.99	4.066	2.13	.902	.023
Parking Facilities	7.19	3.919	1.92	.949	.085
External Atmospheric Clues (Architectural Style, Layout Design and Image)	8.57	3.423	1.92	.729	.138
Internal Atmospheric Clues (E.g: Flooring, Lighting, Air Condition, Music Rest Rooms etc.,)	7.82	3.548	1.91	.867	.253
Hospitality (Food courts & Resting Places)	8.56	4.007	1.96	.876	.258
Entertainment (Multiplex Screening the Latest Blockbusters)	5.96	4.063	1.65	.913	.357
Lifestyle Outlets (Health and Beauty)	9.59	3.778	2.08	.907	.087
Offers and Discounts	7.68	4.126	2.09	.831	.036
Competitive Price	9.62	4.089	2.36	.948	.101
Status Symbol	10.33	4.809	2.35	.980	.146

Level of Significance: 5 per cent

It is evident from the above table that outshoppers' expectation towards shopping malls are very high and it is observed that the retailers at shopping malls have failed to fulfill their customers' needs adequately. Thus it has been found that the respondents' exhibit low level of satisfaction towards services offered by shopping malls that are situated at three prime cities of Tamil Nadu i.e., Coimbatore, Madurai and Trichy.

Table 4.79: Result of Paired Z Test Primary Reasons Stated by the Consumers' for Shopping at Malls and Level of Satisfaction Derived by them

Pairs	Mean	SD	Z	DF	Sig
Availability all Under One Roof	1.924	3.404	13.434	564	.000
Accessibility (Distance of Travel)	5.832	4.184	33.135	564	.000
Retail Tenant Mix	5.837	4.587	30.245	564	.000
Product Range, Merchandise Value	5.232	4.491	27.689	564	.000
Orientation and Infrastructure facilities	5.805	3.960	34.850	564	.000
Better Sales Service	6.860	4.145	39.340	564	.000
Parking Facilities	5.262	3.953	31.637	564	.000
External Atmospheric Clues (Architectural Style, Layout Design and Image)	6.653	3.400	46.519	564	.000
Internal Atmospheric Clues (E.g: Flooring, Lighting, Air Condition, Music Rest Rooms etc.,)	5.912	3.433	40.929	564	.000
Hospitality (Food courts & Resting Places)	6.604	3.875	40.511	564	.000
Entertainment (Multiplex Screening the Latest Blockbusters)	4.313	3.833	26.746	564	.000
Lifestyle Outlets (Health and Beauty)	7.508	3.808	46.863	564	.000
Offers and Discounts	5.589	4.179	31.790	564	.000
Competitive Price	7.260	4.103	42.060	564	.000
Status Symbol	7.984	4.766	39.823	564	.000

Level of significance: 5 per cent

From the above table it has inferred that probability value of 'z' is found to be significant at 5 per cent level. Therefore the hypothesis framed stands accepted and it has been concluded that there exists wide gap between the reasons stated by the outshoppers' for visiting the shopping malls and the level of satisfaction derived by them.

Factor analysis technique has been applied to find the underlying dimension (factors) that exists among 15 variables relating to the outshoppers' level of satisfaction towards leading shopping malls.

Table 4.80: KMO and BARTLETT'S Test Outshoppers Level of Satisfaction at Various Shopping Malls

Kaiser-Meyer-Olkin Measure of Sampling Adequacy	.758
Bartlett's Test of Sphericity Approx. Chi-Square	564.530
DF	105
Sig	.000

Level of Significance: 5 per cent

In the present study, Kaiser-Meyer-Oklin (KMO) Measure of Sampling Adequacy (MSA) and Bartlett's test of Sphericity were applied to verify the adequacy or appropriateness of data for factor analysis. In this study, the value of KMO for overall matrix was found to be excellent (0.758) and Bartlett's test of Sphericity was highly significant (p<0.05). Bartlett's Sphericity test was effective, as the chi-square value draws significance at five per cent level. The results thus indicated that the sample taken was appropriate to proceed with a factor analysis procedure. Besides the Bartlett's Test of Sphericity and the KMO Measure of sampling Adequacy, Communality values of all variables were also observed.

Table 4.81: Cumulative Outshoppers Level of Satisfaction at Various Shopping Malls

Variables	Initial	Extraction
Availability all under one roof	1.000	.509
Accessibility (Distance of Travel)	1.000	.695
Retail Tenant Mix	1.000	.702
Product Range, Merchandise Value	1.000	.766
Orientation and Infrastructure facilities	1.000	.819
Better Sales service	1.000	.650
Parking Facilities	1.000	.600
External Atmospheric Clues (architectural style, Layout design and image)	1.000	.754
Internal Atmospheric Clues (eg flooring, lighting, air condition, music rest rooms etc)	1.000	.726
Hospitality (Food courts & Resting Places)	1.000	.600
Entertainment (Multiplex Screening the latest blockbusters)	1.000	.691
Lifestyle Outlets (Health and Beauty)	1.000	.645
Offers and discounts	1.000	.758
Competitive price	1.000	.773
Status Symbol	1.000	.675

In order to provide a more parsimonious interpretation of the results, 15-item scale was then Factor analyzed using the Principal Component method with Equamax rotation.

Factor analysis attempts to identify underlying variables, or factors, that explain the pattern of correlations within a set of observed variables. Factor analysis is often used in data reduction to identify a small number of factors that explain most of the variance observed in a much larger number of manifest variables.

In the current study rotation factor analysis is performed to measure the association between personality traits of outshoppers' and their preference towards shopping malls.

The significance of relationship between the variables is depicted in the following table.

Table 4.82: Rotated Component Matrix Outshoppers Level of Satisfaction at Various Shopping Malls

Factors	Leading Shopping Malls				
	Brook Field	Fun Republic	Millaneum Mall	Vishall De Mall	Femina Shopping Mall
X_1- Availability all under one roof	-	-	-	-	-
X_2- Accessibility (Distance of Travel)	.566	-	-	-	-
X_3- Retail Tenant Mix	.556	-	.510	-	-
X_4- Product Range, Merchandise Value	.507	-	.627	-	-
X_5- Orientation and Infrastructure facilities	.550	-	-	-	.612
X_6- Better Sales service	.756	-	-	-	-
X_7- Parking Facilities	-	.534	-	-	-
X_8- External Atmospheric Clues (architectural style, Layout design and image)	.704	-	-	-	-
X_9- Internal Atmospheric Clues (eg flooring, lighting, air condition, music rest rooms etc)	.740	-	-	-	-
X_{10}- Hospitality (Food courts & Resting Places)	.589	-	-	-	-
X_{11}- Entertainment (Multiplex Screening the latest blockbusters)	.558	-	-	-	-
X_{12}- Lifestyle Outlets (Health and Beauty)	.512	-	-	-	-
X_{13}- Offers and discounts	-	.697	-	-	-
X_{14}- Competitive price	-	.721	-	-	-
X_{15}- Status Symbol	.549	-	-	-	-
Eigen value	**2.504**	**2.264**	**2.130**	**2.116**	**1.348**
% of Variance	**16.694**	**15.094**	**14.198**	**14.107**	**8.984**
Cumulative%	**16.694**	**31.788**	**45.986**	**60.093**	**69.077**

Level of Significance: 5 per cent

Five factors extracted together account for 69.077 per cent of the total variance (information contained in the original 15 variables). This is good, because the researcher are able to economize on the number of variables (from 15 researcher have reduced them to five underlying factors), while the data lost only about 30.923 per cent of the information content (69.077 per cent is retained by the five factors extracted out of the 15 original variables). Since the idea of factor analysis is to identify the factors that meaningfully summarize the sets of closely related variables, the rotation phase of the factor analysis attempts to transfer initial matrix into one that is easier to interpret. Equamax rotation method is used to extract meaningful factors.

Five factors were identified as being maximum Percentage variance accounted. The variables X_2, X_3, X_4, X_5,X_6,X_8, X_9, X_{10}, X_{11}, X_{12} and X_{13} are grouped as factor I and it accounts for 16.694 per cent of the total variance. The variables X_7, X_{13} and X_{14} constitute the factor II and it accounts for 15.094 per cent of the total variance. The variables X_3, and X_4 are grouped as factor III and it accounts for 14.198 per cent of the total variance. The variable X_5 is grouped as factor V and it accounts for 8.984 per cent of the total variance.

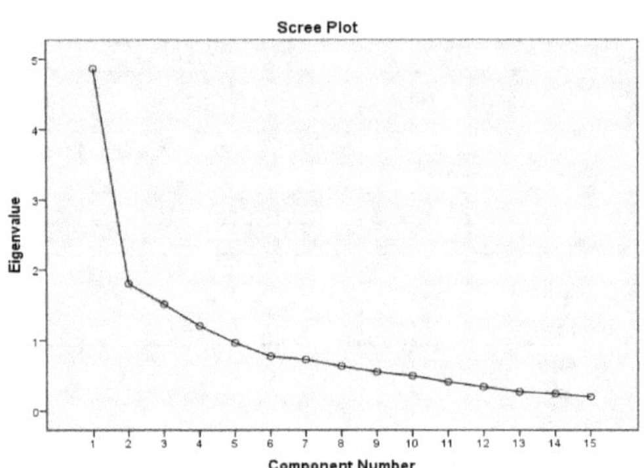

Exhibit 4.11: Scree Plot Outshoppers Level of Satisfaction at Various Shopping Malls

Table 4.83: Summary of Rotation Factor Analysis & Cronbach's Alpha Outshoppers Level of Satisfaction at Various Shopping Malls

Factors	Factor Interpretation	Variables included in the factors	Cronbach's Alpha
F_1	Brook Field	Accessibility (Distance of Travel), Retail Tenant Mix, Product Range, Merchandise Value, Orientation and Infrastructure facilities, Better Sales service, External Atmospheric Clues (architectural style, Layout design and image), Internal Atmospheric Clues (eg flooring, lighting, air condition, music rest rooms etc, Hospitality (Food courts & Resting Places), Entertainment (Multiplex Screening the latest blockbusters), Lifestyle Outlets (Health and Beauty), Status Symbol.	.894
F_2	Fun Republic	Parking Facilities, Offers and discounts, Competitive price.	.839
F_3	Millaneum Mall	Retail Tenant Mix, Product Range, Merchandise Value,	.772
F_4	Visall De Mall	-	.752
F_5	Femina Shopping Mall	Orientation and Infrastructure facilities.	.737

Source: Computed From Primary Data

Factor analysis was used to find out the association between the outshoppers' level of satisfaction towards **leading** shopping malls they had visited. The Cronbach's reliability values (.894, .839, .772, .752 and .737) indicate significant correlation between the variables tested.

Table 4.84: Outshoppers Opinion about Recommending others to buy at Shopping Malls

Sl. No	Opinion	No. of Respondents	Percentage
1.	Yes	438	77.52
2.	No	127	22.48
	Total	565	100

Source: Primary Data

The above table indicates the respondents' opinion about recommending others to buy at shopping malls. Out of the total respondents 565, majority of 77.52 per cent of the respondents have opinioned that they would recommend others to buy at shopping malls. Remaining 22.14 per cent of the respondents have stated that they would not recommend others to buy at shopping malls.

In general, satisfaction has been conceptualized in terms of whether the product/service meets consumer needs and expectations. Satisfaction has been found to significantly affect consumer's attitude, retention behavior and loyalty to the stores and services. It is a vital outcome of marketing activity that leads to revisiting stores, repeat product purchases, and word-of-mouth promotion to friends, relatives and even among colleagues. Based on this theoretical understanding following hypothesis is framed.

H13: Outshoppers' level of satisfaction experienced in the shopping mall to a greater extent determines their recommendation of shopping mall to others infuture.

Discriminant analysis is technique where by researcher can able to distinguish between two or three sets of objects or people. Discriminant analysis is much similar to multiple regression technique. In this section Discriminant analysis is used to determine the outshoppers' level of satisfaction experienced in the shopping mall to a greater extent determines their recommendation of shopping mall to others in future.

Predictor variable considered for the analysis includes the following: X_1- Availability all under one roof, X_2-Accessibility (Distance of Travel), X_3-Retail Tenant Mix, X_4-Product Range, Merchandise **Value**, X_5-Orientation and Infrastructure facilities, X_6-Better Sales service, X_7-Parking Facilities, X_8-External Atmospheric Clues (architectural style, Layout design and image), X_9- Internal Atmospheric Clues (eg flooring, lighting, air condition, music rest rooms etc), X_{10}- Hospitality (Food courts & Resting Places), X_{11}- Entertainment (Multiplex Screening the latest blockbusters), X_{12}- Lifestyle Outlets (Health and Beauty), X_{13}- Offers and discounts, X_{14}- Competitive price and X_{15}- Status Symbol.

Table 4.85: Outshoppers' Level of Satisfaction towards Shopping Mall and their Opinion on Recommendation of Shopping Mall to others in Future (Group Mean Score)

Particulars	Recommendation of Shopping Mall			
	Yes (280)		No (285)	
	Mean	SD	Mean	SD
X_1- Availability all under one roof	1.521	0.644	1.819	0.963
X_2-Accessibility (Distance of Travel)	2.073	0.709	**2.252**	0.756
X_3-Retail Tenant Mix	**2.717**	0.991	2.119	0.722
X_4-Product Range, Merchandise Value	2.071	0.796	1.984	0.678
X_5-Orientation and Infrastructure facilities	1.906	0.847	**2.039**	0.647
X_6-Better Sales service	2.073	0.831	**2.339**	1.093
X_7-Parking Facilities	1.872	0.906	**2.102**	1.068
X_8-External Atmospheric Clues (architectural style, Layout design and image)	**2.134**	0.770	1.858	0.705
X_9- Internal Atmospheric Clues (eg. flooring, lighting, air condition, music rest rooms etc.,)	1.831	0.791	**2.181**	1.050
X_{10}- Hospitality (Food courts & Resting Places)	1.888	0.833	**2.213**	0.973
X_{11}- Entertainment (Multiplex Screening the latest blockbusters)	1.945	1.157	1.564	0.811
X_{12}- Lifestyle Outlets (Health and Beauty)	**2.094**	**0.982**	2.055	0.582
X_{13}- Offers and discounts	2.039	0.772	**2.276**	0.989
X_{14}- Competitive price	**2.622**	0.786	2.285	0.977
X_{15}- Status Symbol	2.288	1.008	**2.551**	0.852

Source: Computed from Primary Data

From the above table it has been inferred that the outshoppers who had visited the primary shopping malls functioning in the three cities of Tamil Nadu have opined that they prefer to recommend these malls to the others for the following reasons: attracted by modern day retail fashion trends, to experiences the shopping malls external architectural style, Layout design and image etc., and to for shopping lifestyle goods at a competitive price. However, the dissatisfied outshoppers have claimed that they would not like to recommend the shopping mall to others due to the following reasons: inconveniences in shopping mall accessibility i.e. distance, dislike with mall infrastructure facilities, poor service quality, inadequate parking facilities, dissatisfaction with interior ambiences, dissatisfaction with food court and rest room facilities, unattractive offers & discounts and also due to low feel of status symbol.

Table 4.86: Outshoppers' Level of Satisfaction towards Shopping Mall and their Opinion on Recommendation of Shopping Mall to Others in Future

Factors	Wilk's Lambda	F	Sig
X_1- Availability all under one roof	.971	16.548	.000
X_2-Accessibility (Distance of Travel)	.989	6.084	.014
X_3-Retail Tenant Mix	.909	56.337	.000
X_4-Product Range, Merchandise Value	.998	1.240	.006
X_5-Orientation and Infrastructure facilities	.995	2.678	.102
X_6-Better Sales service	.985	8.644	.003
X_7-Parking Facilities	.990	5.846	.016
X_8-External Atmospheric Clues (architectural style, Layout design and image)	.975	14.401	.000
X_9- Internal Atmospheric Clues (eg flooring, lighting, air condition, music rest rooms etc)	.972	16.472	.000
X_{10}- Hospitality (Food courts & Resting Places)	.976	13.803	.000
X_{11}- Entertainment (Multiplex Screening the latest blockbusters)	.970	17.628	.000
X_{12}- Lifestyle Outlets (Health and Beauty)	.900	0.177	.008
X_{13}- Offers and discounts	.986	8.099	.005
X_{14}- Competitive price	.978	12.687	.000
X_{15}- Status Symbol	.987	7.192	.674

Level of Significance: 5 Per cent

The key statistic indicating whether or not there is a relationship between the independent and dependent variables is the significance test for Wilks' lambda.

Eigen value	: .255
Percentage of Variation Explained	: 100 per cent
Wilk's Lambda	: .797
Chi-Square	: 127.277
DF	: 7
P	: .000
Canonical Correlation	: .451
Canonical Discriminate Function Fitted	:

$$D=.626X_1+.378X_2+.350X_3+.339X_4+.316X_5+.312X_6+.297X_7+.284X_8+.271X_9+.268X_{10}+.234X_{11}+.210X_{12}+.193X_{13}-.093X_{14}-.035X_{15}$$

In the above table most of the variables are significance at 5 per cent therefore the hypothesis framed stands accepted and it has been concluded that outshoppers level of satisfaction experienced in the shopping mall to a greater extent determines their recommendation of shopping mall to others in future.

Classification of Individuals

Using the discriminate function fitted and the observed predictors' variables of individual, which classified and correct Percentage is presented below

Table 4.87: Determination of Percentage of Correct Classification by using Discriminate Function on the Data

Recommendation of shopping mall	Recommendation of shopping mall		Total
	Yes	No	
Yes	356(81.30)	82(18.70)	438(100)
No	43(33.90)	84(66.10)	127(100)

Source: Computed Data

Relative Importance of Predictor Variable

The relative importance' of each predictor variables in discriminating between the two groups is obtained and the results are presented below:

Table 4.88: Relative Importance of Outshoppers' Level of Satisfaction towards Shopping Mall and their Opinion on Recommendation of Shopping mall to others in Future -Discriminating between the Groups

Influence factors	Importance Value of the variables (I_j)	Relative Importance (R_j)	Rank
X_1- Availability all under one roof	.312	10.08	5
X_3-Retail Tenant Mix	.847	27.36	1
X_4-Product Range, Merchandise Value	.545	17.60	3
X_8-External Atmospheric Clues (architectural style, Layout design and image)	.323	10.43	4
X_{11}- Entertainment (Multiplex Screening the latest blockbusters)	.297	9.59	7
X_{12}- Lifestyle Outlets (Health and Beauty)	.468	15.12	2
X_{14}- Competitive price	.304	9.82	6

From the detailed data analysis it has observed that out of 15 variables took for analysis only seven were considered as the discriminant of level of satisfaction towards the factors at shopping malls. These seven variables mentioned in the above table are considered as important determinant of outshoppers' level of satisfaction experienced in the shopping mall to a greater extent determines their recommendation of shopping mall to others in future.

Table 4.89: Reasons Stated by the Outshoppers for not Recommending Shopping Malls to others in Future

Sl. No	Opinion	No. of Respondents	Percentage
1.	Not worth to be recommended	25	19.69
2.	Let them decide by themselves	102	80.31
	Total	127	100

Source: Primary Data

The above table portrays the reasons stated by the outshoppers for not recommending shopping malls to others in the future. Out of the total 127 respondents 19.69 per cent of the respondents have stated it is not worth to recommend others to shop at shopping malls. The balance 80.31 per cent of the respondents have stated let the person themselves decide about the shopping in malls about themselves.

Table 4.90: Outshoppers Opinion on Feedback Systems in Shopping Malls

Sl. No	Opinion	No. of Respondents	Percentage
1.	Yes	280	49.56
2.	No	285	50.44
	Total	565	100

Source: Primary Data

The above table clearly states that out of the total 565 respondents, 49.56 per cent of the respondents have stated that the shopping malls have adopted the feedback system. On contrary, 50.44 per cent of the respondents opined that feedback system is not adopted in the shopping malls.

Table 4.91: Outshoppers Opinion on type of Feedback Systems Adopted in Shopping Malls

Sl. No	Feedback systems	No. of Respondents	Percentage
1.	Register Method	140	50.00
2.	Direct Interview Method	43	15.35
3.	Questionnaire Method	42	15.00
4.	Online survey Method	37	13.22
5.	Telephone Enquiry Method	18	6.43
	Total	280	100

Source: Primary Data

From the above table it has been inferred that out of the total 280 respondents, 50.00 per cent of the respondents had stated that register method of feedback system is adopted in the shopping malls. Similarly 15.35 per cent of the respondents have agreed that direct interview method of feedback system is adopted in the shopping mall. Consequently 15.00 per cent of the respondents have accepted that questionnaire method of feedback system is adopted in the shopping mall. Further 13.22 per cent of the respondents have agreed that online survey method of the feedback system is used by the shopping malls. Remaining 6.43 per cent of the respondents have opinioned that telephone enquiry method of feedback system is adopted in the shopping malls.

4.2. Conclusion

The study has observed that 54.34 per cent of outshoppers gained awareness about the shopping malls through friends. The study findings declared that there exists no association between outshoppers' level of awareness about a shopping mall and their preference of visit to the malls. The study further, observed that majority i.e., 96.81 per cent of outshoppers have visited all the five malls functioning in the three prominent cities of Tamil Nadu i.e., Coimbatore, Trichy and Madurai. Out of 565 respondents surveyed 21.24 per cent of the respondents have stated that among the five shopping malls Brook field mall the is most preferred and visited shopping mall in Tamil Nadu. About 31.68 per cent of the respondents have stated that they consider shopping malls as means for shopping purpose. The study concluded with the support of statistical analysis that the outshoppers view about the malls differs from one demographic and socio-economic segment of populations to others. Majority of the occasional visitors to malls have commented that they preferred to shop clothing, food and beverage product in the malls. The study findings declared that there exists close association between impulsive/rational nature of consumers' and products brought by them in the shopping malls. Further, the study claims that there exists no association between the demographic and socio-economic status of outshoppers and the products shopped at malls. However, it has been well inferred that there exists rational association between demographic and socio-economic status of the outshoppers and the primary reasons stated by them for visiting shopping malls.

Out of the 565 respondents surveyed 61.24 per cent of the respondents' opinion is shopping in malls are comparatively better than in other retail shops, as all necessary products are available under one roof and they express satisfaction towards the same. And about 61.77 per cent of the respondents have stated that cultural and religious festivals sales periods do influence their shopping behavior in shopping malls. Majority of the respondents claim that shopping malls are adequately modernized these days. The study observed that primary reasons stated by the outshoppers' for shopping at mall greatly influence their perception towards it.

CHAPTER V

Summary of Findings, Suggestions and Conclusion

The final and fifth chapter of this elaborate empirical study aims to present a brief summary of the statement of the problem, the purpose of the study and methodology used in the investigation, the findings, suggestion proposed by the researcher and conclusion are presented.

5.1. Summary of the Study

Organised retailing and mall development is growing at an exponential pace in India. Recent years have witnessed major infrastructural developments coupled with demographic changes. Malls and supermarkets are no longer popular only in metropolitan cities. Increase in income levels in smaller cities has led to changes in consumers' purchasing patterns in malls in Tiers II and III cities. Moreover, Globalisation has brought changes in the purchasing power and income levels in smaller towns. Consumers' mall choice and store selection are influenced by different attributes like: mall image, mall access, atmosphere, pricing, promotions, cross-category assortment, within-category assortment, mall patronage and word of mouth publicity etc. These attributes generates positive emotions adding to exploring personal pleasure and innovative shopping experiences. Based on the above discussion this study aims to analyse shopping experience and satisfaction of outshoppers in shopping malls in selected cities in Tamil Nadu. The study focused on selected shopping malls functioning in tier II cities of Tamil Nadu i.e., in Coimbatore, Madurai and Trichy.

Following objectives are framed for the effective conduct of this study. The first objective of the study focused on collection of data on the demographic and socio- economic status of outshoppers in Tamil Nadu. The second and third objective of the study was framed with the perceptive to measure the outshoppers' level of awareness and perception of outshoppers towards shopping malls and to evaluate the level of shopping experience experienced by the outshoppers in malls. The fourth and fifth objective of the study focused to evaluate the influences of shopping motives on the outshoppers buyer behaviour and to measures the level of satisfaction experienced by the outshoppers and their future loyalty towards shopping malls. The research methodology of the study consists of two stages. First stages of the research were explanatory in nature. This forms the desk research where the reviews of available secondary literature for the study were collected. This exploratory research forms the basis for preparing the questionnaire for the next stage. A descriptive research was carried out at the second stage. It is a fact finding investigation with adequate interpretation. Tamil Nadu is chosen as the study area.

There are 46 mall registered in Tamil Nadu, of which only 30 malls are currently functioning successfully. These 30 malls were considered as the sample malls for the effective conduct of this study. The malls operating in the tier II cities of Tamil Nadu were considered as the primary samples. Coimbatore, Madurai and Trichy are the prominent tier II cities in Tamil Nadu. In total, five malls are functioning in these three regions: Brook Fields, Fun Republic Mall, Vishall De Mall, Millaneum Mall and Femina shopping Mall. The structured self-administered questionnaire was collected by selecting 200 respondents from each city i.e., Coimbatore, Madurai and Trichy. Out of 600 questionnaire distributed nearly 35 questionnaire were found to be incomplete, these 35 questionnaires were deducted from actual sample and thus the study was confirmed to 565 respondents only.

5.2.   Major Findings of the Study

Major findings of the study are discussed in this sub-section.

A.   *Demographic and Socio Economic Status*

The study observed that out of 565 respondents surveyed majority i.e. 60.53 per cent of respondents are male and rest of 39.47 per cent were female shoppers. The study inferred that 49.91 percent of the respondents belong to age group of 21-35 years. It was observed that majority of outshoppers i.e.57.35 per cent of sample populations are married and 28.50 percent of the respondents are found to be post graduates. The study found that 55.60 percent of the respondents are salaried employees and it has been observed that 34.30 percent of the respondents monthly income ranges between Rs. 10001-Rs. 20000. Out of 565 respondents' surveyed 74.69 percent of the respondents family constitutes of 2-4 members. Followed by, it has been observed that 56.46 percent of the respondents' family consists of two earning members. Similarly 48.85 percent of the respondents have opined that their family consist of two dependents i.e., children, aged people or unemployed member.

B.   *Level of Awareness about Shopping Malls*

From the elaborate data discussion it has been inferred that 54.34 percent of the respondents have sourced information about the shopping mall from their friends. Similarly it has been inferred that 19.12 percent of the respondents have gained awareness through internet or social network. The study observed that majority i.e., 86.80 per cent (mean score of 4.34) of the respondents are found to be well aware of Brook Field shopping mall in

Coimbatore. The statistical result of One-Way ANOVA test revealed that there exist no association between out shoppers' level of awareness about a shopping mall and their preference of visit to the malls.

C. *Outshoppers Shopping Experiences at Malls*

With the support of empirical data analysis it was observed that almost i.e., 96.81 percent of respondents have visited all the five leading shopping malls (Brook Field, Fun Republic, Millaneum Mall, Vishall De Mall and Femina Shopping Mall). Further, the study revealed that out of 565 respondents' surveyed, 21.24 percent of the respondents have stated that they often prefer to visit Brook field mall as they feel comfortable and majority i.e., 53.98 percent of the respondents visit shopping malls for fun and entertainment purpose. Results of Chi-Square test revealed that the out shoppers view about malls differ from one demographic and socio-economic segment of populations to others.

The study identified that 69.20 percent of the shopping mall customers' are rational buyers who are very specific in their product choice. The results of Independent 'Z' test indicated that there exists close association between impulsive/rational nature of consumers' and products brought by them in the shopping malls. From the detailed data discussion it has been inferred that 39.12 percent of the respondents visit the shopping malls once in a month and it has been inferred that 61.77 percent of the respondents preferred to buy clothes in the shopping malls. Another test results of Chi-Square analysis revealed that there exists no association between the demographic and socio-economic status of out shoppers and the products shopped at malls.

The study observed that majority i.e., 61.24 percent of the respondents' have a better shopping experience in comparison to the ordinary retail shops. It was observed that 83.27 per cent (mean score of 12.49) of the respondents have stated that shopping malls avail all type of goods under one roof and it is the primary reason for visiting malls. The empirical results of ANOVA test concluded that there exists rational association between demographic and socio-economic status of the out shoppers and the primary reasons stated by them for visiting shopping malls.

The study findings revealed that 61.77 percent of the respondents have stated that cultural and religious festival occasions do influence their shopping behaviour in malls.It is evident from the empirical data analysis that most i.e., 88 per cent (mean score of 4.40) of the sample populations' visit shopping malls on festive occasions like diwali, christmas, ramzan etc. And 49.91 per cent of outshoppers visit shopping malls through the influence of their friends circle.

D. *Outshoppers' Level of Perception towards Shopping Malls*

The study inferred that majority i.e., 86.60 per cent (mean score of 4.33) of the respondents believe that the shopping malls are adequately modernized and avails trending collections. With the conduct of the multivariate analysis results of Multiple Regression analysis it has been concluded that the primary reasons stated by the out shoppers' for shopping at mall greatly influence their perception towards it.

E. *Shopping Motives and Buying Behaviour among Outshoppers*

The elaborate data discussion confirmed that majority i.e., 79.40 (mean score of 3.97) of the outshoppers have stated that shopping stimulates their personality. Further, it was observed that 82 per cent (mean score of 4.10) of respondents' think that shopping malls provide more sales offers. Further it has been inferred that 86.40 per cent (mean score of 4.32) of respondents' have opined that they enjoy while shopping for their family at the time of visiting malls. The study findings revealed that almost i.e., 83 per cent (mean score of 4.15) of sample populations' visit shopping malls to keep up with the new trends and fashions. Followed by, it has been inferred that 78.60 per cent (mean score of 3.93) of respondents' have opined that in their perspective shopping with friends is a social occasion. The study conclusion was complemented by the Multiple Regression Analysis, the results revealed that there exist a great influence of shopping motives on perception of outshoppers towards shopping malls.

F. *Outshoppers Level of Satisfaction to Shopping Malls*

The study observed that almost i.e., 88.20 per cent (mean score of 4.41) of sample populations' exhibit high degree of satisfaction towards the product availability in shopping malls. Whereas, 80.40 per cent (mean score of 4.02) of respondents' exhibit high degree of satisfaction towards Brooke Fields shopping mall in comparison to the other malls in Coimbatore. Similarly, to this conclusion the test results of Paired 'Z' analysis reveal that there exists wide gap between the reasons stated by the out shoppers' for visiting the shopping malls and the level of satisfaction derived by them. The study observed that out of 565 respondents' surveyed, 77.52 per cent of outshoppers intend to recommend others to purchase at shopping malls.

The detailed results of Discriminant Function Analysis reveal that out shoppers' level of satisfaction experienced in the shopping mall to a greater extent determines their recommendation of shopping mall to others in future. Further, it has been found that 19.69 percent of the respondents feel that the shopping malls are not worth to recommend to others, since they fail to satisfy the need of the customers. Further it has been inferred that 50.44

percent of the respondents opined that feedback system is not adopted in the shopping malls. Finally, the study comments that out of 280 respondents' surveyed 24.78 percent of the respondents have stated that register method of feedback system is adopted in the shopping malls.

5.3. Suggestion

The study has observed that as per the opinion of 80 per cent (4 mean score) outshoppers the information systems provided are inadequate in shopping malls. Similarly, 76.60 per cent (mean score of 3.83) outshoppers have claimed that lack of promotional offers are inadequate and 75.60 per cent of the sample shoppers surveyed had inconveniences while billing (3.78 on a mean score of five). On an average 76.40 per cent of the shoppers feel that shopping in malls does not help them in saving their values times and many modern day retail customers feel that purchasing at shopping mall is no more considered as status symbol. Rather it is treated as life-style changes of dual income and higher income families as per the opinion of 73.67 per cent of sample subjects. Moreover, 78.2 per cent of the outshoppers' claim that the retail stores at mall are offers poor custom services. The results of multiple repression analysis also depicts a negative correlation with the service feature of customer services i.e., shopping malls does not provide better customer care services and the study observed that there exists wide gap in customer expectation before visiting the mall and level of satisfaction derived by them after visiting the mall. Based on the above shortfalls observed, following suggestions are proposed for the promotion of both malls and the retail establishments in five malls functioning in the three sample regions i.e., Coimbatore, Madurai and Trichy.

The suggestions are proposed to the Mall Managers and the Retailers functioning in Malls.

A. *Suggestions to the Mall Managers*

Shopping malls have various features like: comfort, entertainment, diversity, mall essence, convenience, and luxury. Unless these features are properly communicated to the shoppers well in advance, the shoppers are deprived of availing these facilities, sophistications and luxury to their optimum usage. Thus, to offer complete shopping experiences to the shoppers in malls, the mall managers are suggested:

- To adhere a promotion information i.e., communication systems, so that the shoppers can learn about the nature of retail outlets that are available in the malls and facilities they can avail inside the malls.

- Like they can install touch screens at the entrance of mall, so that the shoppers can learn about the nature of retail establishments that currently operate inside the malls, their floors of operations, guide manual for easy reach to the stores etc.

- Free Wi-Fi facilities can be offered to the shoppers for easy identification of retail stores and other facilities available inside the malls like lifting, wheel chair facilities, doctors assistance, access to rest rooms, café or food court etc.

- The mall operators or managers can install digital sign boards or Television screen that scroll the retail shops names, its operating time and opening in a week, where by the shopper can gain knowledge about the shops.

- The study findings reveals that on an average 76.40 per cent of the shoppers feel that shopping in malls does not help them in saving their values times and many modern day retail customers feel that purchasing at shopping mall is no more considered as status symbol. To overcome this issues:

  - The mall managers can design their malls with the inbuilt features like: value for shopping, entertainment centric features etc to attract more customers.

  - In order to attract more shoppers to the malls and to offer them they pride and prestige of shopping at malls, the malls managers should hire valuable tents of multi-brands, international reputed brands, who can offer value for shopping and a brand value association with the every single brought by the shoppers at the malls.

  - Malls have to well-designed according to the changing life-style status of the common man i.e.., middle class people in India. So that the common man may be psychologically motivated to visit the malls.

- Entertainment has become an important object for developing positive attitude among target customers, thus. the mall managers are suggested,

  - To incorporate more of hang-out features inside the malls, so that, it may support in attracting more youth in to the malls, like: play stations, indoor auditorium, Pub with non-alcoholic features, yoga theatre, meditation hall, prayer halls and many more to add.

  - To retain the existing shoppers the mall managers can incorporate the concept of theme park or greener provision within the mall provision and charge free play areas for children aside the garden sides with a conceptual theme of garden arrangement, these added features may help in attracting more family customers and elders inside the mall.

- The study observed that there exist wide gap in customer expectation before visiting the mall and level of satisfaction derived by them after visiting the mall. For enhancing the customers satisfaction the mall managers have to:
  - Ensure that various multi-branded products are available under one roof.
  - Make provision for excellent hhospitality services like: Food courts with both local and international cuisines, Resting Places, entertainment themes etc.
  - Provision of more Multiplex, healthy and beauty saloons/spas.
  - Try to earn more reputation (Word of Mouth of Publicity), among the customers and visitors, so that they can ensure a feel of prestige in visiting the malls.

B. *Suggestions to the Retailers Functioning in Malls*

The retailers in the malls are suggested to enhance their sales and to retain their shoppers by following techniques:

- The retailers functioning in mall should understand the fact promotions of their stores and advertisement is very vital for the successful survival in the malls for a long period. The study has observed that the retail stores functioning in malls do not offer more of the sales promotion discounts of fringe benefits to the shoppers. Thus, the retailers are suggested to provide more promotional offers to attract the outshoppers.
  - As it is well understood that the outshoppers are found to be less loyal towards various stores functioning in far distance places, in order to persuade these customers they have:
    - To offer special bonus point on their second purchase.
    - Offer special discount or bonus points that they can redeem, during their future visits.
    - Selling the branded products less than the MRP (Maximum Retail Price).
  - The retailers functioning at malls are also suggested to understand the fact that Indian consumers are very price conscious, even though most of the families new have entered into the scale of dual income, still they are very spectative while buying branded products and spending on valuable goods. Moreover, consumers always have a notion that branded products are always costlier than non-products and in fact the product prices rises, when it is sold in malls. Thus, provision of right combination of offers and discounts throughout the year will keep the customers to step into their stores regularly.

- The study observed that there exist wide gap in customer expectation before visiting the mall and level of satisfaction derived by them after visiting the mall. In order to satisfy the shoppers and meeting out their expected needs on times, it is duty of the various retailers function in malls to focus on:
  - Enhancing the retail store product range, merchandise value according to the shoppers' satisfaction and demand at the time of shopping.
  - The retailers are suggested to offer better sales services:
    1. By enrolling more staff, who can serve the customers on time.
    2. Keeping all billing counters functioning around the clock, for the conveniences of the shoppers.
    3. To offer better sales services to the shoppers of various income class and social status.

5.4. Conclusion

Shopping malls have become a fashion and a new life style among the present generation. So now a day shopping malls contribute to business more significantly than the unorganized traditional markets, which are viewed as a simple means of concentrated supply and demand. Shopping malls attract buyers and sellers, by providing an unmatched ambience, enough variety, and time to make choices as well as a pleasure ways of shopping. Even though the competition from traditional shopping centrs prevails in the market, because of building more excitement and enthusiasm in customers, more and more ordinary people are attracted to the mall. Earlier the mall was visited only by the upper class people. But, these days things have been changed a lot.

More and more middle income class people irrespective of the age, gender, education and occupation, visiting the mall very frequently, since they have changed to be more brand conscious, shopaholic and their spending power has increased in the recent past. Moreover, these shopper consider malls as a convenient place for economic shopping, entertainments and for socialising.

The study concludes by stating that saturation in the growth and number of malls in the metropolitan cities has forced mall operators to explore options in Tier II and III cities. Unless these mall operators and retail establishments functioning in the malls focus their marketing strategies for enhancing shoppers shopping experiences inside the mall, offer value for every single rupee spend by them and extent excellent customer care facilities the future success, sustainment and growth of the malls in these tier II and tier III cities.

5.5.   Future Scope of Research

Through the process of literature survey and at the time of data collection it has been realised that not much studies has been conducted in the past on the concept of outshopping behaviour. Though, outshopping is part of Indian rural and semi-urban consumers' cultures for many centuries, where people had been traveling to far distance or nearby neighbourhood cities for purchase of food articles, clothing, jewels, consumers' durables goods and many more, and this culture of outshopping is still popular among Indians. The prevailing nature of research dearth itself is considered as one of the limitation of this study, which had reflected in data collection, collection of reviews and even while framing conceptual framework of the study. Thus, the study provides a wider scope for future researcher to be conducted in the concept of outshoppers' behaviour and their buying practices in mall. Since, this study had focused on three geographical regions of Tamil Nadu, excluding Chennai. Future researcher can add Chennai in their study. They can even compare the outshopping practices among two regional states like: Tamil Nadu vs. Karnataka, Andhra Pradesh, Telegana or Kerala. Or say they can compare the outshoppers buying behaviour in malls in cities like: Chennai vs. Bengaluru or Vs. Hyderabad or Vs. Cochin.

BIBLIOGRAPHY

Books and Magazines

1) R. Pancholi, "Growth off the Shelf", Hindustan Times, New Delhi, 2006.

2) S.L. Gupta and Sumitra Pal, "Consumer Behaviour–An Indian Perspective, Sultan Chand and Sons", New Delhi, First Edition, 2000.

3) Johan Anselnisson, "Study on Source of Customer Satisfaction with Shopping Malls", A comparative study of different customer segments, The International Review of Retail Distribution and consumer research, Pp. 381-403, 2006.

4) S.L. Gupta and Kaur, Tripat, "The Framing of Promotional Strategies and its Relation with Attributes of Stores as Perceived by Shoppers in a Shopping Mall", Amity Business Review, Pp. 24–32, 2006.

5) Asif Zameer, "Study on Management of Events/Promotions at DLF City Center Mall, Gurgaon", Indian Retail Review, Pp 36-42, 2007.

6) Barry Bermanand Joel R. Evans, "Retail Management A strategic Approach, Tenth Edition, Pearson Prentice Hall", Pp. 207-208, 2007.

Journals

1) Sonu Joseph and Vibhuti Singh, "Changing Lifestyles Influencing Indian Consumers: Conceptualizing and Identifying Future Directions", Global Journal of Management and Business Studies, Vol. 3, No. 8, Pp. 861-866, 2013.

2) Mohammed Ismail El-Adly, "Investigating the Relationship between Shopping Mall Patronage Motives and Customer Satisfaction Using Importance-Satisfaction Analysis", International Journal of Customer Relationship Marketing and Management, Vol. 3, No. 2, Pp. 33-46, 2012.

3) F. Piron, "International outshopping and ethnocentrism", European Journal of Marketing, Vol. 36, No. 1/2, Pp. 189-210, 2002.

4) T.A. Arentze, H. Oppewal and H.J. Timmermans, "A multipurpose shopping trip model to assess retail agglomeration effects", Journal of Marketing Research, Vol. 42, No. 1, Pp. 109-115, 2005.

5) Y.J. Wang, S.K. Doss, C. Guo and W. Li, "An investigation of Chinese consumers outshopping motives from a culture perspective: Implications for retail and distribution", International Journal of Retail & Distribution Management, Vol. 38, No. 61, Pp. 423-442, 2010.

6) D. Jarratt, "Outshopping behaviour: an explanation of behaviour by shopper segment using structural equation modelling", International Review of Retail, Distribution and Consumer Research, Vol. 10, No. 3, Pp. 287-304, 2000.

7) D.J. Burns, J.M. Lanasa and C.L. Lackman, "Outshopping: An examination from a motivational perspective", Journal of Professional Services Marketing, Vol. 19, No. 2, Pp. 151-160, 1999.

8) Amandeep Kaur, "Shopping Malls: The Changing Face of Indian Retailing–An Empirical Study of Cities of Ludhiana and Chandigarh", International Journal of Business and Management Invention, Vol. 2, No. 5, Pp. 30-36, 2013.

9) Rupesh Kumar Tiwari and Anish Abraham, "Understanding the Consumer Behavior towards Shopping Malls in Raipur City", International Journal of Management & Strategy, Vol. 1, No. 1, 2010.

10) V. Lakshmipathy and S. Kareemulla Basha, "Globalisation-Its Impact on Indian Retail Industry - Opportunities and Challenges", International Journal of Marketing, Financial Services & Management Research, Vol. 1, No. 2, Pp. 89-95, 2012.

11) A. Mansurali, R. Swamynathan and Chandrasekhar, Umesh, "Mall Mania: A Study of Factors Influencing Consumers", Preference towards Shopping Malls in Coimbatore City, The IUP Journal of Marketing Management, Vol. 12, No. 4, Pp. 29-41, 2014.

12) S.L. Gupta, "An Exploratory Research on Promotional Strategies and its Relation with Attributes of Stores as Perceived by Consumers in a Shopping Mall", PCTE Journal of Business Management, Vol. 3, No. 2, Pp. 8–17, 2006.

13) Rajaguru, Rajesh, Matanda and Margaret J, "A Study on Consumer Perception of Store and Product Attributes and its Effect on Customer Loyalty within the Indian Retail Sector", ANZMAC Conference, Queensland University of Technology, Pp. 4–6, 2006.

14) A.M. Sakkthivel, "Strategic Placement of Organized Retail Formats in Potential Markets–A Critical Analysis", Indian Retail Review, Vol. 1, No. 1, 2007.

15) C.S. Venkata Ratnam, "A study on Changing Consumer Behaviour and Emerging challenges to the Retail Trade in India", Indian Retail Review, Vol. 1, No. 1, 2007.

16) Mujahid Mohiuddin Babu and Md. Mihiuddin, "Cause Related Marketing and Its Impact on the Purchasing Behaviour of the Customers of Bangladesh: An Empirical Study", AIUB Business and Economics Working Paper Series American International University-Bangladesh (AIUB), 2008.

17) S.V. Pathak and Aditya P. Tripathi, "Customer Shopping Behaviors among Modern Retail Formats: A study of Delhi and NCR", Indian Journal of Marketing Vol. 24, No. 2, 2009.

18) R.K. Tiwari and A. Abraham, "Understanding the consumer behaviour towards shopping malls in Raipur city", International Journal of Management and Strategy, Vol. 1, No. 1, 2010.

19) G. Baltas, P.C. Argouslidis and D. Skarmeas, "The Role of customer Factors in Multiple Store patronage: A Cost Benefit Approach", Journal of Retailing, Vol. 86, No. 1, Pp. 37-50, 2010.

20) Shivakumar R. Sharma, "Customer Attitude towards Shopping Malls in Mumbai", International Journal of Trade and Commerce-IIARTC, Vol. 1, No. 2, Pp. 269-280, 2012.

21) R. Pandyya Amit and J. Bariya Kameshvari, "A Study on Consumer Behaviour of Organised and Unorganised Retail Outlets in Vadodara City", International Journal of Engineering and Management Science, Vol. 3, No. 4, Pp. 466-474, 2010.

22) B. Orme, "Getting Started with Conjoint Analysis: Strategies for Product Design and Pricing Research", Second Edition, Madison, Wis.: Research Publishers LLC, 2010.

23) Sangeeta Mohanty, "Drivers of Retail Shopping: An Exploratory Study", International Journal of Scientific and Research Publications, Vol. 2, No. 3, Pp. 1-6. 2012.

24) Arun Kumar Singh and P.K. Agarwal, "A Study on Shifting Consumer Preferences from Un-organised Retailing Vis-a-Vis to Organised Retailing in Noida", Bookman International Journal of Accounts, Economics and Business Management, Vol. 1, No. 2, Pp. 69-79, 2012.

25) Mohd. Nadeem Abbas, "Consumer Behaviour in India–Post Recession Scenario", International Journal of Scientific and Engineering Research, Vol. 3, No. 12, Pp. 1-7, 2012.

26) Bulakanti and Romala Vijaya Srinivas, "The Most Influential Factors of Consumers Buying Pattern At Organized And Unorganized Retail Stores With Special Reference To Kakinada City", Indian Journal of Marketing, Vol. 43, No. 1, Pp. 14 -23, 2013.

27) Girish K. Nair and Harish K. Nair, "An Analysis on Customer Perception towards Service Quality Variables in Selected Organised Retail Outlets", International Journal of Management and Social Sciences Research, Vol. 2, No. 1, Pp. 56-61, 2013.

28) DipinMathur, Apeksha Jain and Manoj Kumar Sharma, "Analysis of Factors Influencing Consumer Buying Behaviour In Modern As Well As Conventional Retail Stores",

International Journal of Innovative Research and Development, Vol. 2, No. 6, Pp. 409-415, 2013.

29) G. Nandhini Devi, S. Sankaranarayana and Deepak Ashokkumar, "Consumers' Shopping Behaviour of Convenience Goods in Organised Retail Stores", Asia Pacific Journal of Marketing and Management Review, Vol. 2, No. 2, Pp. 87-95, 2013.

30) Vibhuti, Ajay Kumar Tyagi and Vivek Pandey, "A Case Study on Consumer Buying Behaviour towards Selected FMCG Products", International Journal of scientific research and management, Vol. 2, No. 8, Pp. 1168-1182, 2014.

31) Jay Kumar Dewangan, Dr.J.H. Vyas and Imran Nadeem Siddiqui, "Effects of Demographic Variables on Consumer Buying Behaviour: With Reference To Purchase of Household Commodities from Organized Retail Stores in Chhattisgarh", Global Journal of Multidisciplinary Studies, Vol. 4, No. 9, 2015.

32) Robert G.V. Barker, "Towards a dynamic aggregate shopping model and its application to Retail Trading hours and market area analysis", Regional Science, Vol. 79, No. 4, Pp. 413-434, 2000.

33) Sherman, Elaine, Leon G. Schiffman and Anil Mathur, "The Influence of Gender on the New-Age Elderly's Consumption Orientation", Psychology and Marketing, Vol. 18, No. 10, Pp. 1073-1089, 2001.

34) Melody L. Adkins Lehew, Brigetter Burgers and Scarlet Wesley, "Expanding The loyalty concept to include preference for a Shopping Mall", The International Review of Retail Distribution and Consumer Research, Vol. 12, No. 3, Pp. 225-236, 2002.

35) R. Stephen Parket, Charles Pettijohn, linda Petti John and John Kent, "Study on An analysis of consumer perception: Factory outlet Malls versus Traditional Departmental Stores", The Marketing Management Journal, Vol. 13, No. 2, Pp. 29-44, 2003.

36) R. Pancholi, P.K. Sinha, A. Banerjee, E.S. Millam and F. Howard, "Studyon Emergence of Mall Culture in India", International Journal of Retail and Distribution Management, Vol. 32, No. 10, Pp. 482-494, 2004.

37) Janson Sit and BilMersiley, "Understanding satisfaction Formation of Shopping Mall Entertainment seekers: A conceptual Model", Proc. of ANZMAC conference: Retailing, Distribution Channels and Supply Chain Management, Pp. 106-114, 2005.

38) Tammie-Frost Norton, "Study on the future of Mall: Current Trends affecting the future of Market Research in Malls", Journal of Consumer Behaviour, Vol. 4,Pp. 229-301, 2005.

39) Shelja Jose Kuruvilla, "Study on Malls VsKiranas- Challenges and Strategic options", Research Conference at Gurukul University, Haridwar, 2007.

40) Shelja Jose Kuruvilla and J. Ganguli, "Study on Mall development and operations, an Indian perspective", Journal of Retail and housing property Vol. 7, No. 3, Pp. 204-215, 2008.

41) Chung YimYien, Y.S. Sherry and N.G. Hing Cheong, "Space Allocation and tenant placement at high rise shopping malls", Journal of Retail and Leisure Property, Vol. 7, No. 4, Pp. 315-324, 2008.

42) Shelja Jose Kuruvilla, "Study on The River side Mall–A Case Study", Synthesis, Vol. 4, No. 2, 2008.

43) Rajagopal, "Growing Shopping Malls and Behaviour of Urban Shoppers", Journal of Retail and Leisure property, Vol. 18, No. 2, Pp. 99-118, 2009.

44) Zairenl N. Mura and Michael Pitt, "Study on Defining Facilities Management Service Delivery in UK Shopping Centres", Journal of Retail and Leisure Property, Vol. 8, No. 3, Pp. 193-205, 2009.

45) Rajesh Iyer and Jaequeline K. Eastman, "Study on The Fashion conscious Mall Shoppers –An Exploratory Study", The Marketing Management Journal Vol. 20, No. 2, Pp. 42-53, 2010.

46) Hardviner Singh, Swapna Kumar Bose and ViniaSahay, "Management of Indian Shopping Malls: Impact of the patterns of Financing", Journal of Retail and Leisure Property, Vol. 9 No. 1, Pp. 55-64, 2010.

47) Deepak Devgan, and Mandeep Kaur, "Shopping Malls in India: Factors affecting Indian Customers' Perceptions", South Asian Journal of Management, Vol. 17, No. 2, Pp. 29–42, 2010.

48) Swaroop Chandra Sahoo and Prakash Chandra Dash, "Consumers decision making style in Shopping Malls: A Empirical study in the Indian Context", Indian Journal of Marketing, Vol. 40, Pp. 25-30, 2010.

49) Rupesh Kumar Tiwari and Anish Abraham, "Study on Understanding the Consumer Behaviour towards Shopping Malls in Raipur City", International Journal of Management and Strategy, Vol. 1, No, 1, Pp. 1-14, 2010.

50) Zhang, Yan, Chaipoopirutana, Sission, Combs and Howard, "The influence of the Mall Environment on shopper's value and consumer behavior", Proceedings of ASBBS Annual Conference : Las Vegas, Vol. 18, No. 1, Pp. 214-224, 2011.

51) Andrew Newman, Charles Dennis, Len-tiu Wright and Tamira King, "Study on Shoppers Experience of Digital Signage Cross National Quality Study", International Journal of Digital Content Technology and its Application, Vol. 4, No. 7, Pp. 50-57, 2011.

52) Sureshramam Mayyer, "Study on the study on Impact of Shopping Malls on the unorganized retail sector:A case study of Mangalore Region", Indian Journal of Marketing, Vol. 42, No. 9, 2012.

53) Anuradha Devadas and Hansa Lysander Manohar, "Study on A Cross Sectional Study on Shopping Values and Mall Attributes in Relation to Consumer Age and Gender", European Journal of Social Sciences, Vol. 31, No. 1 Pp. 6-16, 2012.

54) Ritu Srivastava, "Study on Mall Motivations in India Aligning Demographics for Segmentations", The International Journal of Social Sciences, Vol. 6, No. 1, Pp. 86-102, 2012.

55) N.H. Mullick, "Study on The Success of Shopping Malls Lies in the Hands of Mall Developers: A study", Indian Journal of Marketing, Vol. 43, No. 6, Pp. 40-46, 2013.

56) Suman Yadav and Sadaf Siraj, "Study on Mall Patronage Behaviour: Understanding the Inter-linkages between Shopping Motives, Shopper Demographics, and Shopping Behaviors", Indian Journal of Marketing, Vol. 44, No. 11, Pp. 36-48, 2014.

57) P. Lalitha Praveena, "A Study on Consumer Buying Behaviour Factors in Shopping Malls In Hyderabad City", International Journal of Engineering and Management Science, Vol. 6, No. 4, Pp. 211-214, 2015.

58) P. Sullivan and S. Ronald, "Store patronage and lifestyle factors: implications for rural grocery retailers", International Journal of Retail Distribution Management, Vol. 25, No. 11, Pp. 351–364, 1997.

59) Michael F. Smith, "Urban versus suburban consumers: a contrast in holiday shopping purchase intentions and outshopping behaviour", Journal of Consumer Marketing, Vol. 16, No. 1, Pp. 58–73, 1999.

60) Denise Jarratt, "Study on Out shopping behavior: an explanation of behavior by shopper segment using structural equation modeling", The International Review of Retail, distribution and Consumer Research, Vol. 10, No. 3, Pp. 287-304, 2000.

61) Caroline Levantis, "Country Towns: Impact of Farmers' Expenditure on Employment and Population in Australian Towns, Sustaining Regions", Vol. 1, No. 1, Pp. 38-42, 2001.

62) F. Piron, "Study on International out-shopping and ethnocentrism", European Journal of Marketing, Vol. 36, No. 1/2, Pp. 189-210, 2002.

63) E. Kim and P. Sullivan, "Study on Cross-border tourism and shopping:Consumer segmentation", e-Review of Tourism Research (eRTR), Vol. 1, No.1, Pp. 14-20, 2003.

64) Kevin M. Elliott and Robert R. Edwards, "Differentiation Based on Service Quality: A Viable Small Business Strategy for Minimizing the Effects of Outshopping", 2004.

65) S. Varshney and A. Goyal, "A review and extension of the out shopping paradigm to the Indian context", Asia Pacific Journal of Marketing and Logistics, Vol. 17, No. 4,Pp. 30-63, 2005.

66) Sanjeey Varshney and Anita Goyal, "Outshopping Behaviour in a Small Indian Town: An Exploratory Study", South Asian Journal of Management, Vol. 13, No. 2, 2006.

67) T. Dmitrovic and I. Vida, "Study on An examination of cross-border shopping behaviour in South-East Europe", European Journal of Marketing, Vol. 41, No. 3/4, Pp. 382-395, 2007.

68) P. Qiu, C. Maksymiuk and E. Bruning, "Factors influencing the frequency of shopping in a neighbourhood food store: A social capital theory perspective", Administrative Sciences Association of Canada (ASAC), Vol. 29, No. 3, 2008.

69) C. Guo and Y. Wang, "A study of cross-border out shopping determinants: Mediating effect of out shopping enjoyment", International Journal of Consumer Studies, Vol. 33, No.6, Pp. 644-51, 2009.

70) Chetan Bajaj and Nandini Bajaj, "Outshopping Behaviour in Rural and Urban Indian Markets, Global Management Review", Vol. 4, No. 1, Pp. 27, 2009.

71) Sanjeev Varshney, "Outshopping Behaviour, Antecedent, Inter-Relationship Classification", 2010.

72) Anuradha Devadas and Hansa Lysander Manohar, "Shopping behaviour of rural consumer migrated to urban area in the Indian context-An emerging market", African Journal of Business Management, Vol. 5, No. 6, Pp. 2276-2282, 2011.

73) Pingali Venugopal, "Urban Orientation of Rural Consumers: Implication for Consumer Goods Distribution", International Journal of Rural Management, Vol. 8, No.1-2, Pp. 107-119, 2012.

74) Johan W. Strydom, "Retail patronage of Sowetan consumers after 1994", African Journal of Business Management, Vol. 7, No. 29, Pp. 2863-2887, 2013.

75) Brain A. Zinser and Gray J. Brunswixk, "Cross Border Shopping: A Research proposal for a comparison of service encounters of Canadian cross-border shoppers versus Canadian Domestic Inshopper", International Business and Economic Research Journal, Vol. 13, No. 5, Pp. 1077-1090, 2014.

76) Piyush Sharma and Ting S. Luk, "Tourist shoppers evaluation of retail service: a study of Cross-border vs. International outshoppers", Journal of Hospitality and Amp Tourism Research, 2015.

77) Sunia Sikri and Dipti Wadhwa, "Growth and Challenges of Retail Industry in India: An Analysis", Asia Pacific Journal of Marketing and Management Review, Vol. 1, No. 1, 2012.

78) Satchidananda Dehuri, ManasRanjan Patra, Bijan Bihari Misra and Alok Kumar Jagadev, "Intelligent Techniques in Recommendation Systems: Contextual Advancements and New methods", Information Science Reference, Pp. 231-233, 2013.

79) Cathy Ashley, Carol Gaumer and Barry Foltors, "The effects of Out shopping on a small rural community the importance of relationships", The Coastal Business Journal Spring, Vol. 8, No. 1, 2009.

80) Blakney, VickiSekely and William, "Retail attributes: influence on shopping mode choice behavior", Journal of Managerial Issues, 1994.

81) A. Coskun Samli, "Strategic Marketing for success in Retailing, Quorum Books", London.

82) H.S. Kim, "Using Hedonic and Utilitarian Shopping Motivations to Profile Inner City Consumers", Journal of Shopping Center Research, Vol. 13, No. 1, Pp. 57-79, 2006.

83) T.E. Higgins, "Value from hedonic experience and engagement", American Psychological Association, Vol. 113, No. 3, Pp. 439-460, 2006.

84) O.T. Ahtola, "Hedonic and utilitarian aspects of consumer behavior: An attitudinal perspective", 1985.

85) D.L. Schacter, D.T. Gilbert and D.M. Wegner, "Psychology 2", New York, NY: Worth Publishers, 2011.

86) Vipulpatel and Mahendra Sharma, "Consumers Motivations to shop in Shopping Malls: A Study of Indian Shoppers", Phd Thesis, Institute of Management, Bangalore, India

87) Emergency of shopping Malls, Chapter Six, 17_Chapter 6.Pdf.

88) Greg Haseth, Laura Ryser and Shiloh Durkee, "Shopping and commuting patterns in Kitimat", Bc, University of Northern British Columbia, 2005.

89) Richard A. Feinberg and Jennifer Meoli, "A Brief History of the Mall", Advances in Consumer Research Vol. 18, Pp. 429-427, 1991.

90) C.A. Ingene, "Productivity and functional shifting in spatial retailing: private and social perspectiveness", Journal of Retailing and Consumer Service, Vol. 60, No. 3, Pp. 15-26, 1984.

91) Van Der Waerden, P. Borgers and H. Timmermans, "The impact of the parking situation in shopping centers on store choice behavior", Geo Journal, Vol. 45, No. 4, Pp. 309-315, 1998.

92) C. Teller and T. Reutterer, "The evolving concept of retail attractiveness: what makes retail agglomerations attractive when consumers shop at them", Journal of Retailing and consumer service, Vol. 15, No. 3, Pp. 127-143, 2008.

93) B. Basu, "India's mall explosion: Sense and direction", Images Retail, Pp. 6-9, 2006.

94) Satishand Pratysuh, "The Growth of organized retailing through shopping malls in India", Current trends in technology and science, Vol. 2, Pp. 146-147, 2012.

95) Rupesh Kumar Tiwari and Anish Abraham, "Understanding The Consumer Behavior Towards Shopping Malls in Raipur City", International Journal of Management & Strategy, Vol. 1, No. 1, Pp. 1-14, 2010.

Published Sources

1) Media Reports, Press Releases, Deloitte report, Department of Industrial Policy and Promotion website, Union Budget 2015–16.

Websites

1) www.rasci.in

2) www.rbidocs.rbi.org.in

3) www.faculty journal.com

4) www.researchgate.net

5) www.indianmba.com.

Other

1) Roberto Fantoni, Femanda Hoefel and Marina Mazzarolo, "The future of the shopping mall", 2014.

2) http://www.mckinseyonmarketingandsales.com/the-future-of-the-shopping-mall,

3) Positioning Strategies of Malls: An Empirical Study.

4) Malls face uncertain future as customers desert them, 2015.

5) http://www.dnaindia.com/money/report-malls-face-uncertain-future-as-customers-desert-them-2087068,19th May.

6) Ramandeep Kaur, "Growing Mall Culture in India – Changing Lifestyles", 2014.

7) http://www.mapsofindia.com/my-india/india/growing-mall-culture-in-india-changing-lifestyles7thSeptember.

8) Chapter 3-Introduction to malls.

9) http://shodhganga.inflibnet.ac.in/bitstream/10603/7381/8/08_chapter%203.pdf.

10) Tamil Nadu, https://en.wikipedia.org/wiki/Tamil_Nadu.

11) Shopping Malls in Chennai.

12) http://www.pacificacompanies.co.in/shopping_malls_in_chennai.html

13) Differences between American and Indian Shopping Habits.

14) Http://www.americanpunjabanpi.com/2014/04/differences-between-american-and-indian.html, 8th April.2014.

15) http://business.mapsofindia.com/india-market/retail.html

16) IRIS Primary Research- India Retail Report 2011.

17) http://gizmodo.com/5114869/the-worlds-first-modern-shopping-mall

18) R. Ravikumar, First mover fails to keep up with times, Business Line (Chennai: THE Hindu), Retrieved 14, 2011.

19) http://www.mapsofindia.com/my-india/india/growing-mall-culture-in-india-changing-lifestyles

20) Source – Economic Times Report/ OUTDOOR MEDIAPLAN.COM

21) RBI, Press release 2006-2007/300, 2006.

22) AT Kearney, The Global Retail Development Index, 2006.

23) http://www.retailcustomerexperience.com/articles/the-elements-that-matter-most-in-the-retail-customer-shopping-experience.

ANNEXURE I

Tamil Nadu

Tamil Nadu popularly referred as a cradle of Dravidian Culture, offers exciting shopping experience to its visitors. It is the second largest contributor to India s Gross Domestic Product. For the year 2014-15 Tamil Nadus' GSDP was 9767 billon and growth was 14.86[1]. It ranks third in foreign direct investment approval constituting 9.12 percent of the total FDI in the country[2]. According to the 2011 census, Tamil Nadu is the most urbanized state in India with 49per cent, accounting for 9.6 per cent of the urban population while only comprising 6 per cent of Indias' total population and most urbanized sate in India[3] Government is the major investor in the state with 51 per cent of the total investments, followed by private Indian investors at 29.9 per cent and foreign private investors at 14.9 per cent. Tamil Nadu has a network of about 113 industrial parks and estates offering developed plots with supporting infrastructure.

Tamil Nadu is subdivided into 32 districts. Among the cities in 2011, the state capital Chennai was the most populated city in the state, followed by Coimbatore, Madurai, Trichy and Tiruppur respectively[4]. On based on the population of the cities, The Reserve Bank of India has classified the cities across India into 6 tiers cities[5] based on its population size and human index rating. The table below shows the classification.

Classification of Centers (Tier Wise)

Population Classification	Population (2001 census)
Tier - 1	100,000 and above
Tier – 2	50,000 to 99,999
Tier – 3	20,000 to 49,999
Tier – 4	10,000 to 19,999
Tier – 5	5,000 to 9,999
Tier – 6	Less than 5000

On based on the above classification Tamilnadu cities are classified into tier-1, tier 2 tier 3 cities. Chennai is classified as Tier-1 city and Cities Namely Salem, Trippur, Coimbatore, Tiruchirappalli, and Madurai are termed as Tier-2 cities[6]. The study covers the area of Tier 2

---

[1]GSDP at current prices 2015.

[2] The Hindu 22nd April 2005.

[3] E censeus India 2002.

[4] The Hindu 2nd June 2003.

[5]http://rbidocs.rbi.org.in/rdocs/content/pdfs/100MCA0711_5.pdf.

[6] http://www.mapsofindia.com/maps/india/tier-1-and-2-cities.html.

cities of Tamilnadu namely Coimbatore, Madurai and Trichy and Salem and Trippur are excluded as there are no shopping malls in the cities.

The study area Tier 2 cities Coimbatore has two shopping malls namely Brook Fields, Fun Republic Mall, Madurai has Vishall De Mall and Millaneum Mall and Trichy has Femina shopping Mall.

Coimbatore

Coimbatore know as Kovai, is a major city in the Indian state of Tamil Nadu. Coimbatore is referred as Manchester of South India, because of cotton and textile industries and known as Pump City as it supplies two third of Indias' requirement of motors and pumps It is the second largest city and urban agglomeration in the state after Chennai and the sixteenth largest urban agglomeration in India. It is one of the fastest growing tier II cities in India and a major textile, industrial, commercial, educational, information technology, healthcare and manufacturing hub of Tamil Nadu[7]

Coimbatore was ranked the best emerging city in India by India Today in the 2014 Annual Indian City Survey[8]. The city has been ranked 4th among the Indian cities in investment climate by CII and 17th among the top global outsourcing cities in Tholons[9] Despite being located at one end of the country, Coimbatore has been identified as one of the fastest growing top 20 centers of economic activity in India. It is the largest non-metro city for e-commerce in south India[10]. The Revenue growth in Coimbatore zone is 65 per cent while the all India revenue growth is only 30 per cent it is almost twice the all India growth[11].

Coimbatore has several merits to qualify for higher spending avenues. It is the second largest economy in the State, consumers in the city have deep pockets and its businesses have international exposures. Coimbatore, with its population and infrastructure, is a sub-metro and tier-two has a huge demand for malls. Shopping malls in these cities should be of quality and should have the right mix of tenants. The location is another important factor. The mindset and aspiration of the consumers regarding shopping have changed they wants value for money,

---

[7]Indian Government Press Release-Press information Bureau Government of India, 31 October 2011, Retrived 31 Jan 2013.

[8] India Today Best City Awards 2014 Chennai bags top honour- India Today.

[9] Confederation of Indian Industry Retrieved 30thAuguest 2011.

[10] Tier II and III cities Driving E-Commerce in India- Siliconindia.Com, December 2011 Retrieved 31 January 2013.

[11] Outreach Programme to New Assessees of Central Excise and Service Tax',- Coimbatore's growth is heartening' The Hindu COIMBATORE, July 26, 2011.

want space to park the car, easily accessible area In tier two cities malls are turn into community centers as consumers come with their family to relax, shop and have food.[12]. There are two major malls functioning in Coimbatore are Brook Field Mall and Fun Republic Mall.

Brook Fields Mall

Brook fields is the first of its kind retail project in the city of Coimbatore during May 2009. With several anchor retail outlets, leading local, national and international brands, hyper markets, food court, family entertainment centre, multiplex, parking – all under one roof, it is the ultimate shopping and entertainment experience! The mall promises something for everyone with its bewildering range of products spread over an area of about 4,50,000 sq. ft.Its great location and connectivity make it a convenient destination for locals and tourists alike. The Mall was constructed by Brookefields Estates Pvt. Ltd., an integrated real estate developer. The mall is located in the heart of the city on Brookbond Road in Coimbatore. There are 120 stores and services. There are 4 floors with parking multistory parking.

The mall has outlets from major clothing and apparel brands and a six screen multiplex cinema, along with a food court serving multi-cuisine dishes. The Mall has a Food Court, Gaming Zone and Wi-Fi Connectivity along with usual facilities like Multistorey, Parking, IOB ATM. Chennai-based SPI Cinemas operate 'The Cinema, a six screen Multiplex cinema on the mall's top floor. Fun City, based within the mall itself, is a prominent attraction for children. The play area offers an arcade, a carousel, bumper cars and a 'scary house'.With several anchor retail outlets, leading local, national and international brands, hyper markets, food court, fine dining, family entertainment centre, multiplex, business centre, health club, hotel and parking – all under one roof, it is the ultimate shopping and entertainment experience.[13]

Brook Fields Mall

---

[12] "Potential high for malls in Coimbator"- The Hindu, August 1, 2010.

[13] http://en.wikipedia.org/wiki/Brookefields_Mall.

The Brooke Fields Mall Directory

Lifestyle, Timex, Wrangler, Levis, Hidesign, Reliance Vision Express, Cookiman, The Body shop, Travelon, Zimson, DAR Jewellery, Nike, Reebok, RmKV, Westdie, Pantloon, Reliance Trends, Okapi, Adidas, Louis Phillippe, Van Heusen, Bata, Mochi, Puma, Lee, Allen Solly, Wills Lifestyle, Tommy Hilfiger, Derby, Provogue, Peter England, Pepe Jeans, V. Neckties & More, Samsonite, Crocodile, Jockey, Denizen, Reliance Foot Print, Max, Reynolds, WriteSite, Indian Terrian, Woodlamds, Blackberrys, Basics Life, LP- Youth, Arrow, Raymonds, Planet Sports, United Colours of Benetton, Reliance Living, Queen's Ethnic Trends, Toonz, Biba, Maybell, W, Sthri, Elite, Fashion Palance, Lilliput, RmKV- kids, Stone N strings, Gini&Jony, Mom & Me, 109 & F, Soch, Diva , Reliance Digital, Spice Route, Welcare, Posch, SavithriPhothours, Sony Vaio, HP – IT World, Crusoe, Poorvika Mobiles, Cocktail Fashions, KFC, Foodcourt, Fun City, Odyssey, Crusoe, Cameras, Archies, Propel Fitness, Global Oasis, Canon, Beauty Works, Planet M, Rathna Video & Audio, Naturals Lounge.

Fun Republic Mall

Coimbatore has branched its second mall Fun Rebulic Mall on 19th August 2012 managed by E-city Ventures of Essel Group. The group straddles across different industrial spectrums like media, entertainment, technology, infrastructure etc. The Mall is located on Avinashi Road in Peelamedu area about 3.5 acres in the city amid a cluster of educational institutions, the mall offers different shopping experience to the denizens. The mall has 6 levels with a total are of 5.25 lakh sq ft.

The mall brings together some of the hottest names in the retail sector – Shoppers stop, Reliance group, a host of other retail brands like Lee, Anita Dongre and fast food giant McDonalds etc from different business segments. Shoppers stop is its anchor store and occupies over 79,000 sq ft. The mall also features a five screen multiplex operated by Fun cinemas with a capacity of 1,119 seats and McDonalds restaurant spread over 3,470 sqft on two floors in addition to its food court.

The significance about the mall is its shape a large dome shaped structure boasts of a beautiful atrium and the frontage of the shops and restaurants in the six level structure has been so designed that they face the 15,000 sqft atrium. The strong demand for the mall space in Coimbatore is reflected in the demand for the retail space in Fun Republic with nearly 100 odd retailers picking up a space of about 3.25 lakhs in the mall, which has come up on about 3.5 acres that belonged earlier to the National Textile Corporation.

The tenant mix plays a pivotal role in the success of a mall and this should be decided taking into consideration the disposable income, spending pattern, shopping style of customers etc. The mall developers have taken great care in deciding on the Zoning mix, like the ground floor of the mall being set apart for very premium brands, the first floor for mens' wear, second floor for women's and kids wear, third floor for room furnishings and home appliances, electronics, gaming and fourth floor for multiplex and foof court etc. The another positive factor is the strategic location that made the mall easily accessible from any part of the city. The Mall has 10,000 sqft gaming area offering different games.

Fun Republic Mall

The Fun Republic runs malls in Mumbai, Lucknow, Chandigrah and Ahmedabad and Coimbatore mall is the first mall outside the state capital. For the group the Coimbatore mall is the fifth mall it has opened in the country[14].

Malls in Madurai

Madurai District is second largest in population of the 32 districts of the state of Tamilnadu is southeastern India. The city of Madurai serves as the district headquarters. It houses the world famous Sri Meenakshi Sundareshwarar temple and is situated on the banks of the river Vaigai. Also Madurai as a city is like a phoenix bird, it raises to its Glory even after a great destruction and this is the city which lives for past 2500 years. The city lived under various rulers which brought different cultures and traditions to the city. Madurai houses the oldest

---

[14]R.Y. Narayanan- Essel Group's Fun Republic mall to open in Coimbatore this month – The Hindu – Business Line, August 22, 2012

mall of the world named Puthumandabam which is a place where we can get everything that is needed for a marriage to your daily life.

Madurai city in the process of a radical shift from conventional trader run shops to organized and large retail mall formats. Madurai is categorized as tier two city is having a populationof 14,62,420 persons per census 2011. Madurai has a very high number of low socio-economic households which constitute almost 50per cent of the city population[15] India retail is expected to grow 25per cent annually. Madurai city has two exclusive malls Vishal Dee Mall and Milaneum Mall.

Vishaal De Mall

Vishaal de Mall is shopping mall in the city of Madurai, Tamil nadu. It is the first large formal mall in southern Tamil Nadu and it is the city's first integrated multi utility mall, located in the heart of the city. The mall was opened on April 2012, byVishall Promoters Pvt Ltd. It was 75 crore project, which took more than two years to complete. The mall is spread over 230,000 square feet (21,000m2).

The mall feature 10,000 square feet (930 m2) play area with games like dashing car and bowling. It has an exclusive 12,000 square feet (1,100m2) food court, which includes Café Coffee Day and Pizza Hut apart from the traditional south Indian Mummy Kitchen and others. The mall has theater with five Inox screen with total capacity of 1,302.

Vishaal De Mall

Vishaal De Mall with no boundaries to separate if from the street, it is open to everyone all income and age groups. The architecture of the complex embodies the spirit of Madura. It tries

---

to cater to every segment of society. Branded stores that outlet branded wears, jewellery shops, coffee shops, department stores and multiplex theatres reach out to visitors along with pizza hut. Heritage, culture and indomitable Madurai spirit are not trampled over by rampant commercialisms a vintage tram: an innetant art wall and an NGO pavilion who showcase products made by the less privileged stake their claim with gently persuasiveness[16].

Milan'en Mall

Milan'en Mall is the first shopping mall in K.K. Nagar, Madurai, India. It was opened on 28th September 2009 and is the first shopping mall in Madurai. Built in a half acre site, the mall has five floors with a total area of 90,000 sq.ft.Milanem Mall was developmed by Milan group.The mall has three movie theaters with a total capacity of 500 seats. The mall has a food court in the third floor along with water zorbing for kids.

The malls building management systems has close circuit security, parking management systems, ATM facility, 100per cent power backups, centralized air conditioning and live music well offered world class ambiance.

The atrium of the mall is used to host cultural events. Events are conducted in vast array of meeting spaces which includes state of the art audio visual equipment. High speed Internet access and an inspiring environment.

Events like Balloon festival, food festival, blood donation drive, Indi's most fuel efficient cars etc are conducted in Milanem Mall[17].

Milan'en Mall

---

[16]http://www.vishapromoters.com/vishall-de-mal.php

[17]"Shopping mall opens". The Hindu *(Madurai). 29 September 2009.* Retrieved 4 November 2012.

Mall Directory

Derby – Mens ware, Mee- costumes and Perfumes, Yuvamotifs – DesingnerSarees, Triumph-Women's Inner wear, Cool colors – Men's casual wears , Music Park – Audio and video CD 's centre, Univercell–mobile phone shop, Estelle–designer costume jewellery, Kidsmart- toyshop, Anita's – designer costumes, V.I.P- travel bags, K.S. Kitchen–Kitchen furnitures , Jansons – men's shirts and pants, Roshan–school and leather bags, Singapore Perfumes – perfumes and body spray, park impexinc–home theatre, S & M–kids wears, Scream–ice creams.

Hotel Germanus – pure vegetarian dishes, FSM Grill Chick – Arabian style chicken foods, Big chick – fries chicken shop, FSM Foodie–chat masala and panipori shop, Hani Chill Zone-Jigarthanda and sweet corn, FSM Green Fresh–Fresh green foods, New Nagalakshmi Annexe-pure vegetarian hotel, VasanDosa–dosa corner, Mart- Readymade showroom, Mochi–The Shoe Shoppe, Archies Gallery – gifts and cards, FSM super - super market.[18]

Trichy

Tiruchirappalli city lies in the heart of Tamil Nadu. It was citadel of early Cholas which later fell to the Pallavas. Tiruchirappalli also called Trichy. It is the fine blend of tradition and modernity built around the Rock Fort. Trichy is the fourth largest municipal corporation and fourth largest urban agglomeration in the state. The district has an area of 4,404 square kilometers. Kaveririver flows through the length of the district and its principle source of irrigation and water supply. The presence of a large number of energy equipment manufacturing units in and around the city has earned it the tile of "Energy Equipment and fabrication capital of India". According to the National Urban Sanitation Policy Tiruchirappalli was listed as the second cleanest city in India in 2015.

Indias' largest public sector manufacturing plant was set up by Bharat Heavy Electrical Limited The city has number of retail and wholesale markets, the most prominent among them being the Gandhi Market which also serves people from other parts of the district. The other note able markets in the city are the flower bazaar in sriringam and the mango market at MamabazhaSalai[19].Though spotting a gaint shopping mall might test the patience.

---

[18] http://www.tamilspider.com/resources/5847-Shopping-Malls-Madurai.aspx

[19] https://en.wikipedia.org/wiki/Tiruchirappalli

Trichy is fast catching up with other metropolitans in terms of commercial evolution. Notwithstanding Trichy offers an exciting set of traditional shopping area, which include Burma bazaar, china kadaiveedhi, singarathope and many other shopping oriented areas[20].

Trichy is fast catching up with other metropolitans in terms of commercial evolution. Retail shopping in Tirchy has undergone a sea change in the recent past. A decade ago, Pick n Pack was 'the big store'. And then came a string of supermarkets and department stores, revolutionizing the middle class shopping experience in the city. There was a radical shift from harried housewives handing shopping lifts over the counter to parents wheeling trolleys loaded with sundry groceries, toys and instant foods, with kids in tow. The mushrooming of the hypermarket or large format stores stocking vegetables, footwear, groceries and electronic appliances all under one roof. They have made shopping a family affair- an experience of sorts, with ambience and adjoining food courts playing up their advantage.

The 'conservative spender' tag can no longer solely describe the average middle class Tiruchiite, claim retailers, though the market is price sensitive and people are more value conscious compared to their counterparts in other tier-two cities. With an increase in the spending capacity of people, sales have doubled, compared to the time of our establishment. People value the shopping experience highly[21]

Femina Shopping Mall

New Femina Shopping Mall is located in Contonment, Trichy. It is officially opened for business and customer from September 2012. This mall infrastructure is very atractive. Its provide the product rate is very reasonable rate. This Shopping mall is one of the largest scale store for product imaginable spanning over a 100,000 square feet, This is biggest shopping single store in Trichy.

Shopping mall is in the centre of the city, in the business district of Trichy, state of Tamil Nadu. Over 40,000 sqft of shopping space, with all products from Jewellery to Chocolates, Clothes, high end Sarees and Garments, a Food Court and children's arcade, most products are imported from various parts of the world. Femina shopping mall is a veritable shopping and entertainment hub in the heart of the city.

The customers preference for the retail shopping has changed due to the rise in income and standard of living.

---

[20]http://www.trichy.com/

[21] "Promotional offers and discounts a selling point for stores"The Hindu, Trichy July15, 2011

Exhibit Femina Shopping Mall

Femina Shopping Mall (FSM), a veritable shopping and entertainment hub in the heart of the city says customer preference for retail shopping has changed due to the rise in income and standard of living. The city holds a lot of potential with recent developments and increasing investment. There is a recent trend of people moving from other cities to Tirchy for work. Retail experience has changed over the couple of years. With people giving priority to the shopping experience, large format stores have potential. It is not merely the experience, but quality and price that people are conscious about too.The store's focus is on developing the fresh and processed food segment.[22]

Catering to clients of all different classes, the Moto of the mall is to make sure everyone enjoys shopping as an experience to actually shop, so that they walk out knowing for certain they have got a good deal, this is made possible by our dedicated purchasing team who go all out to shelf products that are new, attractive and of the highest quality yet affordable. The product list of the shopping mall are Grocery, jewellery and watches, Handicrafts, electrical goods, phones and PDA, Clothes and all garments, shoes, candy's and chocolates, perfumes and cosmetics, electrical goods, sarees, accessories and handbags, health and beauty products, ornaments[23]

---

[22] http://www.trichyonline.in/city-guide/shopping-in-trichy

[23] http://www.smiorg.com/feminashoppingmall.html

ANNEXURE II

Statistical Tools Applied

Statistics is the science of collecting, analyzing and making inference from data. Statistics is a particularly useful branch of mathematics that is not only studied theoretically by advanced mathematicians but one that is used by researchers in many fields to organize, analyze, and summarize data. Statistical methods and analyses are often used to communicate research findings and to support hypotheses and give credibility to research methodology and conclusions. It is important for researchers and also consumers of research to understand statistics so that they can be informed, evaluate the credibility and usefulness of information, and make appropriate decisions.

The data collected through the questioner were classified and tabulated for analysis in accordance with the outline laid down for the purpose of justifying the objective and the hypotheses framed at the time of developing research design. According to the nature of data and interpretations required, appropriate statistical tools have been applied. The following tools have been applied in the study: Frequency distribution, Weighted Average, Likert's Summated scale, Independent 'Z' test, Paired 'z' test, Reliability Analysis, Multiple Regression and Rotated Factor Analysis.

A. *Frequency Distribution*

The frequency distribution of the variables were calculated with help of simple percentage, by writing the formula *FD = F/N x 100*. Where f1 denotes the number of respondents, and n denotes the total number of sample population.

B. *Weighted Arithmetic Mean*

One of the most important objectives of statistical analysis is to get one single value that describes the characteristic of the entire mass of entire data. Such a value is called the central value or an "average" means or the expected value of the variable, what the statisticians call the arithmetic mean. The process of computing mean in case of individual observation (i.e), where frequencies are not given is very simple. Add together the various values of the variable and divide the total by the number of items. The researcher has applied weighted mean, instead of calculating the simple mean to obtain a realistic average.

$$\bar{x} = \frac{\sum W_i X_j}{\sum W_i}$$

where $\bar{X}$ = Weighted mean

Wi = Weight of i th item X

Xj= value of the jth item of X

C. *Summated Scales (Likert's-Scales)*

Summated scales (or Likert- type scales) are developed by utilizing the item analysis approach where in a particular item is evaluated on the basis of how well it discriminates between those persons whose total score is high and those whose score is low. Those items or statements that best meet this sort of discrimination test are included in the final instrument. In a Likert Scale, the respondent is asked to respond to each statement in terms of several degrees, usually five degree of agreement (or) disagreement. Each point on the scale carries a score of 5, 4, 3, 2, and 1. Scaling describes the procedure of assigning numbers to various degrees of opinion, attitude and other concepts.

D. *ANOVA (F-Test)*

Two way ANOVA techniques are used when the data are classified on the basis of two factors ANOVA. The F-test is named in honour of the great statistician R.A. Fisher. The objective of the F-test is to find out whether the two independent estimates of population variance differ significantly, or whether the two samples may be regarded as drawn from the normal populations having the same variance. The formula used in the analysis of variance (ANOVA table) classification model is:

$$\text{The ratio of F} = \frac{Between-column\, variance}{Within-column\, variance}$$

$$\text{i.e., F} = \frac{V_1^2}{V_2^2}$$

E. *Chi-Square Test*

The chi-square test is an important test amongst the several tests of significance developed by statisticians. Chi-square, symbolically written as $\chi 2$ (pronounced as ki-square). As a non-parametric test, it can be used to determine if categorical data shows dependency or the two classifications are independent.

Chi-square as a test of independence enables a researcher to explain whether or not two attributes are associated.

$\chi 2$ are calculated as follows:

$$\chi 2 = \frac{\Sigma (Oij - Eij)2}{Eij}$$

Where o_{ij} =observed frequency of the cell in ith row and jth column

e_{ij}=expected frequency of the cell in ith row and jth column

The $\chi 2$ values obtained as such should be compared with relevant table value of $\chi 2$ and the inference can be drawn. If the calculated value is greater than the table value the hypothesis framed will be rejected, otherwise accepted.

The entire hypothesis test in this study was carried out at 5 percent level of significance. In research we quit often face measurement problem (since we want a valid measurement but may not obtain it), especially when the concepts to be measured are complex and abstract and we do not possess the standardized measurement tools.

F. Independent 'Z' test

The independent Z-test, also called the two sample Z-test or student's Z-test, is an inferential statistical test that determines whether there is a statistically significant difference between the means in two unrelated groups. In this study year of exports and value of cotton yarn exports are considered as two variables.

$$Z = \frac{\bar{x}1 - \bar{x}2}{\sqrt{\frac{s1^2 + s2^2}{n}}}$$

G. Paired Z-Test

Paired Z-test is a way to test for comparing two related samples, involving small values of n that does not require the variances of the two populations to be equal, but the assumption that the two populations are normal and must continue to apply.

For a paired t-test, it is necessary that the observations in the two samples be collected in the form of what is called matched pairs i.e. "each observation in the one sample must be paired with an observation in the other sample in such a manner that these observations are somehow "matched" or related, in an attempt to eliminate extraneous factors which are not of interest in test",

$$Z = \frac{\bar{D} - 0}{\sigma\ diff\ /\sqrt{n}} \text{ with (n-1) degrees of freedom}$$

Where,

$\bar{D}$= Mean of differences

$\sigma\ diff$=Standard deviation of differences

H. *Discriminant Analysis*

Discriminant analysis is a statistical technique that classifies an observation into one of several *a priori* groupings on the basis of observations on individual characteristics under appropriate assumptions. Discriminant analysis helps to identify the independent variables that discriminate a dependent variable for example; those who are high on the variable from those who are low on it.

The classification is done by means of a linear discriminant function and the desired discriminant function is of the form

$$Y= \lambda_1\ V_1 + \lambda_2\ V_2 + \lambda_3\ V_3 + \ldots\ldots\ldots\ldots + \lambda_n\ V_n$$

Where Y = the discriminant score $\lambda_1, \lambda_2, \lambda_3$ .... λ_n are the discriminant coefficients

V_1, V_2, V_3 .... V_n are discriminant variables.

In this research since the primary objective is to find out the specific variables that are important in understanding the role of company executives in channel management, discriminant analysis technique was applied.

Cronbach's Alpha is applicable for an estimate of the internal consistency of items in a model or survey. It assesses the degree of the correlations among a set of variables and is used within this paper to evaluate how well a set of sub-indices measures a single unidimensional object. Cronbach's Alpha is defined as:

$$\alpha = \frac{nR}{1+(n-1)R}$$

Where,

n = number of the components of a (sub-) index

R= mean correlation of the items Cronbach's Alpha is zero if no correlation exists and the sub-indices are independent. If the underlying items are perfectly correlated, it is equal to one. Therefore, a high Cronbach's Alpha is an indication that the underlying items proxy the desired variable well. According to aunnally (1978), a value of 0.7 is an acceptable threshold. The other two measures are related to factor analyses.

The Kaiser-Meyer-Olkin measure of sampling adequacy (MSA) is based on the partial correlations among the input variables, and should be >=0.5 to proceed with factor analysis as described by Kaiser and Rice (1974).Bartlett's Test of Sphericity reveals whether the correlation matrix is not an identity matrix and, therefore, can be factorized. Its test value should be below the 0.05 significance level.

I. *Multiple Regressions*

Multiple Linear Regression Analysis is a technique for modeling the linear relationship between two or more variables. It is one of the most widely used of all statistical methods. The regression model was performed to evaluate (i) There exists association between households preferred avenue of saving & investment and factors that determine their saving & investment behaviour at the time of inflation, (ii) Households' realisation about the impact of inflation on them significantly influences their financial discipline practices and(iii) Households' realisation about the impact of inflation on them significantly influences their saving & investment behaviour.

The general linear regression model, with normal error terms, simply of X variables is shown in equation 1.

$$Y_i = \beta_0 + \beta_1 X_{i1} + \beta_2 X_{i2} + \ldots\ldots + \beta_{p-1} X_{ip-1} + \varepsilon_i$$

Where $\beta_0, \beta_1, \ldots\ldots, \beta_{p-1}$ are parameters, $X_{i1}, X_{i2}, \ldots\ldots, X_{ip-1}$ are known constants, ε_i are independent $N(0, \sigma^2)$, i=1, 2, 3, ……. N.

The entire hypothesis test in this study has been carried out at 5 percent level of significance.

J. *Rotation Factor Analysis*

The factor analysis is another multivariate technique. It is an extremely powerful and useful analytic approach to psychological, behavioral, financial and other types of data. It is a statistical technique for determining the underlying factors or forces among a large number of interdependent variables of measures. It is a method for extracting common factor variances from a set of observations. It groups the number of variables of smaller set of uncorrelated factors potentially conveying a great deal of information.

- Factor: A factor is an underlying dimension that accounts for several observed variables. There can be one or more factors, depending upon the nature of the study and the number of variables involved in it.

- Factor–loading: Factor-loading is those values which explain how closely the variables are related to each one of the factors discovered. They are also known as factors-variable correlations. In fact, factor-loadings work as a key to the understanding what the factors mean. It is the absolute size (rather than the signs, plus or minus) of the loading that is important in the interpretation of a factor.

- Communality (h^2): Communality, symbolized as h^2, shows how much of each variable is accounted for by the underlying factors taken together. A high value of communality means that not much of the variable is left over after whatever the factors represent is taken into consideration. It is worked out in respect of each variable as under:
  - H^2 of the ith variable= (ith factor loading of factor A)^2= (ith factor loading of factor B)^2
- Eigen Value: Eigen value (or Latent Root) is the sum of squared values of factor loadings relating to a factor. It indicates the relative importance of each in accounting for the particular set of variables under study.
- Total sum of squares: When Eigen values of all factors are totaled, the resulting value is called the total of squares. Rotations reveal different structures in the data. If the factors are independent, orthogonal rotation is done, and if they are corrected, an oblique rotation is made. Factor score represents the degree to which each respondent gets high scores on the group of item that load high on each factor. Factor scores are used in several other multivariate analyses.

Appendix

Questionnaire

Objectives

1) To study the socio economic status of Outshoppers in Shopping Malls in selected cities in Tamilnadu

2) To find out the level of Awareness and Perception of Outshoppers towards Shopping Malls

3) To evaluate the level of Shopping Experience of Outshoppers in Shopping Malls

4) To critically evaluate the influences of Outshoppers personality on their Buyer Behavior

5) To Measure the level of Satisfaction experienced by the Outshoppers and their future loyalty towards Shopping Malls.

Interview Schedule

I.   Demographic and Socio Economic Status.

1) Name of the Respondent (optional):

2) Place of Resident (Please Specify district):

3) Gender:

4) Age:
   a) 15-20years
   b) 21-35years
   c) 36-40years
   d) 41-55years
   e) Above 55years

5) Marital status
   a) Married
   b) Unmarried

6) Education Qualification
   a) SSLC/Matric
   b) HSLC
   c) Under graduate
   d) Post graduate
   e) Diploma/technical Education
   f) Professional Qualification
   g) Others

7) Nature of occupation
   a) Salaried
   b) Business
   c) Professional
   d) Retired
   e) Students
   f) Home Maker
   g) Others

8) State your monthly Income
   a) Below 10000
   b) 10000-20000
   c) 20000-30000

d)   30000-40000

e)   above 40000

9)   Size of the family : ______

10) Number of Earning member in the family : _____

11) Number of dependents in the family: ____

II.   Level of Awareness about Shopping Malls.

12) State your source of awareness about Shopping Malls

a)   Sales person

b)   Dealers

c)   Advertisements

d)   Friends

e)   Relatives

f)   Others Specify _____

13) If it is through advertisement specify the media

a)   Radio

b)   TV

c)   Internet (social network)

d)   News paper/Magazine

e)   Posters, Banners, Broachers

f)   Others Specify ________

14) State your level of Awareness about the following Shopping Malls

S.no	Shopping Malls	Very Highly Aware	Highly Aware	Aware	Low Aware	Very Low Aware
1	Brook field					
2	Fun republic					
3	Millaneum Mall					
4	Vishall De Mall					
5	Femina Hyper all					

15) Have you visited Shopping Malls

a)   Yes

b)   No

III.   Level of Shopping Experience.

16) Which of the leading Shopping Malls you have visited the most

a)   Brook field

b)   Fun republic

c) Millaneum Mall

d) Femina Hyper Mall

e) Vishall De Mall

17) According to you Shopping Malls are the place for the

a) Means for shopping

b) Fun & Entertainment

c) Place of Outing with friends

d) Place for Family outing

e) Place for Multi-cuisine Tasting / Eating's

18) State the nature of consumer you are

a) Impulsive

b) Rational

19) Frequency of shopping in a year

a) Very Frequently

b) Frequently

c) Occasionally

d) Rarely

e) Based on the needs

20) State the nature of product you would like to buy in the Malls

a) Food and Beverage

b) Life style

c) Clothing

d) Provisions

e) Watches and Jewelers

f) Stationeries

g) Cosmetics and Beauty

h) Health and Medicine

i) Foot ware

j) Household Appliances

k) Leisure and personal goods

21) Do you feel shopping in Shopping Malls is better than retail shops

a) Yes

b) No

22) State the primary reasons for shopping at Shopping Malls (Rank the variables as 1,2,3,4)

	Reasons	Rank
1	Availability all under one roof	
2	Accessibility (Distance of Travel)	
3	Retail Tenant Mix	
4	Product Range, Merchandise Value	
5	Orientation and Infrastructure facilities	
6	Better Sales service	
7	Parking Facilities	
8	External Atmospheric Clues (architectural style, Layout design and image)	
9	Internal Atmospheric Clues (eg flooring, lighting, air condition, music rest rooms etc)	
10	Hospitality (Food courts & Resting Places)	
11	Entertainment (Multiplex Screening the latest blockbusters)	
12	Lifestyle Outlets (Health and Beauty)	
13	Offers and discounts	
14	Competitive price	
15	Status Symbol	

23) Does cultural & religious festivals influence you to buy at Shopping Malls frequently

    a) Yes

    b) No

24) If yes indicate the level of influence in your purchase

S.no	Festivals	Very High	High	Normal	Low	Very Low
1	Religious Festivals Diwali, Christmas, Ramzan etc					
2	Social Festivals Republic Day, Independence day					
3	Personal Festivals Birthday , Wedding, Annviseray					

25) Who influences you to buy at Shopping Malls

    a) Self

    b) Spouse

    c) Children

    d) Parents & Elders

    e) Friends

    f) Colleagues

IV.   Level of Perception towards Shopping Malls.

26) State your level of Perception towards Shopping Malls

S.No	Statements	Strongly Agree	Agree	Neither Agree nor disagree	Disagree	Strongly disagree
1	Shopping Malls provides better quality of goods and services					
2	Shopping Malls provides better customer care service					
3	Information system provided is adequate in Shopping Malls					
4	Shopping Malls are adequately modernised					
5	Parking facility is adequate in Malls					
6	Promotional offers are provided in the shops at shopping malls					
7	Billing method is convenient					
8	Shopping at Shopping Malls is better than other shops					
9	It helps customers to save time					
10	Purchasing at Shopping Malls is status symbol to customers					

V.   Outshopper's Personality on their Buyer Behaviour.

27) State the nature of shopper you are

Variables	Strongly Agree	Agree	Neither Agree nor disagree	Disagree	Strongly disagree
Adventure Shopper					
I find shopping stimulating					
Shopping is a thrill to me					
Shopping makes me feel like I am in my own universe					
Value Shopper					
For the most part, I go shopping when there are sales offers					
I enjoy looking and hunting for discount when shopping					
I go shopping to take advantage of sales offers					
Role Shopper					
I feel good when I buy things for the special people in my life					
I enjoy shopping for my family members					
I enjoy shopping for around to find the perfect gift for friends					
Idea Shopper					
I go shopping to keep up with the new trends and fashions					
I go shopping to see what new products available in the market					
I go shopping to experience new things					
Social Shopper					
I go shopping with my family to socialise					
I enjoy socializing with others when shopping					
To me, shopping with friends is a social occasion					
Gratification Shopper					
When I am in down mood, I go shopping to make me feel better					
To me, shopping is a way to relieve stress					
To me, shopping is a way to treat myself fresh					

VI.   Level of Satisfaction.

28) State the level of satisfaction towards the following factors at Shopping Malls

S.No	Reasons	Highly satisfied	Satisfied	Neither satisfied nor dissatisfied	Dissatisfied	Highly Dissatisfied
1	Availability all under one roof					
2	Accessibility (Distance of Travel)					
3	Retail Tenant Mix					
4	Product Range, Merchandise Value					
5	Orientation and Infrastructure facilities					
6	Better Sales service					
7	Parking Facilities					
8	External Atmospheric Clues (architectural style, Layout design and image)					
9	Internal Atmospheric Clues (eg flooring, lighting, air condition, music rest rooms etc)					
10	Hospitality (Food courts & Resting Places)					
11	Entertainment (Multiplex Screening the latest blockbusters)					
12	Lifestyle Outlets (Health and Beauty)					
13	Offers and discounts					
14	Competitive price					
15	Status Symbol					

29) Would You recommend others to buy at Shopping Malls

    a)   Yes

    b)   No

30) If No State the reason

    a)   Not worth to be recommended

    b)   Let them decide by themselves

    c)   Other specify ___________________

31) Is there is any feedback system in Shopping Malls

    a)   Yes

    b)   No

32) Which of the feedback system they adopt

    a)   Register Method

    b)   Questionnarie Method

    c)   Telephone Enquiry Method

    d)   Direct Interview Method

    e)   Online survey Method

    f)   Others specify__________

* 9 7 8 9 3 8 6 6 3 8 1 1 3 *